Hiking the Benton MacKaye Trail

Suspension bridge over the Toccoa River

OVERVIEW MAP

Hiking the Benton MacKaye Trail

SECTIONS 1–12

Springer Mountain to Ocoee River

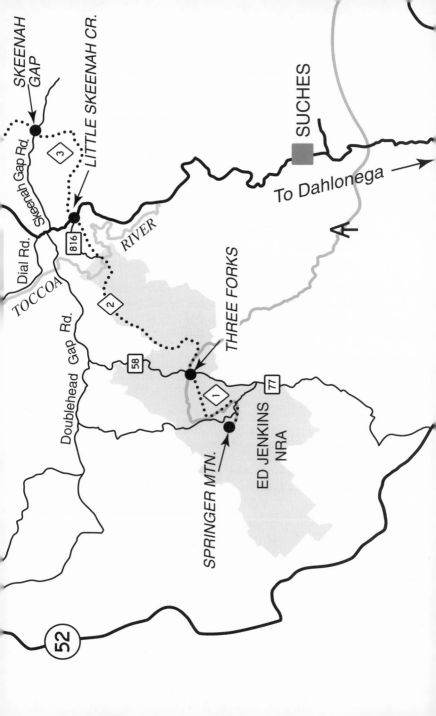

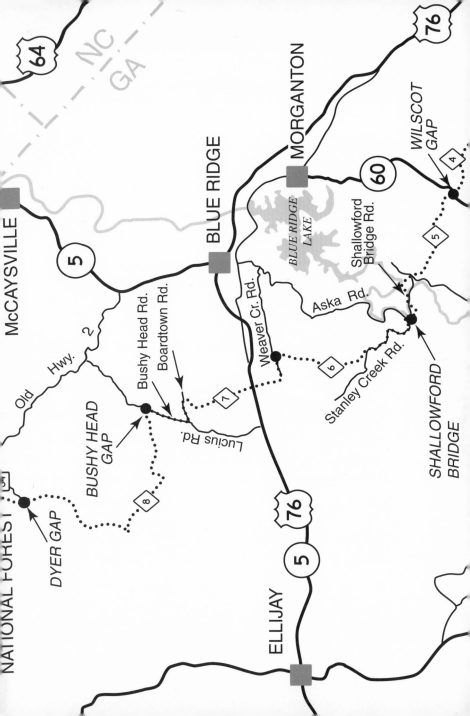

A guide to the Benton MacKaye Trail from Georgia's
Springer Mountain to Tennessee's Ocoee River

Hiking the Benton MacKaye Trail

Tim Homan

PEACHTREE
ATLANTA

Ω

Published by
PEACHTREE PUBLISHERS
1700 Chattahoochee Avenue
Atlanta, Georgia 30318

Interior illustrations © 2004 by Vicky Holifield
Maps page 8 and front foldout © 2004 by Mark Morrison
Section maps created by Ken Jones and Marty Dominy
    with National Geographic's TOPO! software
Book design by Loraine M. Joyner
Book composition by Robin Sherman

Manufactured in the United States of America

10 9 8 7 6 5 4 3 2 1
First Edition

Library of Congress Cataloging-in-Publication Data

Homan, Tim.
    Hiking the Benton MacKaye Trail / Tim Homan.— 1st ed.
        p. cm.
    Includes index.
    ISBN 1-56145-311-0
    1. Hiking—Benton MacKaye Trail (Ga. and Tenn.)—Guidebooks. 2. Benton
MacKaye Trail (Ga. and Tenn.)—Guidebooks. I. Title.

    GV199.42.G46H64 2004
    796.51'09758--dc22

                                                          2004002162

Acknowledgments

I WISH TO EXTEND SPECIAL THANKS to the following people for their help:

- Claire Broadwell, David Acton Brown, Walt Cook, Steve Craven, Gary Crider, Darcy Douglas, Dana Hamilton, Page Luttrell, Maggie Nettles, George Owen, and Charles Ratliff for hiking with me;

- Page Luttrell, my wife, for her typing, computer lessons, and all-around support;

- Vicky Holifield for her editing, artwork, and calming presence;

- Loraine Joyner for her map and design work;

- Mark Morrison for his photography, maps, and patience;

- Marty Dominy for all of the information and data he unselfishly provided for me and this project;

- Darcy Douglas, BMTA liaison, for her enthusiastic support, editing, and writing the section called "History of the Benton MacKaye Trail Association";

- Ken Jones for his work on the elevation profiles and all his efforts to make the full-length version of the Benton MacKaye become a reality;

- George Owen for his unstinting hospitality, his knowledge of the BMT, and his clearing and flagging on Section 8;

- Walt Cook for editing, walking me through Section 2's reroutes, clearing the way on Section 8, and writing the section called "Forests of the Benton MacKaye Trail";

- David Blount for his work in making part of Section 8 easier to hike and measure-wheel;

■ Mike Christison for his wildflower notes and expertise;

■ Edwin Dale, Margaret Drummond, Ken Jones, George Owen, Clayton Pannell, Dave Sherman, Nancy Shofner, and Randy Snodgrass for answering questions concerning the history of the BMTA;

■ Tom Keene for his work as BMTA liaison after Darcy Douglas left;

■ Tony Oldfield for his editing;

■ Rob McDowell for writing the section called "Geology of the Benton MacKaye Trail";

■ And all of the Benton MacKaye Trail maintainers for making the trail such a pleasure to walk.

—*Tim Homan*

Contents

Preface

DURING SPRING, SUMMER, AND FALL of two recent years —mostly on weekends and holidays—I walked all of the BMT sections included in this guide at least once, and all but two of them twice. On the first go-around, I rolled a measuring wheel—a bright orange, incessantly clicking, spoked mechanism that, especially to the jokers, resembles a unicycle. By pushing this wheeled counter, I was able to record distances to the exact foot (for example, Section 1 measured 32,763 feet), then easily crunch the large numbers to the nearest tenth of a mile. If a measurement fell exactly between tenths, I rounded the figure upward; mile 1.65, for example, became mile 1.7.

I measured the Benton MacKaye Trail because I wanted current information on the various reroutes, and because I wanted accurate mileages to all the features I intended to note. I was not the first to wheel the trail. Various BMTA members, especially Marty Dominy, had already wheeled and recorded distances on data sheets, precise to the hundredth of a mile. I thank them for all the information available to me when I started this project.

On the second go-around, I left the wheel at home and walked selected sections, taking comprehensive nature notes during springtime. After close to 200 miles of hiking on the Benton MacKaye—wheeling; nature note taking; wheeling reroutes; showing friends wildflower colonies, big trees, and the suspension bridge over the Toccoa River—I am pleased to report that I did not encounter a single poisonous snake, and I did not get stung by a single hornet or yellow jacket. I came to no harm worse than becoming wetter than I wanted from a couple of thunderstorms. My best wildlife sighting was a very young wild hog, 14 to 16 inches long, yellow streaks still plainly showing on its flanks. It sprang off the edge of the treadway just in front of my footfall and hurtled downslope with astonishing speed for its small size.

I did experience one unforgettable moment of fear. I had walked a mile of Section 8, starting from Bushy Head Gap, when I felt the undeniable need to make a pit stop. I left the trail, walked down a woods road well out of sight, and dropped trousers. I had assumed the squat-and-strain position, both hands holding onto mountain laurel, when something gave my bare backside an emphatic nudge. A jolt of fight-or-flight adrenaline hit me with the instant insistence of an electric shock. I involuntarily hollered, jumped up, and twisted around to see what was behind me. But my adrenaline rush had neither clue nor care that my pants were wrapped around my ankles. As I began to fall, I saw a spooked-eyed hound, perhaps 60 pounds worth, frantic with his own fear.

I toppled onto the roadbed without harm. And as I sat there— letting my heart rate and adrenaline subside, pulling up my twisted trousers—Ranger padded up and properly introduced himself. He sat when commanded, gave me his paw when asked. I scratched behind his ears and told him he had scared the living ...daylights out of me. He trotted ahead of me—snake-sweeper and scout—for nearly three miles before turning back and heading home. This outing was not Ranger's first rodeo; he knew the trail, seemed to know the blazes, and made every turn correctly after only a moment's hesitation. So there you have it, my big moment of fear in the wild mountains did not come from bear or boar or rattler, but from a friendly dog who had a strange way of telling me he wanted to go for a walk.

—*Tim Homan*

The Benton MacKaye Trail:
Questions and Answers, Present and Future

How long?

As of autumn 2003, the BMT's first twelve sections measure 92.8 miles, from Springer Mountain, Georgia, to the path's current end at US 64 in Tennessee. Georgia's share of that length—from Springer Mountain to Double Spring Gap on the Tennessee border—spans 81.6 miles. Tennessee's treadway, which will expand dramatically in the next few years, currently totals 11.2 miles.

How high, how low?

Thus far, Tennessee's relatively short segment features the BMT's highest and lowest terrain, which ranges from yellow birch habitat atop Big Frog Mountain (4,220 feet; Section 11) to river birch habitat in the Ocoee River floodplain (1,120 feet; Section 12). Georgia's two highest BMT points rise to 3,730 feet on the wide ridgeline of Flat Top Mountain (Section 8) and 3,740 feet at the trail's southern terminus on Springer Mountain. The route's covered-bridge crossing of Cherry Log Creek (1,540 feet; Section 7) is its lowest elevation in Georgia.

Where does it go?

Starting at Springer Mountain, the BMT winds northward— over the Toccoa River, across GA 60—for 26.2 miles to Payne Gap (Section 4) before making its first major directional shift. Along the way, the footpath reaches its easternmost point in Georgia on the upper-west slope of Rhodes Mountain. For the next 36.3 miles, from Payne Gap to the top of Fowler Mountain, the treadway heads generally westward, crossing GA 60 again, passing through two corridors of private property, and crossing the four-lane Appalachian Highway south-southwest of Blue Ridge. The trail turns north at Fowler Mountain (Section 8) and continues to work its way in that direction for the remaining 30.3 miles to US 64. Big Frog Mountain is the westernmost point of Sections 1–12.

How wild?

The first five and final five sections range through an almost uninterrupted corridor of public land: the Chattahoochee National Forest in Georgia and the Cherokee National Forest in Tennessee. These two long segments sandwich a narrow slice of private land in the center, part of Section 6 and almost all of Section 7. Of the BMT's 10.3 miles of public-road walking, 3.5 miles occur along Section 6 and 5.1 miles occur along Section 7.

Heading north from Springer Mountain, all of Section 1 and approximately eight miles of Section 2 venture through the 23,300-acre Ed Jenkins National Recreation Area. Continuing to the north, then west, the route does not follow its first open road—Shallowford Bridge Road closely paralleling the shoaling Toccoa River—until it reaches Section 5's westernmost 0.5 mile: a total of 36.6 miles of national forest trail from Springer Mountain to the first road-walk. Beyond Section 7, the Benton MacKaye traverses federal land again. The BMT road-walks only 1.1 miles of its northernmost 36.9 miles (Sections 8–12), and 0.7 mile of that short distance follows remote, dirt-gravel Forest Service roads.

Sections 8 through 11 penetrate the trail's wildest and most remote forests. Beyond FS 793 at Hudson Gap, Section 8 roams 9.8 miles before reaching its next open Forest Service road, FS 64A.

Beyond the 0.3-mile road-walk from Watson Gap, Sections 10 and 11 do not set tread on another open road until the trail crosses FS 221 in Tennessee—a distance of 16.1 miles. Thirteen and six-tenths miles of Sections 10 and 11 zigzag through the 45,059-acre Cohutta–Big Frog Wilderness.

How primitive?

The Benton MacKaye is not the Appalachian Trail: a wide, bare-dirt treadway with a little personal space to either side. Where the BMT threads through national forest, it is a more primitive, much less traveled alternative to the AT. Except where a wide aisle remains on old roadbed, the Benton MacKaye has neither extra-wide tread nor shelters (with the lone exception of Section 7's private-property shelter) at regular intervals. Backpacking this trail requires tent or tarp. On public land, the BMT is more often intimate footpath than sidewalk-wide promenade. The Benton MacKaye Trail Association specializes in sidehill paths—narrow treads constructed into forested slopes, gently winding and gently undulating, easy and pleasant to walk, hard to erode.

In addition to participating in the Association's monthly work trips, BMTA volunteers maintain their own short segments of the trail. Even though all of the route is regularly brushed out by one or more members, there are still places, especially the light gaps of old roadbeds, where vegetation can crowd the trail by late spring. In general, just to be on the cautious side, you should probably wear long pants after early spring, or at least long shorts and tall gaiters.

Why hike the Benton MacKaye?

Because the Benton MacKaye offers an impressive array of

natural and man-made landscapes and experiences—from riparian to ridgetop, from rural to remote, from wide road to wilderness path. Starting at Springer Mountain the white diamonds lead walkers over or through, across, past, or near the southern terminus of the Appalachian Trail, a plaque commemorating Benton MacKaye, fern fields, rock outcrop overlooks, old-growth trees; springs, rivulets, branches, creeks, whitewater rivers, cascades, and waterfalls; wildlife management areas, wildernesses, and a National Recreation Area; wildlife openings, wildflower slopes, flame azalea displays, rhododendron and mountain laurel tunnels; a fire tower, covered bridges, a swaying suspension bridge, rural lanes, Forest Service roads, paved roads, churches, a chapel, ponds, houses, cabins, and split-rail fences; remote second-growth forests, rock outcrops, springtime warblers and orchids, summer lushness and six-foot-tall lilies, fall foliage and beautiful blue skies, winter views and solitude; easy road-walks, tough wilderness grades, and numerous peaks and knobs from 3,000 to 4,200 feet high. That's why.

Where will the trail be routed north of US 64?

When the BMTA finishes the entire route, the rest of the path—some 185 miles more—will become a beckoning combination of scenic streamsides, deep-forest slopes, and rugged ridgelines, up and down, better and better, higher and wilder, as it progresses toward its northern terminus at Davenport Gap.

When the BMT is built as planned, it will follow the course shown on the map on page 8. Heading generally northeastward, the remainder of the treadway will traverse Tennessee's Cherokee National Forest and a small portion of North Carolina's Nantahala National Forest, then will finish with a wild trek through the Great Smoky Mountains National Park.

North of US 64, the map-line BMT follows the western edge of Little Frog Wilderness before rambling past the islands and rapids of the scenic Hiwassee River. Beyond the whitewater, the track rises into the Unicoi Mountains, passing Buck Bald and dipping to Unicoi Gap, where the line of march begins to follow the Tennessee–North Carolina line to Hazelnut Knob, Round Top, and Rocky Top. Through Sled Runner Gap, the walkway leaves the state line and bends back into Tennessee. Here the wildland path parallels Bald River for a short distance, crosses the Tellico River, and climbs Sycamore Creek's watershed further into the large, nearly solid block of Forest Service land, high and rugged, straddling the TN-NC border.

Onward. After leaving Whigg Meadow, the course ascends to the 5,000-foot contour for the first time just south of Little Haw Knob. It crosses the Cherohala Skyway at Beech Gap, then enters the contiguous Joyce Kilmer–Slickrock and Citico Creek Wildernesses. The track swings around the upper-west slopes of the Fodderstacks—Big and Little—travels north to Farr Gap, loses elevation beside Little Slickrock Creek, leaves the wilderness, then crosses the Little Tennessee River (dammed to make Calderwood Lake) on US 129. Beyond lake and US highway, the treadway re-enters the woods and lights out for Deals Gap on the southwestern boundary of the Great Smoky Mountains National Park before turning southward and following Lake Cheoah (Little Tennessee River) to the east, where it crosses into the park at Twentymile Ranger Station. Now traveling through the Smokies—the Southern Highland's largest preserved tract at a little more than half a million acres, most of it de facto wilderness—the Benton MacKaye finishes with a kick: a backpacker's fantasy of roadless forests and backcountry campsites, sharp-ridged mountains and wildflower slopes, clear water and cascades beyond counting.

Once inside the park, the route heads up beautiful Twentymile Creek before intersecting the Appalachian Trail at Sassafras Gap. Now roaming south of the AT, in North Carolina, the wilderness footpath descends with Lost Cove Creek, ascends with Pinnacle Creek, continues through Pickens Gap, then rises beside Hazel Creek and Cold Spring Branch to Cold Spring Gap on Welch Ridge. Next it gains elevation to 4,800 feet on the upper slope of High Rocks, swings south of Bearwallow Bald, roller-coasters on or near the crests of two ridges—Bald and Jumpup—loses elevation alongside Bear Creek, and follows Forney Creek upstream before proceeding through Board Camp Gap. Beyond the saddle, the BMT zigzags down another branch and creek, up Noland Creek, through a second Sassafras Gap, down Pole Road Creek, and over Sunkota and Thomas Ridges to 5,060 feet at Newton Bald. From the bald, the Benton MacKaye's highest point in the western half of the park, the trail descends eastward to where it crosses US 441 and the Oconaluftee River at Smokemont Campground.

Higher and higher, then down to Davenport. Once across the blacktop, the walkway rises beside the swift, clear waters of Bradley Fork and Chasteen Creek, heads up to and over Hughes Ridge, drops down Enloe Creek, fords the Raven Fork, skirts the upper south slope of Hyatt Bald, then advances to 5,070 feet at Beech Gap. Here, on Balsam Mountain's ridgeline, the path climbs into the highcountry. After ascending to 5,680 feet on Balsam High Top, the track follows Mount Sterling Ridge to the crown of its namesake peak—the proposed route's highest point at 5,840 feet. Down it goes from Sterling, losing over 4,000 feet of elevation before crossing Big Creek near its northern terminus at Davenport Gap, where the TN-NC line exits the park's northeastern corner. Completing the figure-eight loop that began at Springer Mountain, the BMT's northern terminus ties back into the good old AT.

Note: *During December of 2003, both the Cherokee and Nantahala National Forests gave the BMTA permission to proceed through their public lands. (See History of the Benton MacKaye Trail Association on page 9 for more information.) Upon completion, the Benton MacKaye will become much more than a long trail alternative to the AT in the Southern Appalachians. The BMT will also become a critical link in the 4,500-mile mega-trail called the Eastern Continental Trail, which will stretch all the way from Florida's Key West to Quebec's Gaspé Peninsula. The ECT is rapidly gaining miles and momentum. When completed, this international route will be the longest foot trail in North America.*

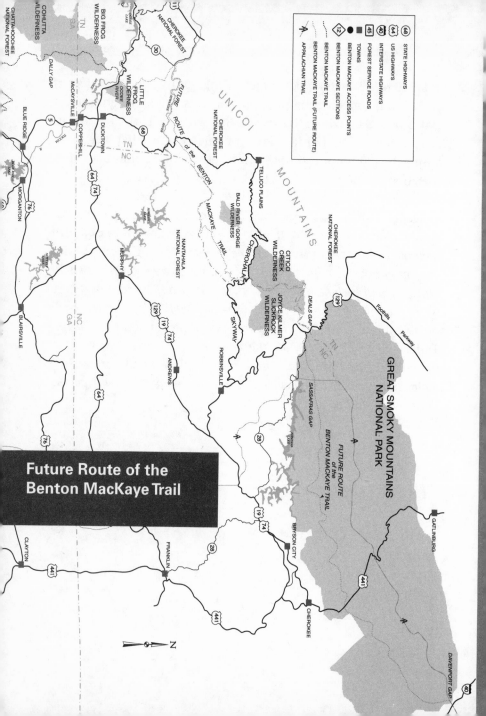

Future Route of the Benton MacKaye Trail

History of the Benton MacKaye Trail Association

IN 1921, THE *Journal of the American Institute of Architects* published Benton MacKaye's visionary proposal—"An Appalachian Trail: A Project in Regional Planning." His grand scheme called for a long trail over the full length of the Appalachian skyline, from the highest peak in the north to the highest peak in the south—from Mt. Washington to Mt. Mitchell. Forester by training, regional planner by aspiration, and mapmaker by compulsion, MacKaye drew his now well-known Appalachian Trail map to illustrate the breadth and boldness of his plan. In addition to the main route, MacKaye recommended a system of branch trails that would link other wild areas to the AT. He planned for two of these long branch trails to begin in southernmost Appalachia, routing them generally northeastward atop both forks of the Blue Ridge—east and west—to their junctions with the AT.

MacKaye's dream caught fire; it quickly drew enthusiastic support and soon expanded in scope and ambition. In 1937 volunteers finished the Appalachian Trail from north-central Maine all the way to north Georgia. Today, after numerous reroutes, the AT spans a spirit-stretching distance of approximately 2,170 miles. The southern extension of MacKaye's original plan, from North Carolina's Mount Mitchell to Georgia's Mount Oglethorpe, roughly followed his suggested branch trail along the eastern crest of the Blue Ridge. His branch trail route atop the western arm of the Blue Ridge was not constructed, at least not until recently.

The outdoor recreation boom that began in the 1970s led to congestion and environmental degradation on the Appalachian Trail. To help relieve this pressure the Forest Service, in conjunction with various hiking clubs, embarked upon a trail-building program in the southern mountains. The Forest Service and hundreds of strong volunteers constructed a system of longer trails—primitive footpaths without shelters or designated campsites—as an alternative to the increasingly bustling AT. Conceived in 1975 by David Sherman, then Georgia's DNR Director of the Office of Planning and Research, the aptly named Benton MacKaye Trail quickly become the most ambitious of the new footpaths located solely within the Southern Appalachians.

As envisioned by Sherman, a Benton MacKaye historian, the new route would stretch approximately 275 miles from its southern terminus atop Georgia's Springer Mountain to its northern terminus at Davenport Gap, located along the northeastern boundary of the Great Smoky Mountains National Park. Passing through Tennessee on its way to North Carolina, the finished treadway will roughly follow the rugged western crest of the Blue Ridge, linking another part of MacKaye's vision to reality. Plotted to join the AT at either end and to cross it in the western part of the national park, the completed Benton MacKaye Trail would create a lopsided figure-8 loop in combination with the AT. This configuration would provide backpackers with numerous permutations for multi-day or multi-month treks, ranging from one long section to both full loops south of Davenport Gap—a major hike of over 500 miles.

With crucial help from Roy Arnold and Steve Bowling, Sherman designed and sponsored a Benton MacKaye concept map. Plan in hand, Sherman sought support for his idea from the Forest Service and the hiking community, especially the Georgia

Appalachian Trail Club. Soon, a small but determined core of believers began to scout the trail and sketch the would-be path more precisely on topographic maps. Sherman left the DNR and Georgia in the fall of 1978. After Sherman's departure, Randy Snodgrass adopted and implemented his idea; he began the ongoing process of working wishful lines into walkable treadway.

IN APRIL OF 1980, a group of nearly fifty hikers, mostly GATC members, flagged Georgia's 80-mile portion of the route in one day. Later that spring, Snodgrass established the Benton MacKaye Trail Association. He and the Association's other founding members—Dave Sherman, George Owen, Margaret Drummond, Nancy Shofner, and Lyman Emerson—expended time, money, and sweat to simultaneously build and gain support for their new trail. The group chose Snodgrass, then Southeast Regional Director of the Wilderness Society, as their first president. He concentrated upon recruiting new members, versatile volunteers able to swing a Pulaski and promote the trail.

The rest of 1980 continued to be a time of productive enthusiasm and fundamental firsts for the newly formed BMTA. The organization opened its first post office box and its first bank account, mailed the initial issue of its monthly newsletter, held its first Association-sanctioned work trip, and opened its first BMTA-built trail segment.

Starting in June of 1980, hard-working members have volunteered for work trips on the second Saturday of every month, hot or cold, come hell or high water. But not high snow. Only two work sessions have been cancelled in twenty-four years; both times heavy snow made the dirt-gravel access roads impassable. The hiking club opened its first segment of treadway—from

Skeenah Gap to Rhodes Mountain, part of today's Section 3—on June 25 of that year.

Randy Snodgrass left Georgia and the BMTA late in the summer of 1981; the steadily growing membership elected Edwin Dale as the group's second president. Dale met with Forest Service officials, forging a working relationship between the Association and that federal agency to coordinate trail construction on public lands. This connection launched the Environmental Assessment process for approval of further BMT construction in Georgia's Chattahoochee National Forest. During the BMTA's early days, the Forest Service provided tools and expertise until the club accumulated enough money to purchase its own trail-building tools.

Today, through the continuing efforts of the Association's leaders, the BMTA maintains its close partnership with the U.S. Forest Service. The trail club and the Forest Service have worked together on numerous projects over the years, including the most impressive of them all—the 260-foot-long suspension bridge spanning the shoals of the Toccoa River.

IN THE EARLY 80s, the Forest Service completed an Environmental Assessment of the proposed Benton MacKaye Trail from Springer Mountain to Davenport Gap. At that time, the Forest Service gave the BMTA permission to build their trail to Double Spring Gap on the Georgia-Tennessee line. In 1982, the BMTA and the Forest Service signed a Memorandum of Understanding: a document that defined responsibilities and provided a formal framework for partnership and cooperation in the construction and maintenance of the Benton MacKaye Trail in Georgia's Chattahoochee National Forest.

Also in 1982, the organization established its first membership mailing list (later converted to computer database by Darcy Douglas), chose its first board of directors, and agreed upon its first by-laws. That same year Jeff Sewell, member of the bar as well as the BMTA, secured Articles of Incorporation and nonprofit tax status for the Association in Georgia. The club held its first weeklong work trip in 1984, on the trail segment between Stanley Creek Road and the Appalachian Highway. Subsequent weeklong work trips have been made to less accessible areas in Georgia and Tennessee. On those trips, hard-core members backpacked in with gear and tools, set up base camp, then worked their associations off without wasting all the time driving and walking to and from trailheads. Now annual events, these trail-building and member-bonding sessions have been successful, fun, and surprisingly well attended. Another annual event is the walk-through. Volunteers meet early in the morning, fan out to their segments, then collectively walk the entire trail, noting problems that need to be addressed in the upcoming year.

The first BMT maps, which appeared regularly in the early newsletters, were hand drawn. Later, engineer and BMTA member Marty Dominy crafted a series of professional-quality maps, and Edwin Dale wrote the text detailing distances, directions, and topographic data. The Association published and sold these maps in regional outdoor recreation stores and Forest Service offices. Updated to reflect reroutes and other changes, the maps are still available today.

Beginning atop Springer Mountain, the southern terminus of the AT, the white-diamond-blazed BMT passes the plaque commemorating Benton MacKaye before continuing north to Three Forks and FS 58. One-tenth mile before FS 58, the BMT turns right and shares the treadway with the Appalachian Trail for nearly a mile. After the BMT and AT split apart and go their separate ways, the Benton MacKaye makes a bridged crossing over Long Creek and joins the Duncan Ridge Trail. The Association's policy of sharing trail segments is a carefully designed arrangement, expeditious and beneficial in numerous ways. It speeds the approval process, saves huge amounts of work in what is already a labor-intensive endeavor, and prevents wild areas from becoming cross-hatched with trails. Sharing and helping to maintain existing treadways enabled the BMT to cross the Cohutta–Big Frog Wilderness and to become a largely primitive, long-distance trail now over the 90-mile mark.

BMTA work trip

Edwin Dale was re-elected every year until 1985, when he resigned and accepted an Outdoor Recreation Planner position with the Chattahoochee National Forest. During his ten-year tenure with the Toccoa Ranger District—the district the Benton MacKaye Trail crossed first—Dale served as a liaison with the BMTA and further cemented the working relationship between the Forest Service and the trail club.

From 1982 to 1989, the BMTA worked its footpath steadily northward: clearing treadway, painting blazes, putting up signs, installing water bars, building bridges, and rocking in steep pitches, all the while rerouting problem areas and maintaining existing trail. George Owen and Marty Dominy served as construction crew chiefs; they were instrumental in this strenuous effort.

In October of 1989, BMTA members and Forest Service employees held an all-day celebration at Dyer Gap to commemorate the completion of Georgia's portion of the trail, the now 81.6 miles from Springer Mountain to Double Spring Gap on the GA-TN border. Nearly a hundred people participated, joining together for speeches, food, music, and a ribbon-cutting ceremony. Shortly afterward, the BMTA entered into an agreement with Tennessee's Cherokee National Forest to begin trail conversion from the GA-TN border northward to the Ocoee River Gorge at US 64. Working together, the Forest Service and the BMTA completed the task by 1992.

As the Benton MacKaye moved northward to completion in Georgia, it began to gain momentum, to receive recognition and publicity for the function it fulfilled: a long-trail alternative to the AT in Georgia. In 1984, an article in *Brown's Guide* described the Rich Mountain Trail (now called Stanley Gap Trail and part of the BMT) between Stanley Creek Road and Aska Road south of Blue Ridge. Tim Homan included the BMT's southernmost 17.5 miles in his second edition (1986) of *The Hiking Trails of North Georgia*. In 1991, The National Geographic Society published *Pathways to Discovery*—a well-written book featuring beautiful photographs of our country's long-distance footpaths. A writer and photographer from the Society spent time with various members, went for a sample hike, and joined the group's work trip in preparation for the Benton MacKaye segment. In 1996, Tim Homan's third edition detailed ten sections of the BMT, from Springer Mountain to Double Spring Gap on the GA-TN line. Numerous other articles concerning the trail have appeared in various newpapers and outdoor-oriented magazines. The late John Harmon, former writer for the *Atlanta Journal-Constitution*, hiked the entire trail—weak from his battle with cancer. He shared the experience and beauty of his last long hike—the Benton MacKaye—in two full Sunday paper pages.

As the trail neared the Tennessee border in the late 1980s, BMTA membership from that state began to increase markedly. New leaders from Tennessee helped reassess and promote the hoped-for route through the Cherokee and Nantahala National Forests. Good-will ambassadors Clayton Pannell and Ken Jones have led a small work party of Tennessee volunteers on trail maintenance missions nearly every week since 1995. This determined crew not only helps maintain trails and trail segments along the proposed BMT route in Tennessee and North Carolina, but it also helps maintain footpaths well away from the Benton MacKaye's intended track. The efforts of Jones and Pannell have proved instrumental; they have also maintained a helpful, friendly dialogue with Cherokee National Forest officials throughout the lengthy approval process.

After the trail descended to US 64, the forward march of the white diamonds stalled in red tape, environmental assessments, and Forest Service reluctance. But the Association kept working, kept up their campaign of good will, and slowly chipped away at the requirements and resistance. Before a treadway can be constructed on public land, the National Environmental Policies Act (NEPA) demands three environmental assessments: archeological, hydrological, and biological, including both flora and fauna components. In the mid-1990s, the archeological and botanical assessments—paid for by the BMTA—were completed and submitted to the U.S. Forest Service. The Great Smoky Mountains National Park granted the Association written permission to complete their quest through the park's preserved lands in 1997, but would not allow any trail conversion to occur before the group gained permission to cross the Cherokee and Nantahala National Forests.

Early in 1998, club members completed a crucial link of tread-way across private property along the Tennessee–North Carolina border, bridging the public lands between the Nantahala National Forest and the Great Smoky Mountains National Park. The BMTA publicly extends its appreciation to the Land Management Division of Alcoa Aluminum for permitting the trail to pass through their holdings.

F OR A VARIETY OF REASONS, the approval process bogged down during the five-year period from 1997 to 2001. The botanical assessment proved especially problematic. As time passed after the first survey, new species were added to the watch list and the mid-1990s survey became outdated and obsolete. The Forest Service agreed to pay for and conduct a second assessment.

During 2002, twenty years after signing its first Memorandum with Georgia's Chattahoochee National Forest, the Association signed a Memorandum of Understanding with the Cherokee and Nantahala National Forests. The Forest Service completed the second botanical survey during the summer of 2003. By late autumn 2003, all of the NEPA assessments were completed; the various reports were written, printed, and submitted. Following a public-comment period, officials from both national forests—Cherokee and Nantahala—gave their final written approval for the extension of the BMT through their public lands in December 2003. A crew led by Ken Jones and Clayton Pannell kicked off the official march to Davenport Gap with a work trip on December 23, 2003.

The year 2004 promises to be one of renewed momentum for the BMTA: the Association will continue trail construction and conversion in Tennessee and North Carolina, and the first Benton MacKaye guide book will be published in the spring. Now that the green light has been given to the full-length version of the BMT, Association members are eager to get out in the woods and finish the job. But don't despair, there is plenty of work for everybody, and we—the BMTA—can always use more volunteers, more good people to help us construct and maintain our soon-to-be 275-mile-long trail.

—Darcy Douglas

Benton MacKaye: A Brief Biography

EMILE BENTON WAS BORN the fifth of six children to Mary and Steele MacKaye (rhymes with sky) in Stamford, Connecticut, on March 6, 1879. Steele, son of the wealthy and distinguished Colonel James MacKaye, expressed his creative talents in a variety of occupations: actor, playwright, producer, promoter, and inventor. While brilliant and hardworking, Steele was often indifferent to the commercial side of show business. Late in the year of Benton's birth, the family began a series of financially motivated moves to large metropolitan areas and various homes throughout southern New England. During the summer of 1887 the family visited the small village of Shirley Center, Massachusetts, which became MacKaye's rural retreat for the rest of his life.

Benton's grandfather died in 1888; through a series of convoluted events, his parents did not inherit a dime of the Colonel's considerable fortune. During the winter of 1890–1891, the hard-pressed family moved to Washington, D.C. There, instead of enrolling him in school, Benton's parents allowed him to spend his days at the Smithsonian Institute, where he attended lectures by John Wesley Powell and Robert Peary and began his lifelong pattern of intense, self-directed study. In Washington, as elsewhere, the MacKaye household was a hub of intellectual activity; the older boys—soon to become author, professor, and playwright—wrote and acted out plays. Most evenings the family read aloud on the subjects of evolutionary philosophy and natural history, Benton's early interest.

The following summer the family purchased—with money borrowed from an aunt—a cottage at Shirley Center, where they spent most summers between recurring financial crises and moves. Young Benton flourished in the freedom of the community's rural surroundings. During the summer of 1892, at age thirteen, he completed a series of geographic rambles, which he described in "Expedition 9," a booklet illustrated with the first of his detailed, hand-drawn maps, one of his lifelong trademarks.

During the next two winters, Benton attended a small private school in New York City, where he embarked on another disciplined program of self-education in zoology, natural history, and geography. In the spring of 1893, Benton's father died shortly after his final grand project flopped, plunging the family further into poverty. The remaining MacKayes moved back to their refuge in Shirley Center, long a hotbed of utopian and spiritual experiments.

At fifteen, Benton enrolled at Boston's Cambridge Latin School to prepare for the entrance examinations at Harvard, where brothers James and Percy were already achieving academic excellence. The school's exacting curriculum interfered with Benton's self-education, so he quit and prepared for the tests on his own. He entered Harvard as a seventeen-year-old freshman in October of 1896. After a lackluster performance his first year, the young scholar discovered his academic niche in courses he found both useful and interesting: geography, geology, and other earth science classes.

At eighteen, after his freshman year, he set out on the first of the numerous treks he would make to the mountains of northern New England, where he first experienced wilderness—and first witnessed the destruction of cut-everything-and-run logging. Every summer from 1897 to 1905, he spent his vacations exploring New England's mountains and forests. After graduating in the spring of 1900, the tall, long-legged adventurer traveled to

Vermont, where he climbed as many peaks as he could with brother Percy and a friend. It was on this trip that he first conceived and discussed his idea for a long-distance, Appalachian-skyline trail linking north to south.

Undecided about his career, Benton tutored wealthy schoolboys in New York City for the next three academic years. In September of 1903, MacKaye suffered an attack of appendicitis. Late at night, by the light of kerosene lanterns, a rural doctor performed an emergency appendectomy while the young man lay on the family cottage's kitchen table. This brush with mortality jolted MacKaye out of his vocational indecision: he would become a forester, affording him the opportunity to manage and protect the New England wilds he had come to love. Within weeks after surgery, MacKaye registered in the program that earned him Harvard's first graduate degree in forestry. He completed his studies in the spring of 1905, just as the 86 million acres of federally owned forest reserves (renamed national forests) transferred from the Interior Department to Gifford Pinchot's division of the Agriculture Department: the United States Forest Service.

BENTON MACKAYE ACCEPTED his first federal government position as a forest assistant, alternating summer forestry assignments, often to remote places such as eastern Kentucky or the Adirondacks, with academic-year teaching at Harvard's forestry school. In 1908, he authored a position paper delivered by Harvard to a congressional hearing, arguing for legislation to create national forests in the East.

By 1909, the year William Taft took office, Benton and his two brothers were at the vortex of the Harvard Socialist Club, a group of left-wing activists headed by Walter Lippmann. That same year he became engaged to Mabel Abbot, a promising, muckraking journalist who specialized in natural resource issues. The now thirty-year-old forestry instructor actively collaborated with his ambitious fiancée in her efforts to expose state and federal corruption in the extraction industries, primarily logging and mining.

In the spring of 1910, he received a letter stating, without explanation, that he would no longer be teaching at Harvard. In all likelihood, his left-wing politics and behind-the-scenes involvement in national conservation issues, often controversial, cost him his job.

In 1911 the Weeks Act authorized the creation of new national forests in the East, and Miss Abbot became the center of a national controversy after she directly implicated President Taft in a corrupt mining scheme. Mabel had her moxie, but the president had his power. Taft quickly broke her rake and ruined her career. Not long after this incident, the two sweethearts went their separate ways.

Unemployed and unattached, MacKaye worked as hard as ever, this time writing a forestry textbook titled *A Theory of Forest Management*. He failed to find a publisher for his work, but he did send the manuscript to the new Forest Service chief, who promptly offered him the position of forest examiner.

When the lanky New Englander began his full-time forestry duties in 1911, the fervent spirit of the Progressive Era was near its zenith. At first, President Taft continued many of Roosevelt's progressive policies, but he became steadily more conservative throughout his administration. Before long MacKaye was entrenched in the political and intellectual circles that included many leaders of the nascent conservation movement, as well as many of Washington's prominent liberal and left-wing activists. MacKaye and his activist colleagues worked behind the scenes, writing legislation and speeches for congressmen, promoting their social and conservation causes within governmental agencies. He wrote progressive legislation for Alaskan development, and although his proxy bill was soundly defeated, it did lead to a congressional compromise that set the important precedent for the lease of mineral rights rather than the outright sale of lands from the public domain.

DURING THE NEXT FEW YEARS MacKaye alternated deskbound duties in Washington with fieldwork—projects such as studying watersheds in the White Mountains of New Hampshire or surveying the conditions of the cutover lands in the Great Lakes states. His research and subsequent report on his findings in the White Mountains rank among his greatest achievements. Congressional opponents of the Weeks Act directed the U.S. Geological Survey (rather than the Forest Service, whose leaders they considered to be empire builders) to undertake a scientific study to determine whether careful management of headwater forests would have a major impact on the flow of navigable waters downstream. The USGS designed the required study, but needed an experienced forester to record measurements in the White Mountains, which were to be the test case. Because of his expertise, his familiarity with the region, and his adamant pro-public ownership stance, the Forest Service loaned MacKaye to the USGS for the summer of 1912. Benton spent those three months carefully collecting hydrological data.

Back in Washington, MacKaye produced an exceptional report—complete with charts, tables, and, of course, his wonderfully detailed, hand-drawn maps. His in-depth analysis became an instrumental part of the Survey's document, which enabled the Weeks Act to withstand numerous court challenges. MacKaye proved that careful watershed management could not only lessen, or in some cases prevent, economically ruinous flooding, but it could also help provide a sustained downstream flow in navigable rivers during the summer months. His accomplishment proved vital to the creation of eastern national forests, without which there would be no Appalachian or Benton MacKaye Trails, no Chattooga National Wild and Scenic River or Cohutta Wilderness, and no public-land hiking in the mountains of North Georgia save in state parks and a very few wildlife management areas.

In 1914, Benton met Jessie Hardy Stubbs, "Betty," who had spent two decades as a lecturer, writer, political campaign worker, and irrepressible advocate for women's suffrage. The two became husband and wife on June 1, 1915. Back in Washington after a second tour in the devastated forests of the Great Lakes region, MacKaye mounted a crusade to reform federal natural resource development policies. He favored increased public ownership and regulation of the nation's forests, and he worried that the Forest Service was becoming an unofficial branch of the timber industry.

With the support from a few key conservationists in the Forest Service, Benton wrote extensively, promoting a sustained-yield forestry that would support stable communities of workers. He persuaded a congressman to sponsor his legislation—The National Colonization Bill of 1916—which never made it out of committee. In that year he also wrote a magazine article recommending a shift toward recreation as a high-priority use of national forest land. In his 1917 essay "The Great Problem of Recreation," MacKaye broached the subject of a long trail connecting the northern and southern Appalachians, complete with a network of tributary trails tying into the main trunk. He also urged the protection of rivers as "scenic highways."

After investigating the squalid forestry conditions in the Pacific Northwest, he completed his 272-page report—"Colonization of Timberlands: Permanent Human Communities on Public Land." His report proposed, once again, sustained-yield logging and permanent communities of timber-industry employees as opposed to the status quo: unlimited clear-cutting and the squalor of transient lumberjack camps. Ahead of his time and sawing against the grain as usual, MacKaye's ideas were increasingly at odds with Forest Service policies. In January of 1918 he was transferred to the Labor Department, where he continued his extensive work on various colonization and land settlement programs. Government interest in large-scale public works and resettlement programs waned after the 1918 congressional election. He resigned from his position with the Labor Department in July of 1919.

A YEAR LATER MACKAYE BECAME an editorial writer for the *Milwaukee Leader*, a socialist newspaper. There he wrote articles protesting a plan to build a dam in Yellowstone National Park, promoting the social importance of recreation, and urging increased public ownership of national parks and national forests. He left the paper late in 1920, returning to New York to pursue his self-designed career as a regional planner. On April 19, 1921, his wife Betty—suffering from depression, exhaustion, and heart problems—committed suicide. MacKaye remained single for the rest of his long life.

After Betty's death, Benton immersed himself in his work. His now famous article, "An Appalachian Trail: A Project in Regional Planning," appeared in the *Journal of the American Institute of Architects* in October of 1921. His proposal, which included one of his hand-drawn maps, called for the construction of a trail along the Appalachian skyline, from the highest mountain in the north to the highest mountain in the south, from New Hampshire's Mount Washington to North Carolina's Mount Mitchell. In addition to the proposed feeder trails, MacKaye resurrected his population redistribution plans in the form of shelter camps, community camps, and food and farm camps.

Benton MacKaye

His long-trail idea won immediate support from numerous influential people, including former head of the Forest Service, Gifford Pinchot. MacKaye attended that year's New England Trail Conference meeting, where his long-trail plan met with enthusiastic approval. For the next few years, Benton MacKaye became the Appalachian Trail's unpaid ambassador, traveling from city to city promoting the project, recruiting strategic individuals and organizations, weaving the network that would eventually comprise the permanent community of trail builders.

Early on, his vision expanded northward and southward, linking Georgia to Maine. By the end of 1922, MacKaye's idea had gained traction; outdoor clubs and public officials were organizing, scouting, and constructing new trails from the White Mountains to the Great Smokies. At the next New England Trail Conference meeting he gave an impassioned speech promoting the AT as the focal point of a publicly owned "super national forest" stretching from Georgia to Maine. He fervently believed the populous East needed a wilderness refuge—for recreation and for a buffer against the metropolitan invasion—to match the extensive public lands in the West.

In 1922 Benton MacKaye became a founding member of the Regional Planning Association of America, a prestigious group whose membership included architect Clarence Stein and author Lewis Mumford, his two most loyal friends, financial patrons, and intellectual sounding boards. The RPAA paid him periodic stipends to support his work as a one-man think tank, writer, and guiding intellect of the regional planning movement. During the next three years he completed regional plans for both the state of New York and the Appalachian Trail. He also helped organize the first Appalachian Trail Conference, which convened in March of 1925.

Despite the obvious lack of support among conference attendees for the socialist aspects of his plan, MacKaye would not jettison his plans for Community Camps and Food and Farm Camps. The increasingly middle-class, professional leadership of the hiking clubs strongly favored the construction of his trail, but they did not endorse the social engineering of his colonies and camps. The thin and still-fit ex-forester was recruited as Field Organizer at this first conference, and plans were made to raise 5,000 dollars to finance his projected efforts in the Appalachians. By design, however, he was not named to the group's executive committee. The fieldwork money never materialized, so Benton moved back to his frugal life at Shirley Center, where he wrote, studied, and continued his unrelenting quest as self-assigned regional planner.

In 1927, MacKaye argued for planned communities incorporating belts of open space following the course of local hills and rivers: greenways. That same year he landed a job with the Massachusetts Governor's Committee on the Needs and Uses of Open Spaces, where he drafted recommendations for an open-space protection program. He submitted a detailed plan for an integrated network of linear "wilderness ways" and open-space belts for all of Massachusetts. Such spaces, he argued, would make the state more habitable, and would control the metropolitan invasion. MacKaye was among the first to diagnose and fight against what we now condemn as urban sprawl. The state's political and economic elite, however, did not accept his ambitious land-acquisition program or the regulatory guidelines he always included. His plan was enacted but never implemented.

A YEAR LATER, HARCOURT BRACE published Benton MacKaye's most important opus—*The New Exploration: A Philosophy of Regional Planning*. The ideas in *The New Exploration*, a series of inspirational essays that included a plea for wilderness preservation, remain central in today's smart growth and new urbanism movements. From 1928 to 1931 Benton toiled "to influence the ecology of the human community" on two fronts: the Appalachian Trail and the Townless Highway. With renewed energy he devoted even more attention to the AT, making inspirational speeches at conference meetings, urging public ownership of the wilderness lands traversed by the trail, and evolving into the footpath's leading philosopher and conscience. At the same time MacKaye envisioned a national program for controlling the automobile's enormous impact on almost every aspect of American life. His Townless Highway plan called for a less invasive national highway program, designed to protect the landscape and foster cultural development. He championed zoning controls and limited access—both important components of today's interstate highway system.

In 1931, Myron Avery was elected ATC chairman, a position he would hold for more than twenty years. Immediately after Avery ascended to the ATC throne, he and MacKaye clashed; resentments quickly built to the boiling point, and soon the two titans were no longer on speaking terms. As is often the case with large-scale, multi-faceted tasks, the completion of the AT from drawn line to cleared treadway required different personalities, different leaders for different phases of the project. The philosopher-idealist MacKaye worked with a broad brush; he supplied the articulated vision, the inspiration, and the charisma to persuade movers and shakers to support the trail. The driven Avery, by all accounts a triple-A personality, worked with nuts and bolts and blazes; he concerned himself with the every-weekend details of organization, trail building, and whip snapping.

After Franklin Roosevelt was elected in 1932, Benton MacKaye pushed his own regional planning ideas for New Deal public works projects, including the super forest from Georgia to Maine as part of an integrated Appalachian development plan. In April of that year, he met and discussed wildland preservation with Bob Marshall, the driving force behind the creation of the Wilderness Society. During a short stint with the Emergency Conservation Work, he worked with fellow wilderness proponent Aldo Leopold in Arizona's Navaho Reservation. In Marshall and Leopold, MacKaye found kindred spirits who were inventing a new philosophical and ethical perspective on wilderness.

In the spring of 1934, Benton MacKaye procured a TVA position, with the long-sought-after title of regional planner, which lasted into the summer of 1936. He soon proposed a grand scheme of public ownership, wilderness belts, hiking trails, working forests, and new communities. During his first summer on the job, he pressed his TVA bosses to create a TVA-managed wilderness in North Carolina's Linville Gorge, now a federally designated wilderness. The pattern of his federal career continued; the small and relatively powerless idealist faction of the TVA lost most of its major battles with the dominant conservative wing. Today the TVA manages a small system of natural areas with hiking trails.

Late in 1934, MacKaye helped draft the Wilderness Society's founding charter. In January of 1935, he met with Marshall and other wilderness advocates to create a more detailed statement of the Wilderness Society's principles. That same year he authored a National Scenic Resources Law, which included the first legislative proposal for a national wilderness system. Neither his first nor his second attempt ten years later ever escaped committee. These

AT plaque atop Springer Mountain

early attempts did, however, help nudge the concept of wilderness preservation closer to the middle of the political spectrum.

During the decade after leaving the TVA at age fifty-seven, MacKaye returned to the federal government twice, working for the Forest Service and the Rural Electricity Administration. When not employed by federal agencies, he visited friends or lived frugally at Shirley Center, planning, proposing, writing, and, as always, searching for work to match his talents and undiluted idealism. Benton MacKaye was elected vice-president of the Wilderness Society in 1937, the same year the AT was completed from Mount Katahdin, Maine, to Mount Oglethorpe, Georgia. He was elected president of the Wilderness Society in 1945, the year he retired from his last government position at age sixty-six. During his five-year tenure, he assumed the same inspirational and oracular role that he had with the ATC. In his articles for the Society's magazine, *The Living Wilderness*, he spoke on the pressing need for a worldwide conservation ethic. The year Benton turned seventy-one, 1950, he left the helm of the Wilderness Society; the organization elected him honorary president, a post he held until his death twenty-five years later.

In the early 1950s MacKaye began an intensive regimen of reading and research, laying the groundwork for what he hoped would be his final masterpiece—*Geotechnics of North America: Viewpoints of Its Habitability*. Continually revised, rewritten, and reinvented, this massive work occupied MacKaye—between speeches, article writing, and activist forays—until the late 1960s, by which time his eyesight had deteriorated severely. The reform-minded journal *Survey* published a series of his articles and essays on geotechnics—the applied science of making the earth more habitable—in 1950 and 1951. In one of those pieces he advocated a global law to regulate commerce and the administration of Antarctica as "a common treasure trove" under United Nations jurisdiction. In still another article he wrote, "We must match nature's ecology with geotechnics, or perish. Is there some rule of thumb for this vast consummation? Verily, the first and simplest rule on earth: Give back to the earth that which we take from her. Return the goods we have borrowed; in short, pay our ecological bills."

The University of Illinois Press reprinted his book *New Exploration* in 1962. The press also expressed interest in his *Geotechnics of North America*. At the end of 1965, Benton sent his manuscript—over 800 pages—to the copy editors; after the ensuing disagreements, a contract was never offered. As he approached ninety, he finally stopped work on the project. It was never published in book form.

BENTON MACKAYE LIVED long enough to witness many of his ideas and efforts become legislative reality. Lyndon B. Johnson signed The Wilderness Act in September of 1964. The National Trails System law passed in 1968, designating the Appalachian and the Pacific Crest as the first two National Scenic Trails. The act provided funding for acquiring a protective corridor for the AT through private property. It was a mere sliver of the super national forest MacKaye had recommended in the 1920s; nevertheless, it was protection for the trail he had long sought. The National Wild and Scenic Rivers Act became law in that same year. During the 1960s, Massachusetts began acquiring land along some of its wilder rivers, the same watercourses MacKaye had proposed preserving as Wilderness Ways forty years earlier.

Benton MacKaye received the Department of the Interior's Conservation Service Award in the summer of 1966. After the ceremony he handed the officials his detailed plan for combining nationwide wilderness trails with nationwide wildernesses, including a Continental Divide Trail, which, unknown to MacKaye, the government was already studying. On that day, seemingly for the first time, the federal government had come up with a recreation idea for wild land before Benton—proof that he was slipping in his old age.

In 1968, the University of Illinois published *From Geography to Geotechnics*, a collection of articles spanning MacKaye's career. And in 1969, on the occasion of Benton's ninetieth birthday, the Wilderness Society published *Expedition Nine* in his honor.

Throughout the 1960s and early 1970s, a steady stream of scholars, journalists, biographers, and AT hikers made the pilgrimage to Shirley Center, to talk to the "living memory of the American Conservation Movement." An activist to the end, he responded to the turmoil of the era with a steady flow of letters and editorials. Even after he was nearly blind, he continued to write and correspond with the help of volunteers.

During the 1950s (Myron Avery died in 1952), MacKaye renewed friendly relations with the ATC leadership, once again making inspirational speeches as he pushed for federal protection of the AT corridor. His caregiver and friend Lucy Johnson delivered his final speech to the ATC meeting in 1975, where his words received a wildly enthusiastic ovation. Benton MacKaye died on December 11, 1975. His ninety-six years spanned the technological bridge between horse and buggy and manned moon-flight. His persistent efforts helped to close the cultural gap between laissez-faire logging and federally designated wilderness.

His ideas continue to improve our culture and our lives. MacKaye called for planned communities and railed against metropolitan invasion long before either concept became popular. Early on, he proposed that the populous states in the East begin systematic open-space preservation. Not long ago, part of his green-space program for Massachusetts was resurrected by Robert Yaro. When Yaro was a visiting professor at the University of

Massachusetts, he discovered MacKaye's 1928 plan to create the Bay Circuit—a belt of parkways, parks, and trails encircling the greater Boston area. In the intervening years MacKaye's corridor, authorized but never funded, had become the Route 128 Super-highway, yet much of the landscape remained unscathed. Working for the state in the late-1980s, Yaro began implementing a modification of MacKaye's plan, purchasing land for trails and conservation, for beauty and tranquility.

Note: *Benton MacKaye spent most of his long life as an immigrant in the realm of ideas: an immigrant who worked extremely hard, played little, and struggled mightily, though often impoverished, to preserve our country's natural resources and to make the earth more habitable for future generations. At first glance, some might think him stubbornly oblivious to political and economic realities, but they would have the wrong measure of the man. Benton MacKaye was no starry-eyed idealist; he knew what he was up against. He knew the odds were almost always stacked against quick and meaningful change. But he never stuck his forefinger up in the air to feel which way the wind was blowing. He courageously and steadfastly clung to his ideals and convictions, though at times it cost him dearly. He knew that ideas, like forests, are transformed through successional change. He knew that Kitty Hawks always come before Cape Canaverals, and that many ideas must be nursed and nudged into the center of public debate. Though his vision of a better world was often tethered to a hundred hindrances, he spoke throughout his life with two positive voices: the insistent and unapologetic voice of an activist, and the hopeful voice of an optimist.*

Benton MacKaye's ninety-six years of people, places, vision, prophesy, environmental and social activism, government reports, articles, essays and books (published or not), lively wit, raconteurial talent, regional planning, Appalachian Trail work, and wildland preservation efforts cannot be distilled adequately into a few pages. His life and intellect were too large for quick categorization. Beyond conservation and regional planning, which included industrial organization, he contributed to many noteworthy social and intellectual causes, including women's suffrage, labor reform, and nuclear disarmament.

*Most of my facts came from Larry Anderson's excellent biography—*Benton MacKaye: Conservationist, Planner, and Creator of the Appalachian Trail, *published by the Johns Hopkins University Press in 2002. The following summation comes directly from Anderson: "Benton MacKaye surmounted many personal and professional impediments during his resolutely unconventional American life, which was zestfully pursued on a plane of extraordinary idealism, hope and vision."*

—T. H.

Geology of the Benton MacKaye Trail

THE BENTON MACKAYE TRAIL lies entirely within the Blue Ridge Province of the Southern Appalachian Mountains. In north Georgia, the Blue Ridge Province consists of moderately metamorphosed rocks that were originally layers of sediment deposited on the ancient continental shelf of North America approximately 600 million years ago. These deposits were much like the ones being laid down on the present-day continental shelf, e.g., sand, silt, mud, and some limey sediments, but were deeply buried, compressed, and turned into metamorphic rocks. They were finally folded, uplifted, and shoved westward into their present location approximately 245 million years ago when Africa collided with North America.

The geological process that converts rocks from sedimentary to metamorphic creates a different kind of layering known as "foliation." That process often turns the minerals in sedimentary materials into different and harder minerals in the metamorphic rocks. Clays in the original sediments turn into micas, and pre-existing micas become larger. These micas are stratified, which gives metamorphic rocks their foliated appearance. Mica flakes range from microscopic (hundredths of an inch) to approximately 1 inch in width. If the original deposit had no clays, the metamorphic rocks won't be distinctly foliated, if at all.

Geologists classify foliated metamorphic rocks by the thickness of their foliations and the size of their crystals. The larger the micas, the shinier the rock. Slate has a dull appearance due to its microscopic micas. Phyllite, which can appear almost waxy, is shinier than slate, and schist sparkles because of its large mica flakes. The foliated metamorphic rock that has alternating bands of light and dark minerals is called gneiss (pronounced "nice"). The micas in gneiss were changed into feldspar, hornblende, and other materials.

All these rock types are found along the Benton MacKaye Trail. For much of the first half of the trail, look for glittering mica flakes in the soil or embedded in small rocks. This sparkle comes from a mica schist. Most of the white or silvery mica flakes come from the mineral muscovite. Black mica is called biotite. Both micas exist in the schists along the trail. You may also find pieces of a yellowish-brown rock—pale, translucent, and sharp-edged—that appears hard and crystalline. This is vein quartz, the mineral that filled cracks in the rocks that opened when the land was uplifted and folded during the last orogeny. In some places, you might encounter a grainy-looking rock that doesn't appear foliated. Under a magnifying glass, it looks like salt and pepper. This is meta-graywacke—a metamorphosed form of sandstone. Occasionally, you might discover a hard, grainy-looking rock that looks like the vein quartz but is actually quartzite, another type of metamorphosed sandstone.

Near Maxwell, where the Benton MacKaye crosses US 76, the trail passes over a nearly vertical bedding of thinly layered schist and phyllite. In some locations, the phyllite appears almost black and slightly glittery on a freshly broken surface. The black rubs off on your fingers. This smudging is due to the mineral graphite, metamorphosed from a dark, organic shale. In this same area, some phyllite exhibits a waxy greenish color with reddish hues. Because the rocks along US 76 are folded into a tight "syncline," or downfold, the layers will be repeated on the northwest side of the highway.

Because they contain so much mica and clay minerals, the rock layers along US 76 are easily weathered. This fact explains why there is a prominent valley here; the presence of the valley explains why the major highway is here. Farther north and south, this valley contains marble, which is metamorphosed limestone.

North of Bushy Head Gap, the trail is again dominated by mica schists, but with more layers of gneiss and a black, crystalline rock called amphibolite. Under a magnifying glass, amphibolite looks like a pile of tiny black needles all lined up in the same direction. The light-colored minerals in the gneiss are composed mostly of quartz and muscovite, and the dark layers consist mainly of biotite. In the rainy Southern Appalachians, biotite weathers away quite easily, leaving glittering muscovite flakes and quartz sand as erosional remnants along the trail.

—Rob McDowell,
Georgia Department of Natural Resources

Forests of the Benton MacKaye Trail

IMMENSELY ANCIENT, never glaciated from the north nor flooded from the south, the Southern Appalachians are refugia for one of the most diverse temperate-zone forests in the world. Your experience on the Benton MacKaye will be enhanced if you observe the impressive array of trees, shrubs, vines, and wildflowers along the trail. If you look closely, you will soon notice that certain species occur in groups closely related to elevation, topography, exposure, and soil type. The species groups that are the easiest to recognize are oak-hickory, oak-pine, cove hardwoods, bottomland hardwoods, northern hardwoods, yellow poplar, white pine, eastern hemlock, and Virginia pine.

The dominant forest type within the Benton MacKaye corridor is oak-hickory. This is a large and varied category, occupying well-drained to dry ridges and south- to west-facing slopes. Major species include white oak, southern red oak, northern red oak, black oak, pignut hickory, and mockernut hickory. On higher, drier, and rockier areas, chestnut oak, black locust, and scarlet oak are common. Minor species in the oak-hickory forest include red maple, sourwood, blackgum, sassafras, and three kinds of pine—shortleaf, Virginia, and white. This forest was formerly dominated by the American chestnut. Once the thickest tree in the Southern Appalachians, the chestnut is still common, but it is limited to sprouts from old stumps, which usually grow to about two inches in diameter before the blight kills them back to the roots. Oak-hickory is important to wildlife since most mammals and some birds feast on acorns and nuts.

Other forest types are intermixed with the oak-hickory matrix, depending largely on soil quality and moisture, elevation, exposure, position on slope, and history of disturbance—logging, agricultural clearing or cultivating, and fire. Yellow poplar, both by itself and as a major component of cove hardwoods, is probably the most extensive of these secondary types. Yellow poplar, also known as tulip poplar and tuliptree, is frequently found in nearly pure stands on rich, well-drained soil in coves and on broad ridges and gaps. Associated species, especially in coves, include white pine, black cherry, black (sweet) birch, northern red oak, yellow buckeye, American beech, white ash, basswood, and red maple.

White pine thrives in Georgia's portion of the Southern Appalachian forest, and sometimes forms nearly pure stands. Barring disease, the white pine will be more abundant in the future. It is currently common in the understory, and since it is more shade tolerant than other pines, it will become a major part of the canopy in the next few decades.

Eastern hemlock is often plentiful where the trail dips down into stream valleys. A notable stand of hemlock is found along the South Fork of the Jacks River; this species also dominates both sides of the Toccoa River by the suspension bridge. Old-growth hemlocks, many 200 to 300 years old, are fairly common near the creeks in the Three Forks area. In most of these lower-slope and bottom sites, it is mixed with white pine.

An early successional species, Virginia pine mingles with oak-hickory on the drier, rockier, south-facing slopes, and it also forms nearly pure stands. But unlike the white pine, the Virginia is intolerant of shade, so it is most common on sites that have been cleared for timber or agriculture. If the forest is left undisturbed, the Virginia pine will gradually be replaced by the more shade-tolerant members of the oak-hickory group.

The northern hardwood assemblage is found along Sections 1 through 12 of the BMT in only one location—the top and upper-north slope of Big Frog Mountain. This group of species, which is common in New England and the Great Lake states, extends southward along the highest elevations of the Appalachian chain to the northern border of Georgia. Major species are sugar maple, yellow birch, and beech; associated species include hemlock, red maple, basswood, white ash, black cherry, and yellow buckeye.

The bottomland hardwood forest, as a distinct type, is somewhat rare beside the Benton MacKaye Trail. Many of the trees in this group are dependent on alluvial soils found on floodplains—a habitat in short supply within the BMT corridor. Nevertheless, you may encounter this interesting mix of broadleafs, a partial list of which includes sycamore, river birch, green ash, boxelder, red maple, sweetgum, and American hornbeam (ironwood). The best example of this forest is near the northern end of Section 12, where the treadway briefly descends into the Ocoee River floodplain.

—Walt Cook

Things to Know Before You Go

Wildland hiking brings many rewards—solitude; views of ancient mountains; slopes covered with spring wildflowers; clear, cold cascading streams—but this kind of hiking also presents challenges. The following information will help dayhikers and backpackers plan for trips and will help them become aware of what to expect on the Benton MacKaye Trail.

Water

Water along the Benton MacKaye Trail—even from high springs, rivulets, and branches, cold and clear and inviting—should be purified before drinking. Giardia and other harmful microorganisms are much more prevalent than they were thirty years ago.

There are three general ways to purify water: boil it, filter it, or treat it. Because of the time and fuel required, boiling is usually considered impractical. A reliable filter that will remove at least all particles larger than 0.4 microns will do the job. If you have had trouble with your filter clogging up and slowing down, try tie-twisting a coffee filter around the pre-filter uptake acorn. You can also use water purification tablets. How-to books and hiking magazines recommend tablets that employ iodine as their purifying agent. The iodine-based tablets are safer and more effective (they retain their potency longer after the bottle has been opened) than the others. Recent publications have expressed health concerns associated with prolonged use of chemical tablets.

Stream Crossings

Under normal to high-water conditions, the Benton MacKaye's southernmost twelve sections do not demand any dangerous stream crossings. The West Fork Rough Creek in the bridgeless Big Frog Wilderness, however, can become too high and swift for safe fording right after heavy rain, especially during the colder seasons when the trees are not taking up water. Section 11 crosses the West Fork three times, and under most conditions you scarcely get your feet wet. But when the West Fork's steep-sided watershed receives inches of rain in a short span of time, it can flood rapidly. As always, it is your call.

Cold-weather Hiking and Hypothermia

Many hikers consider winter, with its solitude, unobstructed views, and snowy landscapes, the best time of the year to hike. For the unprepared and inexperienced, however, winter hiking can be as dangerous as it is beautiful.

Do not underestimate the severity of the weather conditions you will be likely to encounter. Especially at the higher elevations, be prepared for temperatures near or below zero and expect fierce winds on unprotected ridges. Even in mid-March, when high temperatures in the 50s are predicted for the large cities south of the mountains, you may have to contend with freezing temperatures and snow at the higher elevations. Keep in mind that if all other conditions are equal, for every 1,000-foot gain in elevation, the temperature drops from 2.5 to 3.0 degrees.

Use your compass, map, and common sense to find the most comfortable campsite. Gaps, especially the deep ones, are wind funnels when cold fronts whistle through. To take advantage of early morning sun, choose slopes and ridgelines facing from east to south. If a cold wind is coming from the northwest, for example, try slipping down onto a southeast-facing slope or hollow for maximum wind protection and warming from the sun.

All cold-weather hikers should be aware of hypothermia, its symptoms and treatment. Hypothermia is a lowering of body temperature. A drop of only 5 degrees is very serious. Few people whose body temperature drops more than 10 degrees survive.

What causes hypothermia? It is caused by exposure to low temperatures; it can occur in dry air temperatures as high as 41 degrees Fahrenheit. Wetness and exhaustion intensify the effects of the cold. Many people have died of hypothermia because, thinking they could warm up by keeping in motion, they did not stop to take necessary precautions, such as putting on a dry sweater or rain gear. Wet clothes can lead to heat loss and greatly increase your chances of hypothermia.

What are the symptoms? The first symptom is shivering. Continued shivering is serious. Shivering may be followed by slurred speech, impaired judgment, weakness, and loss of coordination. The final symptom is unconsciousness.

What can you do when someone is suffering from hypothermia? Get the person into warm clothes. Make the patient rest. Give him or her hot drinks and food, the more calories the better. If the condition is serious, put the victim in a sleeping bag with another person, the bigger and warmer the bag and snuggler the better. Make a fire. Put up a tent or make a shelter. As soon as possible, transport the person to a hospital for further treatment. Do not continue your trip after one of your party has had hypothermia.

Note: *Hypothermia information courtesy of the United States Forest Service.*

Poison Ivy

Poison ivy grows beside every long-distance trail in the North Georgia mountains. Like many of the other routes, the Benton MacKaye leads you through some memorable gauntlets; these stretches, however, can serve to make the path more challenging, to make your feet more attentive. If you wear boots and long pants, and watch more closely where you step when ivy is flanking the treadway, you should be fine. If you are strongly allergic, carry a pair of gaiters and put them on over your pants when you have to go through a patch.

Yellow Jackets

These fierce, ground-nesting insects reach numerical peak during late summer and early autumn. Just as they reach this peak, bears begin to grub up their nests and eat their larvae. So when the dog days are over and it's time to start hiking again, these winged stingers are numerous, edgy, and on full-pheromone alert. Although you will never be entirely safe from these little warriors, you can take a few practical precautions.

Wear long pants and, if you can stand it, a long-sleeved shirt too. Leave the dogs at home—they are yellow jacket magnets. In their bug brains, anything big and hairy is an enemy—and all dogs are big and hairy to a yellow jacket. Take a few moments to look for insects flying out of the ground before you throw off your pack and plop down on the ground. Develop a low-level, internal alarm that automatically goes off when your eyes see flying insects milling around close to the ground.

Poisonous Snakes

This is the potential problem people always ask about. The copperhead and the timber rattlesnake, both poisonous, inhabit the Benton MacKaye corridor. The sluggish, unaggressive copperhead is more common than the timber rattlesnake. The eastern cottonmouth (water moccasin) does not occur along the BMT's streams. Most of the large, prominently patterned snakes seen in or beside the trail's streams are nonpoisonous northern water snakes, not cottonmouths, as is often assumed.

While it is likely that you will see nonpoisonous snakes along the BMT, your chances of seeing a poisonous snake are somewhat slim. Your chances of being bitten by a poisonous snake are rare—in fact, they are remote. There are records of hikers who have walked the entire Appalachian Trail, from Georgia to Maine, without seeing the first poisonous snake.

More people are killed each year by lightning and by bee and wasp stings than by venomous snakes. There are approximately 8,000 venomous snakebites per year in the United States. Of that number, however, only twelve to fifteen people, mostly the young and elderly, die each year. In 20 to 30 percent of snakebite cases, no venom is injected.

Treatment for rattlesnake or copperhead bite

Don't:
- Cut incisions and attempt to suck the poison out.
- Use a tourniquet.
- Use ice or cold water on the wound.

Do:
- Use a suction device, such as the Extractor by
  Sawyer Products. Studies show that an Extractor
  can remove up to 30 percent of the venom if

applied within three minutes. The suction from
the Extractor is applied without incision.

■ Clean the wound with antiseptic soap.

■ Apply sterile dressing.

■ Remove rings and other constrictive items.

■ Keep limb at or below the level of the heart.

■ Keep patient quiet, hydrated, and comfortable. Treat
for shock as needed.

■ If possible, arrange for safe and rapid transport to a
hospital.

Remember that activity and anxiety accelerate the
absorption of the venom. Walking, however, is
acceptable if the victim feels up to it or if there is
no other alternative.

Snakebite prevention

■ Wear long trousers and hiking boots. The higher the
boots, the more protection you will have against
snakebite. If you cannot see the treadway well, a
pair of gaiters will give you an added measure of
protection.

■ Look before you sit or lie down.

■ Be careful where you put your hands. Do not reach
blindly into holes or crevices. (Do not stick your
face close to look, either.)

■ When a log obstructs your path, step up on it and
take a long stride or look on the other side of it
before crossing.

■ Especially if you are hot-weather camping, wear

shoes and use a flashlight when walking around
the campsite after dark.

Remember that the cooler the weather, the more
sluggish the snake. Winter hikers do not have to
worry about poisonous snakes in the Southern
Appalachians.

Bears

Thus far bears have not become a problem within the Benton
MacKaye corridor. Most often, problem bears are created by problem campers. Backpackers cause habituation problems when they
throw substantial amounts of leftovers in the bushes, purposely
leave food for animals, and worst of all, feed bears. When enough
of these sloppy campers congregate in a small area, it doesn't
take long for bears—intelligent omnivores—to associate power
bars with backpacks and backpacks with tents.

Beyond being a good camper, there are three measures you
can take to help avoid bear problems. The first, quite obviously, is
to avoid camping at heavily used and messy sites. The second is
to actively and aggressively discourage bears from associating
you with easy food. If a bear comes sniffing up to your camp,
holler, bang pots and pans, throw rocks, use pepper spray—do
what you have to do to make the bruin feel extremely unwel-
come. (Remember that in areas where they are hunted, or where
there are hunters, fed bears often quickly become dead bears.)
The third is to hang your food—every bit of it—from a high tree
limb after supper and whenever you are not in camp. This practice will also prevent the mini-bears, mice, from chewing
through your tent or pack to pilfer your food.

Hang your bear bag at least 8 to 9 feet above the forest floor and let it dangle at least 4 feet below the roped limb. Also keep your food at least 4 feet away from the trunk or other branches stout enough for a small bear to shinny out on. If you have found a good limb, but it's not far enough from the trunk, you can employ a second rope to pull the bear bag out of claws' way.

Camping Rules

Unless you receive permission from the landowner in advance, it is illegal to camp on the private property along the trail. Section 7, which traverses private property for nearly all of its length, offers an overnight shelter for backpackers. On Forest Service land, you may make a no-trace tent camp anywhere along the trail unless posted otherwise. (See Environmental Guidelines starting on page 267.)

The Forest Service has established and intends to enforce new rules governing campsites within the Cohutta–Big Frog Wilderness. (See Usage Rules for the Cohutta–Big Frog Wilderness on page 272.)

Trail Usage

While threading through Forest Service land, the Benton MacKaye is a foot-travel only route except where it shares a treadway with another trail that allows more than one method of movement. Section 6 shares 2.3 miles of treadway with the bike-and-hike Stanley Gap Trail. Section 9 shares 1.6 miles of treadway with the horse-and-hike South Fork Trail. In the Cohutta–Big Frog Wilderness, Section 11 shares 5.7 miles of treadway with horse-and-hike Hemp Top and Licklog Ridge Trails. (Horse-riders

seldom use Hemp Top beyond the Penitentiary Branch junction.)
North of the wilderness, Section 12 shares its southernmost 0.4
mile with a mountain bike trail.

Blazes and Signs

Except for the 13.6-mile stretch within the Cohutta–Big Frog
Wilderness, where blazes are no longer allowed, the rest of the
trail—both private-land road-walk and public-land path—is
blazed at regular intervals. A double blaze, one above the other,
means heads up: the route is about to make an abrupt turn. Especially where the track veers sharply from woods road onto path,
the turn is occasionally marked by both double blaze and ar-
rowed sign. Blue is the customary blaze color for sidepaths leading to water off the Benton MacKaye.

Despite the best efforts of vandals, signage along the Benton
MacKaye has improved markedly during the past few years.
Signs usually mark trailheads, major road crossings, trail junctions (including those in the Cohutta–Big Frog Wilderness), and
potentially confusing turns from old roadbed onto path. Signs
increasingly indicate water sources and occasionally pinpoint
geographical locations, such as prominent gaps.

Hunting

Hunting is a legal and somewhat popular pastime along the
Benton MacKaye corridor, both on public and suitable private
lands. Various hunting seasons overlap throughout much of autumn and early winter. In spring, hunters attempt to call turkey
within shotgun range. To further complicate matters for hikers,
the two states—Georgia and Tennessee—have different seasons
and different laws.

Georgia's Chattahoochee National Forest includes both Wildlife Management Areas (WMAs), which have shorter, highly regulated seasons, and non-WMA lands, which follow the much longer, general statewide seasons. All of Section 1 and most of Section 2 are located within the Blue Ridge WMA. Section 3's treadway traverses Coopers Creek WMA. North of Fowler Mountain, Section 8 runs along the perimeter of the Cohutta WMA. All of Sections 9 and 10, as well as Section 11 north to Double Spring Gap at the Tennessee border, are surrounded by Cohutta WMA land.

North of Double Spring Gap, Sections 11 and 12 wind through Tennessee's Cherokee National Forest. The 625,000-acre Cherokee WMA encompasses all of the Cherokee National Forest. This national forest, and therefore the WMA, is split into southern and northern sections by the Great Smoky Mountains National Park. Tennessee's segment of the Benton MacKaye Trail lies within the South Cherokee Portion, Ocoee Unit.

For more information, contact the following offices:

Blue Ridge and Coopers Creek WMAs

Game Management
2150 Dawsonville Highway
Gainesville, GA 30501
(770) 535-5700

Cohutta WMA

Wildlife Resources
2592 Floyd Springs Road
Armuchee, GA 30105
(706) 295-6041

Georgia websites
- www.gohuntgeorgia.com
- www.georgiawildlife.com
- www.dnr.state.ga.us/dnr/wild

Cherokee WMA

Tennessee Wildlife Resources Agency
464 Industrial Boulevard
Crossville, TN 38555
(931) 484-9571
www.tnwildlife.org

How To Use This Guide

THIS GUIDEBOOK DETAILS the Benton MacKaye Trail's southernmost twelve sections, a distance of 92.8 miles from Springer Mountain, Georgia, to US 64 in Tennessee.

Section Descriptions

Each section begins with a map, followed by an elevation profile and a concise, at-a-glance summary of essential trail information. You can quickly refer to a section's location, length, difficulty rating (for both dayhiking and backpacking), and its starting and ending points with elevations given. Also provided here are trail junctions, blaze descriptions, topographic map names, DeLorme map references, counties, nearest cities, ranger districts and national forests, plus a brief listing of some of the section's outstanding features.

Note: *The elevation profiles are visual aids only; because of slight inaccuracies in the computer program used to generate the profiles, the distances shown on the graphs do not always match the wheeled mileages in the text, which are accurate to the nearest tenth of a mile.*

Following the information header, you will find a complete description of the route from south to north, with special attention given to forest types, views, trail junctions, stream crossings, grade difficulty, abrupt turns, and interior mileages to prominent physical features, such as mountaintops and gaps.

After the in-depth south-to-north narratives, a Nature Notes segment lists and describes some of the many wildflowers, ferns, shrubs, and trees you will encounter while walking that particular section. The emphasis on spring wildflowers in the Nature Notes is by design. Fall color is widely heralded and hard to miss in season. Over the years, many hikers have asked me, "Where are all the wildflowers?" Invariably, those who asked the question were already too late for the best of the show. The better question is, "When and where are all the spring wildflowers?" The answer to the first part of the question is, "Earlier than most people think." Many spring wildflowers have already bloomed or are in bloom when the hardwoods first shade the forest floor.

Additionally, this emphasis is intended to help spread trail usage over more of the year and to give hikers an incentive to get off their duffs during early spring—when days are often surprisingly warm, streams are full, winter views remain, life is stirring, and wildflowers are popping up in their perennial round of beauty.

At the conclusion of the Nature Notes, a truncated, north-to-south description—a short list of mileages to help you keep track of where you are—is provided for those wishing to walk the sections in that direction.

The last entry in each chapter provides detailed driving instructions to the section trailheads from several different points on the compass. Mileages and turns for setting a shuttle between trailheads are provided at the end of the directions.

When using this guide, keep in mind that trail sections often change; they are often rerouted by nature or man. Contact the BMTA or the appropriate ranger district for current conditions.

Trail Ratings

Difficulty ratings are inherently subjective and relative; there are no standardized norms that fit all the possibilities. Useful systems, however, are those that achieve consistency by limiting this subjectivity and relativity to a single region and a single source. To this end, I have walked and rated all of the BMT sections described in this guide. Even if you do not agree with my ratings, I hope that you will find them consistent and, after a trip or two, useful.

The ratings utilized in this guide were based upon the usual criteria: the rate and length of elevation change, the way that elevation change is accomplished, the difficulty of a section compared to others, the length of the section, etc. In general, to reflect the cumulative effect of the grades, the longer sections were usually rated as slightly more difficult than shorter sections with roughly the same elevation change per mile. Occasional rough footing and stream crossings, while mentioned in the narratives, were usually given only minimal consideration: they are simply part of wildland walking.

The ratings employed in this guide apply only to the Southern Appalachians. They have been compared and calibrated only to other trails in the southern mountains—from the Cohuttas to the Southern Nantahalas, from Shining Rock to Slickrock. Thus, an easy-to-moderate rating means that I think the section is easy to moderate for a Southern Appalachian Trail, not one from Florida or one from the Colorado Rockies. Also, keep in mind that I rated these sections while I pushed a measuring wheel, carried a heavy daypack, and stopped frequently to look and write notes.

This rating system is also based on two assumptions. The first is that this scheme, or any other, does not apply to either end of the fitness-spectrum bell curve—those in excellent condition and those in poor condition. Hikers who are able to run long distances with little effort already know that ratings are meaningless for them. Conversely, people who become winded after climbing a flight or two of stairs would find difficulty classifications equally inaccurate, although much harder to ignore.

The other assumption is that a very high percentage of the people who hike or want to hike in the mountains exercise, at least occasionally. If you rarely exercise, it probably would be unwise to attempt a route ranked more difficult than easy to moderate. This approach is designed to accommodate those people who exercise, at least sporadically, and who fall somewhere in that broad, general category between slightly below fair condition and slightly better than good condition.

This guide utilizes three categories of difficulty: Easy, Moderate, and Strenuous. As you will notice, many sections have been assigned two designations. These split ratings are used to help bridge fitness levels when trail difficulty falls between obvious gradations. For instance, a section may be rated "Dayhiking: Easy to Moderate." A person in good cardiovascular condition would consider this hike to be easy. A hiker in fair shape would probably rate the route as easy to moderate, and a walker with a poor fitness level would probably judge it moderate, perhaps even harder.

The decision to hike a certain BMT section is a commonsense personal judgment. When planning a trip, you should be aware of the trail's difficulty, not intimidated by it; you should think of the rating as a recommendation, not a warning. If you keep the intended mileage reasonable, walk at a comfortable pace, take frequent rest stops, and are energized by mountain beauty, you will often be surprised at what you can accomplish.

Plaque commemorating
Benton MacKaye

Springer Mountain
to Three Forks

1

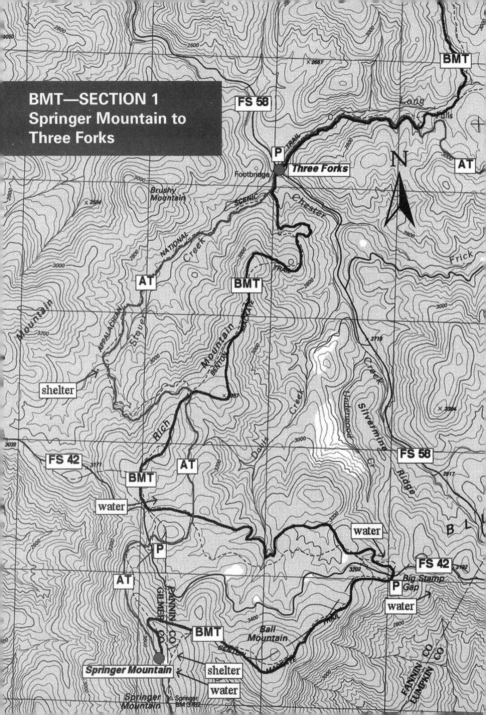

BMT—SECTION 1
Springer Mountain to Three Forks

Benton MacKaye Trail, Section 1

Southern terminus of the Benton MacKaye Trail at its Springer Mountain junction with the Appalachian Trail to Three Forks at FS 58

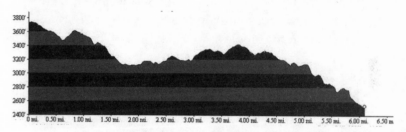

LENGTH 6.2 miles (see description)

DAYHIKING (SOUTH TO NORTH) Easy to Moderate

BACKPACKING (SOUTH TO NORTH) Moderate

VEHICULAR ACCESS AT ONE END ONLY Southern terminus atop Springer Mountain, 3,740 feet, does not have vehicular access. Access to the AT-BMT junction requires a 0.7-mile walk on the Appalachian Trail or a 1.8-mile walk on the Benton MacKaye Trail from FS 42. The northern end at FS 58, 2,510 feet, has vehicular access.

TRAIL JUNCTION Appalachian (see description)

BLAZES White diamond for Benton MacKaye; white rectangle for Appalachian

TOPOGRAPHIC QUADRANGLE Noontootla GA

DELORME MAP GA-14

COUNTIES Gilmer GA, Fannin GA

NEAREST CITIES Ellijay GA (W), Blue Ridge GA (N),
Blairsville GA (NE), Dahlonega GA (SE),
Dawsonville GA (S)
RD/NF Toccoa/Chattahoochee
FEATURES Southern terminus for both the Benton
MacKaye and Appalachian Trails; Springer Mountain;
winter views; rock-outcrop overlooks; Three Forks;
extensive fern colonies

SPRINGER MOUNTAIN. Although Springer's summit, rocky and oak wrapped, is not lofty by southern standards, it is held in high esteem: it is a hiker's Mecca. Sooner or later, every serious Southern Appalachian hiker makes the short pilgrimage to the rock-outcrop overlook, the lone-hiker plaque, the southernmost white blaze. While Springer is technically the southern terminus of the Appalachian Trail, the mountain is hallowed by the yearly round of ritual—by handshakes, hugs, and kisses; toasts and lingering farewells; hoisted backpacks, determined smiles, and the first northbound footfalls—as the beginning. The overwhelming majority of thru-hikers—those intrepids who attempt to walk the entire 2,170-mile odyssey in one year—start at Springer and strike out north with late winter or early spring. They hope to avoid the worst of southern cold—a task more difficult than many imagine—to outlast summer heat, to beat the northern cold to Maine.

Springer is a mountain born for beginnings. From the south, a lone ridgeline leads to Springer's crown: an Appalachian outpost, the southernmost island of its elevation. At Springer the single ridge forks into two curving crests: the eastern Blue Ridge and the western Blue Ridge. Two-tenths mile north of the outcrop where the bronze backpacker revels in the year-round view, the first step of the Benton MacKaye Trail splits away from the Appalachian. Here, like the first branch of a family tree, the father's trail (the AT) and the descendant named after the AT's founder—the Benton MacKaye—diverge with the two crests of the Blue Ridge.

In Georgia, the AT generally accompanies the eastern crest of the Blue Ridge north from Springer Mountain. With the exception of its first 1.8 miles to Big Stamp Gap, where it rides the eastern crest, the Benton MacKaye (once it reaches the ridgetop on Section 6) generally tags along with the western crest of the Blue Ridge through northernmost Georgia.

The shortest route to the BMT's southern terminus on top of Springer is a 0.7-mile walk on the AT from FS 42 (see directions). Once you have reached the AT-BMT junction, however, you will find it difficult to resist the nearly flat, 0.2-mile stroll to the Appalachian Trail's southern terminus. So while this section's length is 6.2 miles, you must stride a minimum of 6.9 miles to hike its entire length, and you will hike 7.3 miles if you make the side tour out to the Appalachian Trail's terminus and back. But don't let the additional mileage intimidate you. Trekked as described, from south to north, most of Section 1 is easily walked. This section—with fern fields, wildflower slopes, and silverbell ridgelines, with its own plaque and rock outcrop overlook—provides an excellent warm-up hike in spring, especially in late April and early May.

Starting from Springer, the much easier way to walk this section, the Benton MacKaye circumscribes a lumpy, lopsided, three-quarters oval—open to the west—before straightening out to the northeast along Rich Mountain to Three Forks. BMT-1 has four points of contact with the AT along its 6.2-mile length. The entire section is protected within the 23,300-acre Ed Jenkins National Recreation Area; it also lies within the sprawling

38,900-acre Blue Ridge Wildlife Management Area.

Hiked from south to north, the trail loses a significant amount of elevation. From its intersection with the AT atop Springer (3,740 feet), the track descends to 3,120 feet just across FS 42 at mile 1.9, then gradually rises to 3,450 feet on Rich Mountain at mile 3.8. The remainder of the walkway steadily loses 940 feet of elevation to Three Forks.

Because of its proximity to Springer Mountain and the AT, this stretch is one of the most popular BMT sections. Compared to the AT, however, this path remains scarcely trod. Section 1 is heavily used only where the two trails share the same course for the final 0.1 mile before Three Forks.

STARTING AT ITS SIGNED JUNCTION with the AT, the Benton MacKaye forks to the right away from the parent trail and blazes its journey's beginning through Springer Mountain's predominantly oak forest, squat and wind honed. After slightly less than 0.1 mile of nearly effortless walking, you will pass a plaque embedded on the face of a low line of outcropped rock to the right. The plaque pays tribute to Benton MacKaye, whose vision became a geographical and spiritual reality.

Beyond the plaque, the track begins a half-mile descent (a short easy-to-moderate grade is the most difficult) to a shallow saddle west of Ball Mountain. The BMT's first conifers, a few white pines, stand out in the otherwise deciduous forest at the upper end of the downgrade. At 0.2 mile the route curls to the right off the ridgecrest, continuing the scenic cakewalk on rich, north-facing slope. Excellent winter views span the short horizon from north to east. In season, the dark tread wends through a lacy, sweet-smelling colony of hay-scented fern, upslope and down as far as the eye can see.

By 0.4 mile the footpath gains the top of the eastern crest of the Blue Ridge, and remains on or near the famous keel down to the slight gap. Along the way, views through winter's hardwoods to the right showcase Springer's impressive bulk. These views come, in part, courtesy of a New York fern colony. Hay-scented and New York ferns produce their own herbicides: they poison many other plants. Where their colonies are especially large and dense, they change the character of the woods. A forest above ferns is more open and has fewer trees per acre; its shrub layer is also significantly reduced.

After ranging through the unnamed gap (3,470 feet) at 0.6 mile, Section 1 ascends (two short easy-to-moderate grades) with the ridge to the east. It bisects a hardwood and white pine forest for slightly more than 0.1 mile before slabbing to the right and skirting the uppermost southern sidehill of 3,660-foot Ball Mountain. (This dip to the south of Ball's crown is actually the southernmost point of the BMT.) At mile 1.0 the trail tops out at approximately 3,600 feet, then loses elevation all the way to Big Stamp Gap (occasional short easy-to-moderate dips the most difficult). BMT-1 quickly bends back to the spine, where it remains on or near the crest of the Eastern Blue Ridge. Here it heads through another fern field and past stands of small sassafras and American holly, their leaves as shiny as rain on rhododendron.

A double blaze and "view" sign mark the sidepath to the right at mile 1.4. A 65-yard walk leads to the Owen Overlook—a rock outcrop open straight out to the southeast. Deeply furrowed Jones Creek valley falls away at your feet. To the right and further in the distance, the outlying humps of Whissenhunt and Campbell Mountains rise above much lower land at 110 and 130 degrees respectively. In winter the view expands to include the higher peaks of the eastern Blue Ridge rolling toward the east before bending away, their high crests sanctuary for the AT. Sassafras Mountain, at 70 to 75 degrees, stands closest, followed in outward line by Justus, Hogback, and Long.

Back at the Benton MacKaye's first double blaze, the course steadily descends with the ridgeline to its usually signed crossing of FS 42 at Big Stamp Gap (mile 1.8; 3,145 feet). Here, across the road, the BMT and the eastern crest of the Blue Ridge go their separate ways; they do not meet again. The downhill run continues on upper-hollow slope before swinging left into a grove of tall yellow poplar. Slightly more than 0.1 mile beyond FS 42, the long grade ends as the treadway rises beside a ravine, curves to the right across the furrow, then doglegs up and to the left onto a drier oak-hickory spur. Here the trailside forest is composed of American holly, white pine, and broadleafs, including blackgum, sourwood, red maple, and several hickory species mixed in with the oaks.

Across the broad spur, Section 1 heads down again, this time on the wide walkway of an old roadbed tunneling through evergreen arches of mountain laurel and rosebay rhododendron. Mile 2.3 dips to and rock-steps a branch, a Davis Creek feeder, before rising to a drier slope with tall white pine. The undemanding upgrade advances westward on the woods road beneath an oak-hickory canopy. At mile 2.6 the trail proceeds over a small spur, then descends (a short easy to moderate grade the most difficult) to its wide, rock-step crossing of another Davis Creek tributary (mile 2.7).

Now the hiking veers up and to the right above the brook, levels, and coasts downhill, where it crosses a smaller feeder branch at mile 2.8. Along the way, during or after the right amount of rain, you will pass by a fast chute sliding white over worn rock. Still traveling generally westward, the woods-road treadway gains elevation, easy overall, to the top of a spur fingering eastward from the main ridge that runs from Springer to Rich Mountain.

BMT-1 pushes forward up the spur, through a drier forest where chestnut oaks are abundant, until it reaches a low knob and drops to its first four-way junction with the AT at mile 3.2 (3,360 feet).

Beyond the intersection, the white diamonds lead you through a stand of Virginia pine: a short-needled, often short-lived, early-succession species that requires disturbance and plenty of light to gain a roothold in most habitats. The footpath leaves the spur, losing elevation to mile 3.4 (3,300 feet) before changing course to the right and down near FS 42. This usually signed sharp turn is now known as Crosstrails, named for the

Carolina silverbell

AT shelter that once stood nearby. Following a tenth-mile of no-strain walking, Section 1 starts a short upgrade (easy to moderate) to the keel of Rich Mountain. Here the trail roller-coasters with the main crest—up to a knob, down the other side, most of it easy—for the next 1.5 miles.

Rich Mountain is aptly named; it is fertile and unusually lush for its relatively low elevation. Here silverbells, both saplings and maturing trees, dominate much of the mid-canopy and understory. Their white bell-shaped blossoms, which sway in the spring breeze, normally open sometime between April 15 and May 1.

The mountain's north-south orientation is another of its interesting characteristics, one you will notice many times as you follow the white diamonds toward Tennessee and beyond. North-south-running ridges lead hikers through the driest exposure, south, on one side of their knobs and the moistest exposure, north, on the opposite side. If you walk Rich Mountain from south to north, the uphills are south facing and the downhills are north facing. As you can readily see, the sweet birch and the stands of yellow poplar, the crest's dominant canopy tree, are more common in the saddles and on the downgrades, and the oaks and hickories are more prevalent on the rises.

The route ascends to the summit of Rich Mountain (3,450 feet) at mile 3.8 before dropping steadily (very short moderate the steepest grade) to a shallow gap (3,300 feet), where it crosses the wide and usually signed track of the AT again at mile 4.1. White pine and an occasional hemlock are the only conifers in the largely hardwood forest. The way through the woods undulates to the topknot of the next knob (3,360 feet) at mile 4.3, then descends (nearly 0.2 mile of easy to moderate) again. BMT-1 marches over its last slight bump (3,160 feet) at mile 4.8. Looks through winter's latticework afford views left and right; Buckeye Mountain is the first peak to the west.

By mile 5.1 the course curls to the right and down off the main fold onto fern slope and old roadbed, beginning the steady, overall easy downgrade to Three Forks. After threading through yet another fern colony, the walkway gains the top of a spur and resumes its elevation loss with a short easy-to-moderate down-ridge run. The trail swings to the left and down onto the open aisle of a woods road, and into the riparian green of rhododendron and hemlock at mile 5.7. Now you can hear Chester Creek, one of the forks, entrenched out of sight down the steep slope to the right. Here the nearly level hiking, shady and leaf cushioned, is particularly pleasant. The moist downslope forest, largely hemlock and hardwood, holds its crown gracefully high.

The track rounds a slight hollow with an intermittent spring at mile 5.9. A yellow poplar over 10 feet around is rooted (if it is still alive) beside the trail just to the right of the hollow's downhill cleft. Approximately 70 yards beyond the notch, look down into the hollow. A lunker hemlock 12 feet 4 inches in circumference rises like a column (again, if it is still alive) just uphill across the crease.

The mild downgrade continues to its usually signed, three-way junction with the Appalachian Trail at mile 6.1. The Benton MacKaye turns right and shares the gravelly tread with the AT to Three Forks and FS 58. Section 1 finishes with a flourish; it crosses the sturdy 40-foot bridge over Chester Creek—a clear, cold, rippling run flanked by rhododendron and hemlock. Section 2 begins straight ahead, across FS 58.

THE FOUR POINTS OF CONTACT between Section 1 of the Benton MacKaye and the Appalachian Trail form three loops, one atop the other from south to north, from Springer Mountain to Three Forks. With four possible vehicular access points, the two trails and three loops offer a wide variety of distances and configurations. The following three routes, all starting from the AT parking area off FS 42, will lead you along all three loops, plus two short, doubleback side trips.

Route 1 (southernmost loop, 4.6 miles): From the Appalachian Trail parking area (fee-pay), walk the AT across FS 42 to the BMT-AT junction atop Springer Mountain. Continue straight ahead on the AT to its southern terminus, marked by a rock-outcrop overlook and two plaques. Backtrack to the BMT-AT junction, then follow the BMT (white diamonds, cross FS 42) to its next meeting with the AT, this one a four-way intersection. Turn left (200 degrees) onto the southbound AT and finish the short distance to the AT parking area.

Route 2 (the southernmost two loops, 6.2 miles): From the Appalachian Trail parking area (fee-pay), follow directions for Route 1 to the first four-way junction of the two trails north of FS 42. There, where the trails cross, proceed straight ahead on the Benton MacKaye to its next four-way intersection with the AT, this one on Rich Mountain at the top of the second loop. Turn right (130 degrees) onto the AT and travel south—straight through the first four-way junction—back to the AT parking area.

Route 3 (all three loops, 10.6 miles): From the Appalachian Trail parking area (fee-pay), follow the directions for Route 1 to Springer Mountain and the southern terminus of the AT. Backtrack to the BMT-AT junction, then hike all of Section 1 of the BMT (cross the AT twice) to Three Forks and FS 58. The two trails share the final 0.1 mile of treadway to Three Forks, which you will recognize by the bridged crossing of Chester Creek followed immediately by FS 58. Backtrack the 0.1 mile to where the trails split apart, then tramp the AT straight ahead, generally southward, all the way (cross the BMT twice) back to the AT parking lot.

Unlike the Springer Mountain plaques, the routes of the two trails are not set in stone. Varying lengths of treadway are rerouted from time to time for varying reasons. Check with the Benton MacKaye Trail Association or the Georgia Appalachian Trail Club to learn if the loops have changed significantly.

In addition to its shelter, Springer Mountain offers two overflow camping areas, designed and developed to disperse tent campers away from the immediate vicinity of the shelter and other overused spots, which the Forest Service and trail clubs wish to restore. If you walk the Appalachian Trail southward (toward its southern terminus) from the AT-BMT junction atop Springer, you will pass, after slightly less than 0.1 mile, the signed, blue-blazed sidepath leading a little more than 0.1 mile to the Springer Mountain shelter: a deluxe, two-story, A-frame cabinlike structure with a loft and picnic table. One hundred and twenty yards down the well-worn treadway toward the shelter, you will come to a prominent path bending backward to the left.

This track leads to a large camping area—open and roughly oval in shape—with numerous designated sites, many tucked into the woods. Additional designated sites, rock lined and tucked into evergreen heath, are located across the spring beyond the shelter. The Forest Service and the two trail clubs request that you stay on existing paths as much as possible and camp at one of the two designated tenting areas.

NATURE NOTES

SEGMENTS OF Section 1 from Springer Mountain down to FS 42 and along the Rich Mountain ridgeline are a fairyland of fern and wildflower in spring. If you walk BMT-1 from April 15 to May 10, you have a good chance of spotting—in bud, bloom, or leaf—dwarf and crested dwarf iris, bloodroot, Catesby's and

lousewort

painted trilliums, lousewort (several large colonies just above Big Stamp Gap) and toothwort, mayapple, foamflower, halberd-leaved violet, blue cohosh, yellow star-grass, giant chickweed, Solomon's seal, sourgrass (an oxalis or sorrel species with purple rimmed leaves), trailing arbutus, and pink lady's-slipper. You'll find the maximum number of bloomers in early May. Before the Benton MacKaye plaque, just after Section 1 dips for the first time, an extensive lily-of-the-valley colony graces Springer's crest to the right of the tread. Rich Mountain's spine has a good aster display in late summer and early fall.

Over the past thirty years, the two most noticeable changes in forest composition near the Benton MacKaye Trail have been the

eastern white pine

dramatic decline in flowering dog-woods due to disease and the rapid in-crease in the numbers of eastern white pine. White pine saplings are much more abundant and widespread in the oak-hickory uplands than they were in the 1970s. The reason for this conifer's recent proliferation is twofold: fire suppression and the tree's shade toler-ance. Especially when young, white pines cannot tolerate fire, but unlike most other eastern pines, they can tol-erate shade and readily grow up through a hardwood canopy.

There is no mistaking an eastern white pine in the Southern Blue Ridge. Everything about this evergreen—its growth rate; its height; its needles, cones, branches, and bark—is distinctive. It is the only five-needled pine in eastern North America. The slender needles, soft bluish green and 3 to 5 inches long, spray out five to a bun-dle or sheath. Its skinny cones are 4 to 8 inches long, tapering at either end, and often slightly curved. The branches spoke from the trunk in pronounced whorls, one whorl per year, a useful aid in estimating age.

The fast-growing and long-living (recorded maximums between 500 and 550 years) white pine is the tallest tree east of the Rockies. Mature specimens can often be recognized from a distance by their graceful, upward-sweeping tiers of branches, which tower pagodalike above the hardwoods. In eastern North America's now legendary virgin forests, many of these giants once ranged from 200 to 220 feet in height and 4 to 6 feet in diameter. The current Georgia state champion (an old-growth tree in Rabun County) is 12 feet 7 inches in circumference and soars skyward for 193 feet.

rattlesnake fern

The distinctive rattlesnake fern is unusually common along the Rich Mountain ridgecrest. Most ferns reproduce from spores located on the undersides of their pinnae (their leafy parts). A few species, however, produce fertile fronds, stems that bear only the sporangia (clusters of spores). The native rattlesnake fern is readily recognized by its fertile frond and by its obviously forked stem. One branch of the fork holds the fertile stalk; the other the sterile blade (the entire leafy segment). The fertile stalk continues straight up from the split, while the leafy blade leans away from the reproductive stalk at an approximate 45-degree angle.

Usually 8 to 24 inches in height, the deciduous fronds unfurl in April and last until frost. Branching from the sterile blade, the conspicuous, 6- to 14-inch-long fertile stalk withers earlier in the fall than the rest of the plant. The sporangia clump on short alternate stems. This fern's reptilian name came from a fanciful resemblance of its reproductive clusters to the noisy end of a rattler.

NORTH TO SOUTH Three Forks to Springer Mountain

Mile 0.0—From FS 58 at Three Forks, Section 1 immediately crosses the bridge over Chester Creek and shares the wide treadway with the AT.

Mile 0.1—At its usually signed, three-way junction with the AT, the BMT turns up and to the left, forking away from the gravelly AT.

Mile 0.5—Doglegs up and to the right away from the open aisle of the woods road.

Mile 1.1—Curls to the left and up onto the Rich Mountain ridgecrest.

Mile 1.4—Rolls over its first slight knob.

Mile 1.9—Reaches the high point of the next knob.

Mile 2.1—Descends to the shallow saddle, where it crosses the wide and usually signed AT at the first four-way junction with that trail.

Mile 2.4—Rises to the crown of Rich Mountain before descending.

Mile 2.8—Makes the usually signed sharp turn to the left and up at Crosstrails near FS 42.

Mile 3.0—Arrives at the second four-way junction with the AT.

Mile 3.5—Rock-steps across a Davis Creek tributary.

Mile 3.9—Rock-steps across another Davis Creek feeder branch.

Mile 4.4—Crosses FS 42 at Big Stamp Gap.

Mile 4.8—Passes a usually marked sidepath to the left, which
leads to Owen Overlook.

Mile 5.2—Slabs to the left of the ridgecrest as it begins to skirt
the upper southern slope of Ball Mountain.

Mile 5.6—Regains the ridgetop through a gap on the west side
of Ball Mountain.

Mile 6.1—Passes the Benton MacKaye plaque to the left.

Mile 6.2—Section 1 ends at the BMT-AT junction on Springer
Mountain, the southern terminus of the BMT.

DIRECTIONS

Section 1's Springer Mountain Trailhead is located off FS 42,
south of GA 60 and north of GA 52. A short walk from this trailhead leads to the southern end of Section 1, the southern terminus
of the Benton MacKaye.

Approach from the west: From the US 76–GA 2–GA 282–GA 5
intersection in East Ellijay, Georgia, take the short (less than 0.1
mile) "To 52" spur to the T-intersection with GA 52 across the
bridge. Turn right onto GA 52 East and travel approximately 5.2
miles before turning left (from a turning lane) onto signed Big
Creek Road. Once on Big Creek Road, continue straight ahead on
Big Creek–Doublehead Gap Road (Big Creek Road turns to the
left, Doublehead Gap Road proceeds straight ahead). Follow Big
Creek Road and then Doublehead Gap Road straight ahead for
approximately 12.5 miles to the signed right turn onto the wide
gravel entrance of FS 42. Forest Service 42 is additionally designated with prominent signs for Springer Mountain and the Blue
Ridge WMA.

Approach from the south: From the GA 52–GA 183 junction west of Dahlonega, Georgia, follow GA 52 West approximately 11.5 miles to the signed right turn onto Roy Road. Slow down when you see the power apparatus on the left side of the highway. The entrance to Roy Road runs between a church and the old and new Stanley's stores. Remain on Roy Road for approximately 9.4 miles to its T-intersection with usually unsigned Doublehead Gap Road, then turn right onto that road and advance approximately 2.1 miles to the right turn onto the wide gravel entrance of signed FS 42. Forest Service 42 is additionally marked with prominent signs for Springer Mountain and the Blue Ridge WMA.

Approach from the northeast: From the US 76–US 129 intersection in Blairsville, Georgia, where US 129 North crosses US 76 and leaves Blairsville, continue on US 76 West or turn onto US 76 West. If you approach this junction from the south, on US 129 North, circle three-quarters around the Blairsville Square, turn right to stay on US 129, then head 0.4 mile to an all-way stop. Turn right at the stop sign and gas station, follow US 129 for 0.1 mile, then turn left onto US 76 West. Travel 0.1 mile on US 76 West, then turn left onto signed Blue Ridge Highway (also known and signed as Old Blue Ridge Highway). After remaining on this road for approximately 7.5 miles, turn left onto signed Skeenah Gap Road and follow it for slightly less than 8.0 miles to its T-intersection with GA 60. Turn right onto GA 60, proceed 0.2 mile, then turn left onto signed and paved Doublehead Gap Road. Stick to Doublehead Gap Road for approximately 8.5 miles (approximately 4.7 miles of good dirt-gravel road until more is paved) to the signed left turn onto the wide gravel entrance of FS 42, also marked with signs for Springer Mountain and Blue Ridge WMA.

From the entrance of FS 42: Drive dirt-gravel FS 42 for approximately 6.5 miles to where the well-marked AT crosses FS 42. A very short distance beyond the trail crossing, you will see a large gravel parking area (fee-pay) to the left of the road. The AT crosses through the far end of the parking area. To reach Springer Mountain, walk the AT across FS 42 from the parking area.

If you wish to walk to Springer via the Benton MacKaye Trail, drive approximately 1.7 miles farther on FS 42 from the AT parking area to the BMT's usually signed and always blazed crossing at Big Stamp Gap (pull-off parking). Springer Mountain is uphill and to the right from this direction of travel.

Approach from the southeast: From the GA 52–GA 9 junction west of Dahlonega, Georgia, take GA 52 West for approximately 4.5 miles before turning right onto signed Nimblewill Church Road, further marked with a Forest Service sign on the left side of the highway. Follow Nimblewill Church Road for approximately 2.2 miles, then turn right onto signed dirt-gravel FS 28-1, also marked with a Forest Service sign for the Bull Mountain parking area. Travel slightly more than 7.0 miles to the four-way FS 42– FS 58–FS 77 junction at Winding Stair Gap. After approximately 2.1 miles the road forks; head up and to the left onto FS 77. Forest Service 77 is narrow and often winding.

Turn left onto FS 42 and proceed 1.0 mile to Big Stamp Gap (pull-off parking), where the signed Benton MacKaye Trail crosses the road, or 2.7 miles to the Appalachian Trail parking area (fee-pay) to the right of the road. The AT crosses through the far end of the parking area. To reach Springer Mountain, walk the AT across the road from the parking area.

Shuttle: If you followed the approaches from the west or south to Springer Mountain, a backtrack shuttle is about as good as any more complicated route. From the AT parking area continue approximately 2.7 miles farther on FS 42 before turning left and down onto FS 58 at a prominent, three-way intersection forming a triangle inside the roads. Follow FS 58 approximately 2.7 miles to the Three Forks Trailhead, then backtrack.

If you approach Springer from the northeast, or any route involving GA 60, however, your shuttle will be significantly shorter if you turn left onto FS 58 from Doublehead Gap Road. Follow directions for Section 2 (see page 93) to Three Forks, leave a vehicle there, then proceed approximately 2.7 miles farther on FS 58 before curling up and to the right onto FS 42. From here, it is 1.0 mile to the Benton MacKaye's crossing at Big Stamp Gap or approximately 2.7 miles to the AT parking area.

If you approach Springer from the southeast, via FS 77 to Winding Stair Gap, turn right onto FS 42, then immediately turn down and to the left onto FS 58. Follow FS 58 approximately 2.7 miles to the Three Forks Trailhead before backtracking to the FS 42–FS 58 junction. Finish the shuttle by turning to the right onto FS 42 and traveling either 1.0 mile to Big Stamp Gap, where the usually signed BMT crosses FS 42, or 2.7 miles to the AT parking area (fee-pay) to the right of the road.

*Suspension bridge high over
the Toccoa River*

Three Forks to
Little Skeenah Creek

2

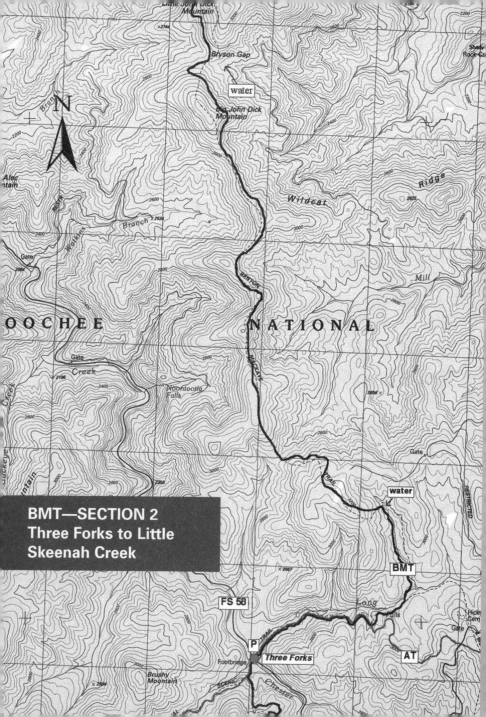

BMT—SECTION 2
Three Forks to Little Skeenah Creek

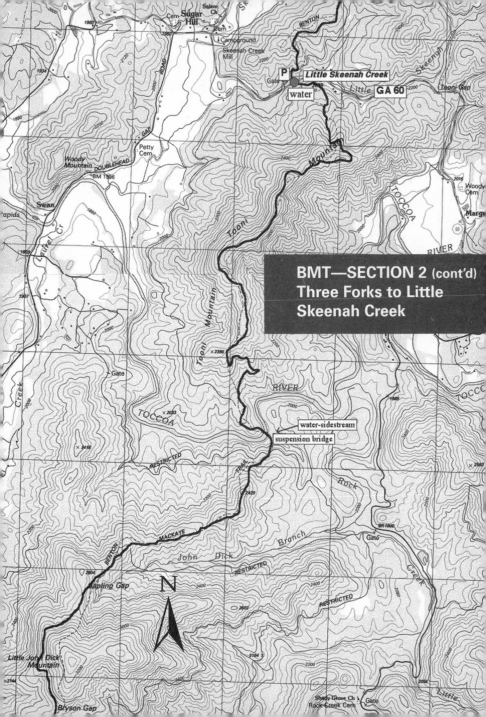

BMT—SECTION 2 (cont'd)
Three Forks to Little Skeenah Creek

Benton MacKaye Trail, Section 2

*Three Forks at FS 58
to Little Skeenah Creek at Highway 60*

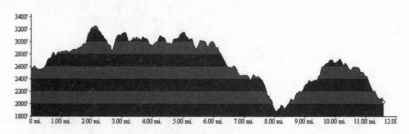

LENGTH 12.2 miles

DAYHIKING (SOUTH TO NORTH) Easy to Moderate

BACKPACKING (SOUTH TO NORTH) Moderate

VEHICULAR ACCESS AT EITHER END Southern end at FS 58,
2,510 feet; northern end at GA 60, 2,015 feet

TRAIL JUNCTIONS Appalachian, Duncan Ridge (see description)

BLAZES White diamond for Benton MacKaye; white
rectangle for Appalachian; sporadic blue rectangle for
Duncan Ridge

TOPOGRAPHIC QUADRANGLES Noontootla GA, Wilscot GA

DELORME MAP GA-14

COUNTY Fannin GA

NEAREST CITIES Ellijay GA (W), Blue Ridge GA (NW),
Blairsville GA (NE), Dahlonega GA (SE)

RD/NF Toccoa/Chattahoochee

FEATURES Long Creek Falls; mountain streams;
wildlife opening with year-round view; old-growth trees;
Toccoa River; suspension bridge

ECTION 2 IS LONG, LONELY, and often scenic. At 12.2 miles, it is the third longest BMT segment from Springer Mountain to the Ocoee River. Beyond the Three Forks area, where the Benton MacKaye shares its treadway with the heavily used AT, this stretch is lightly trod except in the immediate vicinity of the Toccoa River. Winding south to north, this section leads hikers past old-growth trees, cascades, Long Creek Falls, small mountain streams, a wildlife opening, and over a bridge suspended high above the shoaling Toccoa River. Most of BMT-2's corridor south of Tooni Mountain's southernmost knob is protected within the 23,300-acre Ed Jenkins National Recreation Area. All of this section south of the Toccoa River ventures through the 38,900-acre Blue Ridge Wildlife Management Area.

This section shares its southernmost 0.9 mile with the Appalachian Trail. Starting at mile 1.0, where the BMT bends 90 degrees to the left and bridges Long Creek, the Benton MacKaye shares its treadway with the Duncan Ridge Trail all the way to GA 60.

Beginning at FS 58 and Three Forks—where Stover, Long, and Chester Creeks flow together at right angles to form a fourth, Noontootla Creek—Section 2 follows a wide, heavily used former road up the south side of Long Creek's sheltered valley. Long Creek is a shallow, small-volume stream, clear and often cascading. At first the route remains within easy eyesight of the creek's calm lowermost end, but it soon pulls up and further away from the steeply entrenched cascades. While it usually remains within earshot until you reach the bridge, beyond the first half mile the brook often flows entirely out of sight or is a brief flash of white through downslope rhododendron.

Here the BMT gradually gains elevation to the east as it parallels Long Creek. All of the grades, both up and down, for the first mile are easy. The woods-road trail is cut into a north-facing slope where trees grow large quickly. This section's first mile features far more tall specimens in the 9- to 13-foot-circumference range than any other similar-length stretch of the Benton Mac-Kaye. The forest is largely riparian: hemlock, white pine, and moist-site hardwoods. Many of the white pines are towering tall for their relatively young ages (one branch whorl to the next equals a year's growth). Downslope toward the creek stand old-growth hemlocks—graceful giants rising straight and scarcely tapering out of the rhododendron.

Both upslope and down, the occasional yellow poplar has grown to girths of 10 to 13 feet. Tall red maples, shaggy barked and unusually thick-trunked for North Georgia, have won elbowroom in the overstory. At 0.8 mile, slightly less than 0.1 mile before the usually signed sidepath to the falls, the thickest white pine I have ever seen beside North Georgia's trails—11 feet 5 inches around—is rooted (if it is still alive) 13 long paces downslope from the margin of the roadbed. Seventy yards beyond the impressive pine, and 85 yards before the sidepath, a magnificent hemlock—12 feet 10 inches in circumference—spires up through the rhododendron 30 to 35 yards downslope from the trail (again, if it is still holding heartwood and bole together when you pass by).

By 0.9 mile a usually signed, blue-blazed tread to the left leads 0.1 mile to Long Creek Falls, a 35- to 40-foot-high, two-tiered drop. Rock is falling from the wide face faster than the water can wear it smooth; the vertical white rushes over the horizontal dark of the stair-step ledges, creating an intersecting weave of overlapping lines and colors.

Immediately past the sidepath to the waterfall, the two trails split apart at the sign; the AT travels to the right, toward Maine;

the BMT forges straight ahead, through a scenic area of tall trees and long cascades below. (When the Benton MacKaye Trail Association completes its treadway, the trails will cross paths one more time—at Sassafras Gap inside the GSMNP's southwestern boundary—before the northern terminus of the BMT ties into the AT at Davenport Gap.) At 1.0 mile the walkway bends 90 degrees to the left, crosses the bridge over Long Creek, and lights out to the north, closely following the creek and its branch-sized tributaries for much of the next 0.7 mile. This segment is undemanding, most of it mild as milk. Here the underwood is often a shrub layer of mountain laurel, rhododendron, and deciduous heath. Especially where the passage rises slightly up and away from a watercourse, the drier forest becomes more deciduous; sassafras, hickory, sourwood, and blackgum join the oaks.

BMT-2 angles away from its last Long Creek feeder and begins a steady upgrade (a few easy-to-moderate stretches) at mile 1.8. Much of this initial ascent slants up north-facing slope, where chestnut saplings are conspicuously common and New York ferns pattern the forest floor between widely spaced trees. The track crosses a roadbed at mile 2.0, pushes uphill a little harder, then rises atop an oak-pine ridgecrest. Mile 2.1 levels as it crosses a clearing, section high point at 3,250 feet. Originally cleared as a U.S. Army Ranger helicopter training site, the area was enlarged to serve as a wildlife opening in 1989. For now, until the trees grow taller, the opening offers a year-round view to the south-southwest and southwest: Rich, Buckeye, and Locust Mountains from left to right. You may camp in the clearing; you may not build a fire or a fire ring.

Beyond the sunny field, the well-marked footpath makes a long downridge descent to the northwest beneath the shade of mixed hardwoods and white pine. At mile 2.3 the dark tread tilts down a short pitch of at least moderate difficulty, followed by longer easy-to-moderate grades. The course slips onto upper slope, rounding a rich, north-facing hollow furrowed with the run of a wet-weather spring. After more steady, easy-to-moderate downhills and another short moderate dip, the Benton MacKaye

veers back to ridgeline and quickly bottoms out at an unnamed gap (mile 2.7; 2,860 feet).

Once through the saddle, the route starts back up, making a ridgetop run (two moderate grades, the longer nearly 0.1 mile) to the next knob on the lead. Here the forest, which includes an occasional tall black locust, is drier; scarlet and chestnut oaks are more common. The trail levels through an open stand of yellow poplar

scarlet oak

atop the wide and fertile peak (mile 3.0; 3,170 feet).

From the crown of the unnamed knob to mile 4.9, BMT-2 rides the top of the fold northward, roller-coastering up and over each high point along the way. Elevations range from 2,980 to 3,180 feet. Pignut hickory, four species of oak, and yellow poplar control much of the canopy; here and there, sapling white pines spire toward the day when they will overtop them all. The wildwood path descends to a long shallow saddle at mile 3.4, then elevates toward the next bump. The trail slabs onto the uppermost sunrise slope, reaching its high point (3,180 feet) before quickly regaining the crestline. Mile 3.6 begins a grade (short moderate, overall easy) that, with one exception, proceeds downhill to the next slight gap (2,980 feet) at mile 4.1. The walkway porpoises up and down as it heads toward the highest and westernmost peak of Wildcat Ridge (the route reaches 3,130 feet) at mile 4.4. It then loses elevation through the trough of the next gap at mile 4.7, and ascends toward the next named mountain—Big John Dick.

After rising with the ridgeline for 0.1 mile, Section 2 swings to the right onto sidehill, beginning its near half-loop around the upper northeastern slope of Big John Dick. The narrow cut-in footpath gently undulates, through mountain laurel in places, to its high point on the peak (3,180 feet) before starting a steady, easy downgrade through hardwoods shading ferns and wildflowers. The treadway switchbacks to the right and down at mile 5.5; the undemanding descent advances to usually signed Bryson Gap (2,900 feet) at mile 5.7. A faint sidepath (also usually signed) leads to a spring approximately 100 yards to the right (east) of the gap.

Once through the saddle, the track quickly bears onto the sunset slope of Little John Dick Mountain. From here the no-sweat hiking, level or barely down, follows the wide grade of an old road as it threads around the western shoulder of the mountain. Beyond the large rock outcrop to the right at mile 6.1, views through winter's dormancy reveal the rolling swell of mountains, supple and sinuous, in the distance. The two nearest nubbins, ancient and eroded beyond easy comprehension, are 2,400-foot Rall Mountain, slightly north of west two miles away, and 3,000-foot Wilson Mountain, highest point just south of west four miles away.

After winding below more outcrop rock and curving to the northeast, the course roams above an upper hollow moist enough for basswood at mile 6.4. One-tenth mile farther, back on the keel, the trail levels through Sapling Gap (2,770 feet) and begins its long, undulating 850-foot descent to the Toccoa River bridge. The upgrades along the way are short and easy, gaining no more than 50 feet of elevation. The sometimes steep downgrades are much longer; the final 0.9 mile to the river drops approximately 570 feet.

Traveling toward its next white diamond, the Benton MacKaye leaves Sapling Gap on a woods-road walkway. At mile 6.7 the footpath doglegs to the right off the crest; at mile 6.8 it makes a short, easy-to-moderate downslope run, tunnels through an archway of mountain laurel, then regains the spine. Section 2 surges down a short moderate grade at mile 7.1 before crossing a roadbed in a slight saddle (mile 7.3). Beyond the shallow notch, the BMT rises into an oak-pine forest that includes shortleaf pine.

The hiking remains nearly effortless until mile 8.0, where, following a short sharp pitch, the route swerves to the right and down onto slope. The track loses more elevation (moderate at its worst), angling onto a spur ridge and continuing the downhill run on an old road cut darkened by hemlock and tall white pine. It then drops increasingly harder (easy to moderate followed by steady moderate) to the wide erosion-bar steps above its crossing of FS 333 (2,050 feet) at mile 8.4. Across the system road, the sound of the river pulls you down the cross-tied trail, heavily used by fishers, campers, swimmers, sightseers, and occasionally, even hikers. The treadway dips to a road grade at mile 8.5 and turns left, quickly arriving at section low point (1,920 feet): the picturesque suspension bridge—260 feet long, shifting enough for fun, but safe—is pulled tight from bank to bank high above the shoaling Toccoa River. Below the bridge, the normally clear mountain stream ripples into a fast Class 1 run when there is water enough. Riddle: how can the Benton MacKaye cross this river three times, yet only cross the Toccoa twice? Answer: the Toccoa becomes the Ocoee River where it enters Tennessee. Toccoa is the anglicized

Cherokee word for Catawba place, signifying a former settlement of that tribe along the river.

ONCE ACROSS THE MEMORABLE BRIDGE, the Benton Mac-Kaye ascends the well-worn treadway beneath the tall white pines flanking the river. The grade quickly lessens as it continues through an oak-pine forest with occasional tall shortleaf pines in the canopy. Two-tenths mile beyond the Toccoa, the course crosses a former road leading a short distance to the left to the parking area at the end of FS 816. After passing over a minor spur probing southeast from Tooni Mountain, the public land path gradually loses elevation on dry southern slope for nearly 0.1 mile before bending to the north back onto the rising spur.

At mile 9.0 the route turns to the right onto slope and old roadbed, following the nearly level grade past an intermittent spring just to the left of the walkway. Mile 9.2 switchbacks to the left off the woods road onto a hand-graded sidehill footpath. One-tenth mile farther, the trail curls to the left across a narrow ravine, the first of three similar crossings in the next 0.1 mile. At mile 9.5 Section 2 swings up and to the right, working its way to the eastern edge of Tooni's southernmost knob. The BMT levels atop the ridgecrest before starting a 0.4-mile ridgetop run, pleasant and gently rolling, through an oak-hickory forest, where you can readily recognize five species of oak in season.

At trail mile 10.0 the long brown tread slants to the left of the fold, gradually gaining elevation on sidehill path for 0.1 mile, then descending for 0.1 mile before angling up and to the right onto old road grade. Here the undemanding ascent offers several good winter views (still open on April 22 of a recent year) out to the left—to Rich, Buckeye, and Locust Mountains along the Blue

Ridge to the south-southwest. After advancing on the roadbed for 0.1 mile, the track bears up and to the right onto cut-in footpath, rising steadily toward the crest, which it reaches at mile 10.4. Atop Tooni Mountain's ridgeline again, the walking heads uphill into a largely hardwood forest to the top of a small knob (2,720 feet) at mile 10.5. From here, the trail makes a downhill run to the northeast through a predominantly deciduous forest supporting pole-timber yellow poplar and sweet birch on the moister northwestern slope and an oak-hickory forest on the drier southeastern slope (winter views to both sides).

The route steadily loses elevation to mile 10.7, where it slabs onto the western pitch, ascends, gains the keel again for a couple of rods, then drifts back onto the sunset side of the mountain. Now the Benton MacKaye drops steadily as it swings around the western side of another unnamed knob. North of the high point, the course regains the crest before dipping to a shallow hardwood saddle (2,660 feet) at mile 10.9. It then half-loops around the northwestern shoulder of the next knob before topping the ridge and ramping down to another slight gap (2,580 feet) at mile 11.1. The treadway gently climbs beneath an oak-hickory canopy shading white pines as it makes an end run around the high point of the final knob before cresting Tooni Mountain again at mile 11.3. After roller-coastering with the keel for 0.1 mile, the hiking slants to the right of the ridgeline and descends. At mile 11.5, where the trail doglegs to the left (northwest), the approximately 540-foot drop in elevation to Highway 60 begins in earnest. This stretch affords excellent bare-branch views of Wallalah and Licklog Mountains to the right across Highway 60.

The long downgrade, occasionally moderate in difficulty, begins on a moist, northeast-facing slope that is lush with ferns and wildflowers, then rounds a hardwood hollow sheltering tall yellow poplar at mile 11.7. It parallels the notch of the hollow before crossing its furrow into a forest where hemlock and white pine join the broadleafs. At mile 12.0, if you are paying attention, you can spot a concrete catch basin a short distance downslope to the left. This basin catches the flow of the hollow's rivulet; you can filter water here. If you are continuing to the north on Section 3, the next nearby source of water, Little Skeenah Creek just across the highway, is considered unpotable even when filtered. The downhill run continues, recrosses the rivulet, then enters the belt of mountain laurel and white pine above the highway. Section 2's northern end dips to the entrance of FS 816 before ending at GA 60. Blazed and signed, Section 3 picks up the treadway across the blacktop.

Many hikers know Tooni Mountain by another name: Toonowee. For whatever reason, current topographical quadrangles—Noontootla and Wilscot—label the modest mountain as Tooni.

crested dwarf iris

If you are continuing northward on the Benton MacKaye, you may want to stock up on calories at the country store 0.3 mile to the right on GA 60 South.

NATURE NOTES

SECTION 2 OFFERS A GOOD spring wildflower display beginning around April 20 and lasting with the mountain laurel until late

May. The best time to see the largest variety of blooming plants is from April 23 through May 8. A fairly complete roll call of species in bud, blossom, or leaf during that seventeen-day period includes three trilliums—painted, Catesby's, and large-flowered—at least five violets—halberd-leaved and birdfoot are the easiest to identify—dwarf and crested dwarf iris, Solomon's seal and false Solomon's seal, foamflower, trout lily, Indian cucumber-root, whorled loosestrife, bellwort, giant chickweed, yellow star-grass, bloodroot, mayapple, pink lady's-slipper, sour-grass, cinquefoil, bluets, trailing arbutus, tooth-wort, rue anemone, and doll's eyes.

New York fern

Silverbell bloom along Long Creek during late April. Flowering dogwood whiten several stretches of woods in the last half of April, and mountain laurel usually reach peak at the higher elevations near the middle of May. Several segments of BMT-2 from the suspension bridge to Highway 60 flaunt excellent flame azalea displays that should be in full fire around May 1.

Only two fern species, the New York and hay-scented (see page 197 for description), form extensive colonies within the Benton MacKaye corridor. These nonflowering plants frequently occur in dense monocultural beds that cover the forest floor. Growing at even intervals beneath widely spaced trees, they are similar in uniformity to an agricultural crop. There are two reasons for this homogeneity. First, these ferns spread from perennial underground rhizomes, often generating evenly spaced, cloned colonies. Second, these two ferns apply herbicide: they poison would-be competitors.

The New York is not only the most abundant fern you will find near the BMT, but it is also one of the easiest of all the ferns to identify. The mostly alternate pinnae (leafy foliage) of this species taper gradually to nearly nothing at either end. The lowermost pinnae of this deciduous, 12- to 24-inch-tall fern resemble tiny wings.

The diminutive size of the eastern hemlock's needles and cones makes it one of the easiest of all trees to identify throughout the year. Its flattened needles are a miniscule ⅓ to ⅔ of an inch long, with two whitish stripes on the undersides. This conifer's roughly oval cones, averaging just ¾ of an inch in length, are significantly smaller than those of any other native Southern Appalachian pine, fir, or spruce. No naturally occurring fir or spruce grow beside the Benton MacKaye, Sections 1–12. Every tiny-needled tree you find near the wild portions of the BMT is a hemlock.

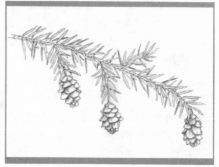

eastern hemlock

In most parts of its extensive range the eastern hemlock is a medium-sized tree—60 to 80 feet in height and 2 to 3 feet in diameter. But at the rainy southern end of the Appalachians, this evergreen can reach impressive dimensions, up to 175 feet in height and 5 to 5½ feet in diameter. These giant, slow-growing conifers are the Methuselahs of the mountain forests of the eastern United States. The record age, rings actually counted, is nearly 1,000 years.

NORTH TO SOUTH Little Skeenah Creek to Three Forks

Mile 0.0—From the usually signed Little Skeenah Creek Trailhead off GA 60, follow Section 2 to the south side of the highway, the side opposite the bridged crossing over Little Skeenah. Skirt the left edge of FS 816 for a few feet before turning left into tall white pine and mountain laurel.

Mile 0.2—Section 2 passes a concrete catch basin a short distance downslope at the rivulet. (Except during drought, you can filter water here.)

Mile 0.5—The trail rounds a hardwood hollow sheltering tall yellow poplar.

Mile 0.8—Ascends to and gains the crest of Tooni Mountain, where it remains on the ridgeline for 0.1 mile before dropping onto slope.

Mile 1.3—After holding course through a slight gap at mile 1.1, the track dips to a shallow hardwood saddle at mile 1.3.

Mile 1.7—Rises to the top of a small, unnamed knob, then descends.

Mile 2.3–2.7—Follows the nearly level crest of Tooni Mountain.

Mile 3.0—Switchbacks to the right off sidehill footpath onto woods road.

Mile 3.4—Crosses former road leading a short distance to the right to the parking area at the end of FS 816.

Mile 3.6—Loses elevation to the suspension bridge over the shoaling Toccoa River.

Mile 3.8—After crossing the bridge, the Benton MacKaye turns right, ascends, then crosses FS 333 at mile 3.8.

Mile 4.9—Crosses a roadbed in a slight saddle.

Mile 5.7—Coasts through Sapling Gap.

Mile 6.1—Passes large rock outcrop to the left of the route.

Mile 6.5—Dips to usually signed Bryson Gap. (A sidepath leads approximately 100 yards to a spring to the left, east, of the gap.)

Mile 6.7—Switchbacks up and to the left.

Mile 7.2—After a steady upgrade from Bryson Gap, the treadway rises to 3,180 feet on the northeast slope of Big John Dick before descending back to the crest at mile 7.3.

Mile 7.3 to 9.2—The BMT follows the ridgeline southward, roller-coastering up and over each high point along the way. The route crosses the highest and westernmost peak of Wildcat Ridge at mile 7.8.

Mile 9.2—Section 2 levels through an open stand of yellow poplar atop a wide, unnamed knob.

Mile 10.1—Crosses a wildlife opening.

Mile 10.4—Descends to a Long Creek tributary, the beginning of easy, scenic hiking that continues to the southern end of the section at Three Forks.

Mile 11.2—Crosses the bridge over Long Creek before bearing to the right onto the woods road paralleling the stream.

Mile 11.3—The AT and BMT converge to share the same treadway at the sign. The usually signed, blue-blazed path to the right leads 0.1 mile to Long Creek Falls.

Mile 12.2—Section 2 ends at FS 58 at Three Forks.

DIRECTIONS

Section 2's Three Forks Trailhead is located off FS 58, south of GA 60 and north of GA 52. This trailhead is the northern end of Section 1 and the southern end of Section 2.

Approach from the east: From the US 19–GA 60 junction at Stonepile Gap north of Dahlonega, Georgia, travel GA 60 North slightly over 22.5 miles before turning left onto signed Doublehead Gap Road. Look for this turn 0.2 mile beyond Skeenah Gap Road, which is to the right of the highway.

Approach from the northeast: From the US 76–US 129 intersection in Blairsville, Georgia, follow the directions for Section 1 (see page 73) to the left turn onto signed Doublehead Gap Road.

Approach from the north: From Morganton, Georgia, where GA 60 South turns 90 degrees to the right a short distance past the post office, take GA 60 South slightly less than 11.0 miles to the right turn onto signed Doublehead Gap Road.

From Doublehead Gap Road: Proceed approximately 5.7 miles on Doublehead Gap Road (pavement ends after 1.6 miles for now) before turning left onto dirt-gravel FS 58, marked with one or more signs. Continue approximately 5.4 miles to Three Forks, where the Benton MacKaye and Appalachian Trails, sharing the same treadway, cross FS 58. This trailhead is difficult to miss: hiker signs are posted on the edge of the road, a pull-in parking area with blocking logs is to the right of the road, and a woods road with low, vehicle-blocking posts is on the left of the road.

If you start out on the old road, the one with entrance-blocking posts across FS 58 from the small pull-in parking area, you will be walking on Section 2 toward GA 60 and the Little Skeenah Creek Trailhead. If you walk in the opposite direction, through the back of the pull-in parking area and across the bridge, you will be on Section 1 heading toward Springer Mountain.

If you just want to reach Three Forks, the southern end of Section 2, and plan an in-and-back-out hike with no shuttle, Section 1's directions (see page 73) from East Ellijay or the GA 52–GA 183 junction west of Dahlonega will also work quite well. Instead of turning onto FS 42, continue straight ahead on Doublehead Gap Road another 2.8 miles before turning right onto FS 58.

Shuttle: If you plan to hike Section 2 from south to north, from Three Forks to GA 60, and plan to set a shuttle, you will want to leave a vehicle at GA 60 first. Follow directions for Section 3 (see page 109) to its Little Skeenah Creek Trailhead off GA 60, then drive GA 60 North for 1.0 mile before turning left onto Doublehead Gap Road.

If you would like to shorten this section to a little over 8.5 miles, you can leave a vehicle at the parking-area end of FS 816. The entrance to FS 816, slightly more than 3.0 miles long and passable but rough for regular cars (as of now), is located opposite the Little Skeenah Creek Trailhead off GA 60. From the far end of the parking area, follow the wide track for 95 yards to where it intersects the BMT, then turn right onto the BMT and walk 0.2 mile to the swinging bridge over the Toccoa River. Coming from the other way, from Three Forks, you will walk 0.2 mile past the bridge before angling to the left onto the former roadbed that leads to the parking area.

A new tradition: thru-hiking the BMT

Little Skeenah Creek
to Skeenah Gap 3

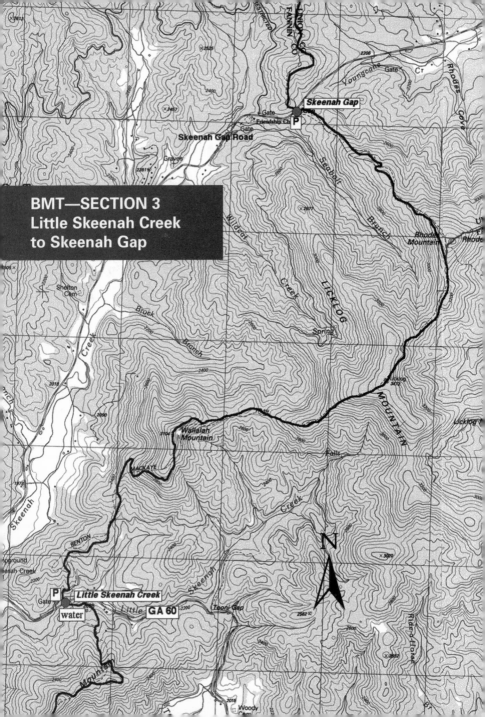

**BMT—SECTION 3
Little Skeenah Creek
to Skeenah Gap**

Benton MacKaye Trail, Section 3

*Little Skeenah Creek at GA 60
to Skeenah Gap at Skeenah Gap Road*

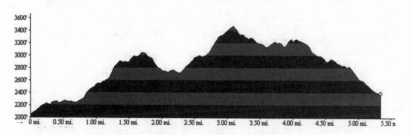

LENGTH 5.7 miles

DAYHIKING (SOUTH TO NORTH) Moderate to Strenuous

BACKPACKING (SOUTH TO NORTH) Strenuous

VEHICULAR ACCESS AT EITHER END Southwestern end at
GA 60, 2,015 feet; northeastern end at Skeenah Gap
Road, 2,380 feet

TRAIL JUNCTION Duncan Ridge (see description)

BLAZES White diamond for Benton MacKaye;
blue rectangle for Duncan Ridge

TOPOGRAPHIC QUADRANGLES Wilscot GA, Mulky Gap GA

DELORME MAP GA-14

COUNTIES Fannin GA, Union GA

NEAREST CITIES Ellijay GA (W), Blue Ridge GA (NW),
Blairsville GA (NE), Dahlonega GA (SE)

RD/NF Toccoa/Chattahoochee

FEATURES Winter views; year-round views (see
description); three mountains in the first 4.2 miles

ECTION 3'S ELEVATION PROFILE bares a couple of sharp teeth. Climbing up to and over two mountains—Wallalah and Licklog—and rising almost to the top of a third peak named Rhodes, BMT-3 ranks as the Benton MacKaye's steepest stretch in feet gained, or lost, per mile of treadway. Although this segment is not nearly as rugged as many trails further north in the Southern Appalachians, it does boast two respectable pulls for this far south in Highland Dixie.

Starting near Little Skeenah Creek, the track ascends to the highest point on Wallalah Mountain (3,100 feet), dips to a gap (2,730 feet), then heads to the top of the taller tooth—Licklog Mountain at 3,470 feet. Beyond Licklog, the wildwood path sinks to another saddle (3,140 feet) and gently ramps up to 3,260 feet on the upper southern ridgecrest of Rhodes Mountain before beginning its often steady, nearly 900-foot downgrade to Skeenah Gap (2,380 feet).

Section 3 shares its treadway with the blue-blazed Duncan Ridge National Recreation Trail from GA 60 to Rhodes Mountain, where they split apart to wander their solitary ways. The BMT does not complete the hat trick of mountains, but you can follow a short, steep piece of the Duncan Ridge Trail to the rock-capped crown of Rhodes and backtrack before proceeding downward on Section 3. Shaped something like a drunken question mark, the route mountain-climbs to the northeast from Highway 60 to Rhodes, where it bends to the northwest, then maintains that heading downhill to Skeenah Gap. BMT-3 skirts the western boundary of the 30,000-acre Coopers Creek Wildlife Management Area.

From its edge-of-the-blacktop beginning, Section 3 enters the vertical haven of the forest, immediately dipping to and crossing the bridge over Little Skeenah Creek, section low point at 2,010 feet. (The creek's water is suspect even when treated or filtered.) Here the path starts its meandering ascent to Wallalah Mountain through red maple, American holly, mountain laurel, and tall white pine. A short, stair-step steep climb up erosion bars is the first grade worth mentioning. At 0.1 mile the route swings to the right, continuing up (easy to moderate, then easy) a south-falling slope supporting a low-elevation oak-pine forest: shortleaf, Virginia, and white pine mixed with scarlet, chestnut, and southern red oak.

After gaining the crest of a spur, the course heads up a little harder again (easy to moderate) to 0.3 mile, where it drops to the right below ridgeline, gently descending above a small hollow before rising again. Here on this dry slope the dogwoods have escaped, for now, the anthracnose disease that has proven so deadly in the moister areas of the mountains. Following a short downgrade at 0.5 mile, the treadway gains elevation easily before leveling on uppermost slope. The presence of an occasional bracken fern indicates a sunny, southern exposure almost as reliably as a compass. The trail dips, then flattens at 0.7 mile before continuing the slow-climbing ascent—a steady upslope run (a short easy-to-moderate grade the most difficult) on narrow sidehill path. Along the way, winter views through hibernating hardwoods provide a peek at your first goal: Wallalah Mountain, nearly straight ahead at 30 degrees.

The white-blazed walkway doglegs up and to the left onto the main ridge leading to Wallalah at mile 1.0, then quickly turns 90 degrees to the right onto roadbed. The top of the fold affords winter views of the Skeenah Creek valley to the west (left). After less than 100 yards atop the crest, the track slips to the left off the rapidly rising ridge onto sunset slope, sustaining the uphill gradient. Here the Benton MacKaye holds its course on the wide woods road to mile 1.2, where it makes a rounded switchback to the right onto narrow tread. Now the walking angles upward across Wallalah's broad southwestern ridgeline beneath an oak and yellow poplar ceiling. Past a short moderate stretch, mile 1.3 switchbacks to the left and slants back across the rocky keel. Rather than running the route straight up the steep crest, like trail builders did in the old days, the BMTA snaked the footpath up the spine, reducing both leg strain and erosion.

The rocky ascent ratchets up to moderate to strenuous for a short distance, then backs off to moderate before bending to the right. Until late April, the prospect straight out to the right through the cold season's skeletal hardwoods looks out upon Tooni Mountain, south of Highway 60 at 200 degrees. Now the hike ranges through an increasingly rugged and scenic landscape: the forest is open and generally oak-hickory; boulders and rock outcrops block straight-line passage. Mile 1.4 veers up and to the left over and between low rock, continuing the climb. Above the abrupt turn, a slab of outcrop rock to the right offers, especially in winter, an open vista of Tooni Mountain to the south.

Beyond the outcrop overlook, the path curves upward on mild grades. Up here, near the 3,000-foot contour, white oaks are noticeably more abundant than along the beginning of the section. The treadway soon slants onto uppermost southeastern slope, affording another bare-limb view at the next high point on the tour: Licklog Mountain to the east at 80 degrees. It then pops back up to the top of the fold at mile 1.6 before gradually rising on narrow crest to Wallalah's crown (3,100 feet) at mile 1.8.

Once over Wallalah, the white diamonds lead you down the ridge through a stand of yellow poplar. Here on the moister northeastern side of the mountain more sweet birch mingle with the other hardwoods. Beyond the sharp 130-yard pitch, the walking becomes progressively less demanding until it reaches a saddle

(2,730 feet) at mile 2.2, then ventures up 0.1 mile to the next low knob on the ridgeline (2,790 feet). After descending to and crossing a woods road in the next shallow gap (2,730 feet) at mile 2.4, the Benton MacKaye climbs again, this time making a 0.3-mile up-ridge run—becoming progressively harder to moderate, tapering to easy, then gearing up to moderate again—before leveling out atop a higher unnamed knob (3,010 feet). The peak provides a good leaf-off look to nearby Licklog Mountain.

yellow poplar

Section 3 extends its arch-and-roll ride down through the next slight scallop (2,980 feet) at mile 2.8, prior to beginning the unabated ascent to Licklog Mountain. The grade starts out easy, shifts to a short moderate-to-strenuous pull, then throttles back to moderate before making a modified switchback to the left at mile 3.0. A second rounded switchback, this one to the right, winds below a line of outcrop rock. The uphill hiking finishes with a steady, easy elevation gain under small ridgetop timber, largely hardwood, mostly yellow poplar and oak. The track levels on Licklog's flat crown (3,470 feet) at mile 3.3.

Licklog is a common Southern Appalachian place name. The term comes to us from the pioneer days, when farmers ran free-range cattle in the lush summer highcountry of the mountains. The herdsmen chopped holes in deadfall logs and dropped salt blocks in the slots. The cattle licked the blocks until they were gone, then licked the salt-impregnated logs.

From Licklog's summit, the route descends with the ridge a short distance before slanting to the right onto sunrise slope and traveling down slightly harder on cut-in path. To the right, through traceries of wintertime branches, you can see the remains of ancient orogenies—the old rumplings of Appalachia—humped up to a short horizon. The overall easy downgrade, shaded by chestnut oak and mountain laurel, regains the crest and sinks to a gap at mile 3.6. Above the bottom of the saddle, a "water" sign points to the blue-blazed sidepath that drops sharply to the right (east) less than 0.1 mile down a hollow to a normally reliable spring. The BMT levels, then dips to the stand of ramrod-straight yellow poplar in the next gap at mile 3.9.

PAST THE SECOND SADDLE (3,140 feet), the lower of the two between Licklog and Rhodes, the treadway slabs to the left of the rising ridgeline onto western slope and swings right back up to the spine where winter views focus on nearby Rhodes Mountain, almost straight ahead. After a short stretch of nearly effortless walking, the BMT makes an upridge run, easy to moderate at the end, to the usually signed Benton MacKaye–Duncan Ridge junction (3,260 feet) at mile 4.2. Here, just south of Rhodes, the Benton MacKaye and Duncan Ridge Trails split apart. Section 3 follows its white diamonds almost 90 degrees to the left; the blue-blazed Duncan Ridge rambles to the top of Rhodes Mountain and beyond.

If you feel cheated out of the chance for another peak, if you would rather stretch a double into a triple, finish the climb—a steep, straight-up-the-crest grunt of a little more than 0.1 mile—on Duncan Ridge to the rock-capped summit of Rhodes Mountain (3,420 feet). For now, a gap in the trees affords a glance to the southeast off Rhodes: Rocky Mountain presses against the sky at 130 degrees. Rock outcrops to the left of the crown provide good winter and partial summer views to the southwest.

Advancing solo again, our trail slowly loses elevation as it skirts the upper-west slope of Rhodes Mountain. By mile 4.5 the mild grade regains the ridgecrest: the lead stretching from the topknot of Rhodes to Skeenah Gap. From here the track bears off to the northwest, descending (easy to moderate, then moderate, for slightly over 0.1 mile) amidst a predominantly hardwood forest. The gentle downhill run enters a stand of Virginia pine, often short lived and always short needled, at mile 4.7. Following a short easy upgrade, the wildland path swerves to the left at mile 4.9 and continues the steady downhill through an oak-pine woods with mountain laurel and deciduous heath in the underwood.

The tread drifts down and to the right off the keel of the ridge at mile 5.0, makes several blazed turns onto roadbed, then proceeds downhill on northeast-facing slope. The young trees, especially the yellow poplars, are much taller than those on the drier crest. The roadbed hiking heads down harder (easy to moderate) for a short distance prior to becoming a nearly effortless stroll above a steep downslope. At mile 5.3 the BMT begins a 0.3-mile, easy-to-moderate descent. Mountain laurel often flanks the aisle of the former logging road, which loses elevation atop a ridgeline blanketed with young, third-growth forest. Section 3 flattens out to a mild downgrade at mile 5.6, comes to the top of the bank above Skeenah Gap Road, turns left and angles down the power cut before climbing steps to its end at Skeenah Gap. Section 4 picks up the tread straight across Skeenah Gap Road.

Note: *A country store is located 0.3 mile from the southern, GA 60 end of Section 3. If you are walking this section from north to south, from Skeenah Gap Road to GA 60, turn left onto GA 60 South and walk the short distance to the store, which is on the right side of the highway.*

NATURE NOTES

SPRING IS A PARTICULARLY ENJOYABLE time to explore BMT-3. The views, the rock outcrops, and the high points of at least two mountains are enhanced by the vernal colors—the greening of the hard-

wood forest and the blossoms of wildflowers. This stretch has a good spring wildflower display, which includes flame azalea and pink lady's-slipper. Others on the early bloomer's list include trailing arbutus, bloodroot, halberd-leaved violet, dwarf and crested dwarf iris, Solomon's seal and false Solomon's seal, toothwort, Catesby's trillium, mayapple, yellow star-grass, foamflower, Indian cucumber-root, and violet wood sorrel. Spring wildflower color ends with whorled loosestrife, galax, fairywand, and firepink (in bloom on June 12 of a recent year). The firepink's narrow red petals, arranged like five propellers notched at their outward tips, are all you need to make an accurate identification.

firepink

Flowering dogwood finish blooming in early May; the occasional flame azalea lights up the forest in late April and early May. Mountain laurel, the most common showy-flowered shrub, usually starts blooming at the lowest elevations by May 5.

Thriving throughout the Southern Appalachian region except at the highest elevations, the red maple is common to abundant beside much of the BMT's treadway from Springer Mountain to the Ocoee River. In fact, this hardwood—with its vivid red leaf stems, flowers, early fruit, and fall foliage—is the most numerous and widespread tree in eastern North America. The red maple is at least a minor component in nearly every forest east of the Mississippi. In the South, its elevational reach currently extends from sea level to slightly over 6,000 feet. With a boost from global warming, it may well climb higher still in the next century or two.

red maple

Foresters call this highly successful maple a "super generalist" because it now prospers in nearly every forested habitat within its huge range. Once considered primarily a swampland species, the red maple has adapted so well to current forest conditions over much of the East—logging, heavy deer browsing, fire suppression, and gypsy moth defoliation—that it has aggressively spread into uplands where it was rare a century ago. The numbers of this resilient, stump-sprouting broadleaf have increased most dramatically in disturbed woodlands, where it has often displaced oaks in the process. Red maple foliage contains chemicals that discourage deer and many insect pests. And, to further ensure survival, it sends its whirlygig seeds, too small to offer larger mammals much sustenance, spinning to the forest floor during spring, when they are not in great demand by wildlife.

You can often spot this species from a distance in spring as well as in fall. During late winter and early spring, its numerous flowers appear before the leaves break bud. Where these trees occur in large, sunlit stands, the red blush of its blooms is almost as dazzling as their bright red fall foliage.

This maple's leaves are readily identified, even though they vary somewhat in size and shape. Opposite and coarsely toothed, the leaves have three prominent, short-pointed lobes. Often two smaller lobes (for a total of five) jut outward near the base of the 2½- to 5½-inch-long leaves.

Like other trees that inhabit a wide range of sites, the red maple's size depends upon where it is rooted. On dry, thin-soiled ridges, where many hardwoods don't grow at all, this maple usually remains a stunted understory tree beneath the pines and oaks. But in coves and along stream corridors, the red maple grows into the canopy tall and straight.

NORTH TO SOUTH Skeenah Gap to Little Skeenah Creek

Mile 0.0—From the Skeenah Gap Trailhead, follow the BMT to the southeast of the road, down the steps and up into the power cut.

Mile 0.7—Section 3 swings up and to the left onto the crest of a Rhodes Mountain spur.

Mile 1.0—Exits a stand of Virginia pine.

Mile 1.5—Reaches the Benton MacKaye–Duncan Ridge junction near the top of Rhodes Mountain.

Mile 1.8—Passes through a saddle.

Mile 2.1—Advances through another saddle. (Just beyond the bottom of the gap, a blue-blazed sidepath drops sharply to the left, east, less than 0.1 mile to a spring.)

Mile 2.4—Levels atop Licklog Mountain's crown.

Mile 2.9—Ranges through a slight saddle.

Mile 3.3—Crosses a woods road in a shallow gap.

Mile 3.9—Tops the rise of Wallalah Mountain.

Mile 4.3—Passes near a rock outcrop that offers open vistas, especially during the bare-branch season.

Mile 4.7—Doglegs 90 degrees to the left, then turns down and to the right off the main ridge leading to Wallalah.

Mile 5.7—Section 3 ends at GA 60 just beyond the bridge over Little Skeenah Creek.

DIRECTIONS

SECTION 3'S LITTLE SKEENAH CREEK Trailhead is located on the north side of GA 60, northwest of the US 19–GA 60 junction at Stonepile Gap and southeast of Morganton, Georgia. This trailhead is the northern end of Section 2 and the southern end of Section 3.

Approach from the southeast: From the US 19–GA 60 junction at Stonepile Gap north of Dahlonega, Georgia, travel GA 60 North slightly less than 22.0 miles to where the Benton MacKaye crosses the highway. Pull-off parking to the right, several hiker-symbol signs, and white blazes mark the trailhead. The entrance to dirt-gravel FS 816 should be on your left, opposite the pull-off parking.

Approach from the northwest: From Morganton, Georgia, where GA 60 South turns 90 degrees to the right a short distance beyond the post office, follow GA 60 South approximately 11.8 miles (0.8 mile beyond Skeenah Gap Road, which is to the left of the highway) to where the Benton MacKaye crosses the highway for the second time traveling in this direction. Pull-off parking to the left, several hiker-symbol signs, and white blazes mark the trailhead. The entrance to dirt-gravel FS 816 should be on your right, opposite the pull-off parking.

Approach from the northeast: From the US 76–US 129 intersection in Blairsville, Georgia, where US 129 North crosses US 76 and leaves Blairsville, proceed on US 76 West or turn onto US 76 West. If you approach this junction from the south, on US 129 North, circle three-quarters around the Blairsville Square, turn right to remain on US 129, then head 0.4 mile to an all-way stop. Turn right again at the stop sign and gas station, continue 0.1 mile, then turn left onto US 76 West. Once on US 76 West, drive 0.1 mile, then turn left onto signed Blue Ridge Highway (also known and signed as Old Blue Ridge Highway). Travel this road for approximately 7.5 miles prior to turning left onto signed Skeenah Gap Road.

Stay straight ahead on Skeenah Gap Road for slightly less than 8.0 miles to its three-way intersection with GA 60. Turn left onto GA 60 and proceed 0.8 mile to the Little Skeenah Creek Trailhead.

If you walk the Benton MacKaye to the north side of the highway, across the bridge over Little Skeenah Creek, you will be following Section 3 toward its northern end at Skeenah Gap. If you hike to the south of the highway, the FS 816 side, you will be on Section 2 heading toward its southern end at Three Forks.

Shuttle: Setting a shuttle to hike this section from south to north—from Little Skeenah Creek at GA 60 to Skeenah Gap—is short and straightforward. If you are traveling from the southeast (Stonepile Gap), continue driving on GA 60 for 0.8 mile beyond the Little Skeenah Creek Trailhead before turning right onto Skeenah Gap Road. Follow Section 4's directions—approach from the southeast (see page 123)—to the Skeenah Gap Trailhead, then backtrack to the Little Skeenah Creek Trailhead.

If you are traveling from the northwest (Morganton), follow Section 4's directions—approach from the northwest (see page 123)—to the Skeenah Gap Trailhead. Backtrack to GA 60, turn left onto the highway, and proceed 0.8 mile to the Little Skeenah Creek Trailhead.

If you are traveling from the northeast (Blairsville), follow the directions already given in this section. While driving Skeenah Gap Road, leave a vehicle at the Skeenah Gap Trailhead (see Section 4, approach from the northeast, on page 123) before continuing to the Little Skeenah Creek Trailhead.

NOTES

Summer view from the BMT

Skeenah Gap to Wilscot Gap

4

**BMT—SECTION 4
Skeenah Gap
to Wilscot Gap**

Benton MacKaye Trail, Section 4

*Skeenah Gap at Skeenah Gap Road
to Wilscot Gap at GA 60*

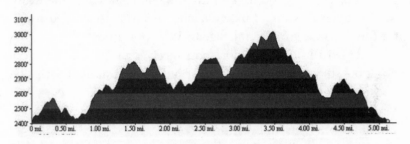

LENGTH 5.3 miles

DAYHIKING (SOUTH TO NORTH) Easy to Moderate

BACKPACKING (SOUTH TO NORTH) Moderate

VEHICULAR ACCESS AT EITHER END Eastern end at Skeenah
Gap Road, 2,380 feet; western end at GA 60, 2,430 feet

TRAIL JUNCTIONS None

BLAZE White diamond

TOPOGRAPHIC QUADRANGLE Wilscot GA

DELORME MAP GA-14

COUNTIES Union GA, Fannin GA

NEAREST CITIES Ellijay GA (SW), Blue Ridge GA (NW),
Blairsville GA (NE)

RD/NF Toccoa/Chattahoochee

FEATURES Winter views; flame azalea display

STARTING AT SKEENAH GAP, section low point at 2,380
feet, BMT-4 runs north along the Union–Fannin
County border before bending west toward the crest of

Deadennen Mountain. This change in compass heading represents a major directional shift; beyond this long curve, the Benton MacKaye meanders generally westward for the next 36 miles. The route rides the long ridgeline westward to the top of Deadennen Mountain, section high point at 3,040 feet, where the treadway switches the line of march again, this time to the southwest for the remainder of the mileage to Wilscot Gap.

Provided the trail corridor soon receives protection, this section's best days are in the future. At present, substantial path-side tracts are regenerating from relatively recent timber cuts, but these trees will grow rapidly, self cull, and quickly acquire a diversity of bole heights and widths.

Walked from Skeenah Gap, Section 4 immediately climbs the steps up the northwestern road bank and enters the primal forms and symmetries of the forest. The initial grade—easy to moderate for a little over 100 yards—ascends below the eaves of an oak-pine canopy, dominated by three pines—white, shortleaf, and Virginia—and at least five species of oak, including southern red. Mountain laurel and deciduous heath (blueberries and huckleberries) are common in the understory. After the length of a football field, end zones included, the walking reaches a minor spur, dips with the crest, and starts an easy up-ridge run at 0.1 mile. The mild grades, both up and down, proceed northward on the ridgetop roadbed along the Union–Fannin County line. Mile 0.4 descends moderately for a short distance as it slants to the right and down off the ridgeline onto a predominantly hardwood slope controlled by the oaks, especially the chestnut oak, which greatly benefited from the demise of the American chestnut.

Following an easy-to-moderate downgrade, the woods-road route regains the crest briefly at 0.5 mile before slabbing to the right and down off the backbone. It then rounds the uppermost cleft of a hollow, rises, then levels on a southeast slope supporting evergreen colonies of galax, the herbaceous plant that emits the peculiar sweet skunky scent often associated with the mountains. The track crosses over a spur at 0.6 mile and undulates gently on uppermost slope. Along this stretch, you can find some of those stubborn chestnut saplings: root-sucker clones offering the species no chance for randomly selected resistance to the blight.

bracken fern

At 0.8 mile the cut-in path begins a 0.2-mile ascent (easy to moderate the most difficult) in the shade of an oak-pine assemblage where a dense growth of deciduous heath occasionally flanks the tread. The upgrade regains the spine, rising with the ridge for nearly 0.1 mile to the top of an anonymous knob (2,700 feet) at mile 1.0. After a short dip off the knob, the BMT roller-coasters again (easy to moderate down the steepest) on or near the crest to mile 1.4, where it slips down and to the left onto the uppermost pitch. Along the way, the footpath runs through a sunny patch of woods where bracken fern and blackjack oak, a tree species uncommon above 2,000 feet in the Southern Appalachians, indicate dry conditions. As the route starts to skirt the upper southern pitch of a 2,900-foot knob, the Benton MacKaye bends to the west at mile 1.4.

Section 4 dips and rises as usual, ties into roadbed and ridgecrest, then heads down progressively harder to moderate until it levels in a slight saddle (2,740 feet) at mile 1.7. The next 0.4 mile gains elevation easily beneath the overhang of a an oak-hickory forest to the high point of a 2,850-foot knob at mile 1.9 before dropping to Payne Gap (2,630 feet) at mile 2.1. The downgrade, which switchbacks near the midpoint, reaches moderate difficulty at least twice. To the right of the gap (north), a blue-blazed path leads a little more than 0.1 mile to a spring.

ROVING STRAIGHT AHEAD across the woods road in Payne Gap, BMT-4 follows a former logging road as it porpoises up and over the next two small bumps on the ridgeline. Mile 2.5 begins an overall easy upgrade alongside a colony of hay-scented fern to a prominent but unnamed knob (2,860 feet) at mile 2.7. Looks through dormant hardwoods to the left, across the Skeenah Creek valley, reveal Tooni Mountain (180 degrees) south of GA 60, and Wallalah (175 degrees) and Licklog (150 degrees) Mountains on the same fold north of the highway.

Inside a forest largely clothed with yellow poplar and oak, the ridgetop-roadbed loses elevation (overall easy) until it crosses FS 640A in a gap (2,700 feet) at mile 3.0. On the other side of the road, the walking resumes its arch-and-roll pattern on or near the keel of the ridge nearly due west to Deadennen Mountain. Here the hiking heads up gradually, switchbacks to the left, then climbs moderately for a short distance before leveling atop a minor knob (2,890 feet) at mile 3.2. From here the walkway threads through a shallow saddle, makes an easy-to-moderate ascent to the next knob (3,010 feet) at mile 3.5, slides to the next saddle at mile 3.6, and rises again.

The elevation gain to Deadennen Mountain is gradual—a short easy-to-moderate stretch the most difficult. Here the trail leads through hay-scented fern colonies; a steady warm breeze occasionally sweetens the air with their scent. Mile 3.7 flattens out on the summit of Deadennen Mountain—section high point at 3,040 feet. Deadennen's name may have originated from the pioneer practice of girdling trees as the first step in clearing new land.

The path makes a steady, easy descent to the south from Deadennen Mountain to Lula Head Gap. From Deadennen's crown, where the slope drops precipitously toward a beginning branch, the track turns to the left and down toward a south-running spur. At mile 3.8 the treadway gains the crest of the spur. One-tenth mile farther, the route veers to the left with a woods road onto the eastern slope; after another tenth-mile, it switchbacks to the right with the roadbed above a sheltered hardwood hollow. The mild downgrade proceeds—often near spurs until it returns to the main ridge—to Lula Head Gap (2,580 feet) at mile 4.4.

Now venturing to the southwest, the Benton MacKaye gradually rises on ridgetop roadbed, slabbing to the left onto the slope and skirting the upper southeastern pitch of Wilscot Mountain. The remaining segment of Section 4 swings over a spur descending southward from the mountain at mile 4.7 before starting the steady downhill run (easy with one very short exception) south of the fold. The course ranges through a grove of white pine at mile 5.1, and continues the undemanding descent to Highway 60 at Wilscot Gap (2,430 feet). The trail angles to the right across the highway; Section 5 begins beside the "road closed" sign, the gate, and the guiding white diamond.

NATURE NOTES

ALTHOUGH THIS STRETCH DOES NOT traverse moist, north-facing hollows and slopes—the best habitat for herbaceous wildflowers—it does support a fair number of spring ephemerals. Section 4's flowering shrub display, however, more than makes up for its relative lack of forest-floor color. On May 6 of a recent year, mountain laurel was just beginning to bloom and the flame azalea was perhaps a day or two past perfection. Especially beyond mile 4.0 (south to north) this azalea is abundant and stop-you-in-your-tracks beautiful during a good year.

flame azalea

A tall heath in the same genus as rhododendron, the flame azalea is almost as inconspicuous without its flowers as it is conspicuous with them. In peak bloom this species is the most strikingly colored deciduous shrub found in the Southern Highlands, and it is immediately recognized by all who know its name. But as soon as the fire has faded and fallen, the small, pale green leaves blend in with the rest of the foliage in the summer understory, and the plants go largely unnoticed until the following spring.

Known to many old-timers as wild honeysuckle, mature azaleas are usually only 4 to 10 feet tall. Occasionally, in rich habitats, this shrub attains a treelike height of 15 to 18 feet. The blossoms often appear before the leaves are fully grown. Clusters of five to seven corollas near branch ends range from light orangish yellow to dark orangish red.

Before the blight, the American chestnut was the most massive, most numerous, and most important tree—to wildlife and humans alike—in the Southern Appalachian forest. Its destruction was an ecological disaster. The species once crowned as the queen of the forest ranged from 80 to 130 feet tall, with a large, spreading crown easily recognized from a distance in winter. Slowly, year after rainy year, it grew to a now scarcely believable thickness: a maximum of 10 to 13 feet in diameter. Written reports described even larger specimens, from 14 to 17 feet in diameter.

In 1540, one of Hernando de Soto's chroniclers, the gentleman of Elvas, wrote: "Where there are mountains, there are chestnuts." The chestnut once flourished in a variety of habitats, from near riverside to extremely dry ridges. In some areas of the Southern Blue Ridge, this prolific mast producer constituted 25 to 40 percent of the forest. It sometimes occurred in nearly pure stands on ridgetops up to approximately 5,000 feet in elevation. Regarded as hardy and disease resistant before the imported blight, chestnuts occasionally lived as long as 600 years.

American chestnut

Thus far the chestnut has refused to succumb completely. Ever since the blight, root sprouts have grown into small saplings, only to be mowed down in turn by the fungus. Since these root-sprout saplings are genetic clones, they offer the species no chance of selective resistance to the fungus. Occasionally, a sapling will reach 4 to 6 inches in diameter, very rarely 10 inches in diameter, before being killed by the bark-ripping blight.

Chestnut saplings still remain occasional to common along much of the BMT corridor. If you see a sapling (especially one next to a slightly larger dead sapling) that has long, relatively narrow leaves with large, pointed saw teeth on the margins, you are probably looking at a chestnut. If the underside of the leaf is pale green and smooth, you are absolutely looking at what remains of the once mighty American chestnut.

NORTH TO SOUTH Wilscot Gap to Skeenah Gap

Mile 0.0—From the Wilscot Gap Trailhead off GA 60, follow the BMT from the back end of the parking area on the east side of the highway.

Mile 0.6—Section 4 swings over a spur.

Mile 0.9—Ranges through Lula Head Gap.

Mile 1.6—Flattens out on the peak of Deadennen Mountain.

Miles 1.8, 2.1—Rolls over minor knobs.

Mile 2.3—Crosses FS 640A in a gap.

Mile 2.6—Reaches high point of a knob.

Mile 3.2—Crosses a woods road in Payne Gap (spring located slightly over 0.1 mile to the left, north, of the gap).

Mile 3.4—Rises to the crown of a knob.

Mile 3.6—Dips to a shallow saddle.

Mile 3.9—Regains the crestline after swinging around the southwestern flank of a knob.

Mile 4.3—Tops a knob.

Mile 5.3—Section 4 descends to and ends at Skeenah Gap on the northwestern side of Skeenah Gap Road.

DIRECTIONS

SECTION 4'S SKEENAH GAP Trailhead is located off Skeenah Gap Road immediately before the Union County sign when you are traveling Skeenah Gap Road north from GA 60. This trailhead is the northern end of Section 3 and the southern (actually eastern) end of Section 4.

Approach from the southeast: From the US 19–GA 60 junction at Stonepile Gap north of Dahlonega, Georgia, travel GA 60 North approximately 22.5 miles before turning right onto signed Skeenah Gap Road. Proceed approximately 3.5 miles on Skeenah Gap Road to where the Benton MacKaye crosses the pavement just before the signed Union County line. Uphill steps to the left side of the road, pull-off parking to the right of the road, blazes, and one or more Benton MacKaye signs mark the trailhead.

Approach from the northwest: From Morganton, Georgia, where GA 60 South turns 90 degrees to the right a short distance beyond the post office, remain on GA 60 South approximately 11.0 miles to the left turn onto signed Skeenah Gap Road. (Follow directions for the previous approach, from the southeast, for the remainder of the distance.)

Approach from the northeast: From the US 76–US 129 intersection in Blairsville, Georgia, where US 129 North crosses US 76 and leaves Blairsville, continue on US 76 West or turn onto US 76 West. If you approach this junction from the south, on US 129 North, circle three-quarters around the Blairsville Square, turn right to stay on US 129, then head 0.4 mile to an all-way stop. Turn right again at the stop sign and gas station, follow US 129 for 0.1 mile, then turn left onto US 76 West. Once on US 76 West, travel 0.1 mile, then turn left onto signed Blue Ridge Highway (also known and signed as Old Blue Ridge Highway).

After advancing approximately 7.5 miles on this road, turn left onto signed Skeenah Gap Road. Follow Skeenah Gap Road a little less than 4.5 miles to where the Benton MacKaye crosses the pavement just beyond the Fannin County sign. Uphill steps to the right side of the road, pull-off parking to the left of the road, blazes, and one or more Benton MacKaye signs mark the trailhead.

If you walk the Benton MacKaye to the northwest side of Skeenah Gap Road, the side with the rising steps, you will be on Section 4 heading toward GA 60 at Wilscot Gap. If you follow the white blazes to the southeast side of the road, the side with the descending steps and power cut, you will be hiking Section 3 toward GA 60 at Little Skeenah Creek.

Shuttle: If you plan to set a shuttle and hike this section from south to north (actually east to west), from Skeenah Gap to Wilscot Gap, your shuttle is fairly short and straightforward. If you are traveling from the southeast (Stonepile Gap), follow Section 5's directions, approach from the southeast (see page 139), to the Wilscot Gap Trailhead, then backtrack approximately 3.5 miles on GA 60 before turning left onto Skeenah Gap Road.

If you are traveling from the northwest (Morganton), follow Section 5's directions, approach from the northwest (see page 139), to the Wilscot Gap Trailhead, then continue approximately 3.5 more miles on GA 60 South before turning left onto Skeenah Gap Road.

If you are traveling from the northeast (Blairsville), follow Section 5's directions, approach from the northeast (see page 139), to the Wilscot Gap Trailhead, then backtrack to the Skeenah Gap Trailhead, which you passed on your way to GA 60.

Morning mist

Wilscot Gap to Shallowford Bridge 5

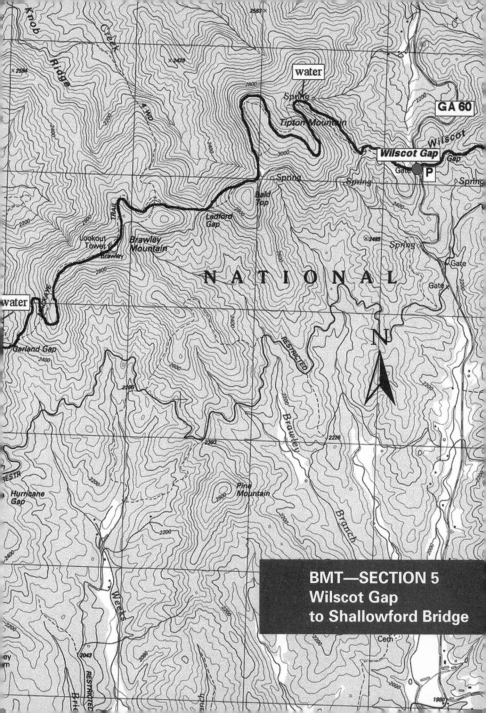

water

Spring

Tipton Mountain

GA 60

Wilscot Gap

Wilscot Gap

Gate P

Spring

Spring

Spring

Bald Top

Ledford Gap

Gate

Lookout Tower

Brawley Mountain

Gate

Brawley

N A T I O N A L

water

Garland Gap

TRAIL

RESTRICTED

N

Brawley

RESTR

Hurricane Gap

Pine Mountain

Branch

Weeks

Cem

RESTRICTED

**BMT—SECTION 5
Wilscot Gap
to Shallowford Bridge**

Benton MacKaye Trail, Section 5

Wilscot Gap at GA 60 to Shallowford Bridge over the Toccoa River at Aska Road

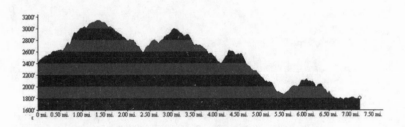

LENGTH 7.7 miles

DAYHIKING (SOUTH TO NORTH) Moderate

BACKPACKING (SOUTH TO NORTH) Moderate to Strenuous

VEHICULAR ACCESS AT EITHER END Northeastern end at GA 60, 2,430 feet; southwestern end at Aska Road, 1,760 feet

TRAIL JUNCTIONS None

BLAZE White diamond

TOPOGRAPHIC QUADRANGLES Wilscot GA, Blue Ridge GA

DELORME MAP GA-14

COUNTY Fannin GA

NEAREST CITIES Ellijay GA (SW), Blue Ridge GA (NW), Blairsville GA (NE)

RD/NF Toccoa/Chattahoochee

FEATURES Hardwood coves and spring wildflower displays; winter views; year-round view from base of Brawley Mountain Lookout Tower; wildlife opening; Toccoa River

ECTION 5 OFFERS HIKERS A DIVERSITY of habitats, ranging from mid-elevation oak-hickory ridgecrests and botanically rich hardwood coves to low-elevation oak-pine forests lit with flame azalea in spring and a riverine strip flanking the Toccoa River. BMT-5 also wanders past a wildlife opening, climbs to a fire tower atop Brawley Mountain (the only tower still in existence beside the BMT; it is not open for public use), and ends with a 0.5-mile road-walk that closely parallels the shoaling Toccoa.

From Wilscot Gap, the trail winds to the southwest over or around the crowns of four named peaks—Tipton Mountain, Bald Top, Brawley Mountain, and Garland Mountain. The route is significantly less difficult hiked as described, from northeast to southwest, from Wilscot Gap to Shallowford Bridge. Either way you walk it, however, this segment's 7.7-mile length and its approximately 4,100 feet of elevation change (either up or down) offer a challenge that only those in at least fair physical condition should attempt to meet.

Beginning on the west side of GA 60 at Wilscot Gap (the side opposite the parking area), Section 5 angles up and to the left onto an oak-hickory slope with shade-tolerant white pines advancing steadily in the understory. The trail undulates (a few short easy-to-moderate grades) to 0.3 mile, where it passes the first of a series of moist north- to northeast-facing hollows—surprisingly rich for their relatively low elevations. Following a short easy-to-moderate ascent, the treadway ties into a woods road and rounds the head of the next hollow at 0.4 mile. The hollows and the slopes between them support an impressive second-growth hardwood forest: green fountains held high above a lush tapestry of wildflowers and ferns. Basswood, yellow poplar, white ash, and northern red oak share sunlight in the canopy.

Heading northwest, the easygoing walkway winds around the notch of another hollow nearly every tenth mile to mile 0.9. At 0.7 mile the upgrade steepens for 0.1 mile; a short moderate ascent is the toughest pull. A sidepath to the right at 0.8 mile leads to an intermittent spring visible from the trail. If you can't find water at the spring, search down the hollow until you find the seep. Several decent-sized yellow poplars in the 9- to 10-foot-circumference range stand (if they are still alive) in the spring hollow. The track doglegs hard to the left around a slight hollow at 0.9 mile, rising into an open deciduous forest as it doubles back on itself to the southeast, higher on the same slope. By mile 1.1 the treadway curls to the right onto Tipton Mountain's ridgeline and travels to the northwest again.

Here the mild rise gains elevation to the top of Tipton's tiny crown (3,170 feet; section high point) at mile 1.3 before starting down to the right of the ridge. The sidehill path descends gradually through a grove of yellow poplar, the thickest 10 feet 8 inches in circumference, on a rich, northeast-facing wildflower slope. At mile 1.6, as the course curves to the left over the crest and swings south, partial summer views to the right provide peeks at Brawley Mountain's fire tower (220 degrees) and Rocky Knob Ridge to the west. The route sticks to the steady downhill run on a rocky, oak-wooded slope to mile 1.9, where a very short sidepath leads up and to the left to a wildlife opening and FS 45, the road that leads to the fire tower. You may camp in the clearing; you may not build a fire or a fire ring.

Beyond the drop-your-pack-and-lounge-in-the-grass opening, the Benton MacKaye ducks down sharply for 30 yards to rock steps, then eases to the gap (mile 2.0; 2,790 feet) between Tipton Mountain and Bald Top. Across the saddle, Section 5 slabs to the right onto the slope, skirting Bald Top's upper north pitch before dropping more steeply. The last 0.2 mile of the downgrade, over-all easy to moderate with a rock-step switchback, sinks into an oak-hickory forest where sassafras and red maple are common in the mid-canopy. At mile 2.3 the BMT dips to signed Ledford Gap (2,620 feet), turns to the right onto FS 45, follows the road for 40 yards, and bends to the right back into the woods at the double white blaze and carsonite sign.

THE CLIMB TO Brawley Mountain begins with a very short moderate grade before gaining elevation more gradually through a forest—a thicket-growth of small trees beneath scattered mature boles, mostly yellow poplar—heavily impacted by Hurricane Opal in the mid-1990s. By mile 2.4 the woodland walkway follows a roadbed and starts up easy to moderate as it advances westward across the north slope of an unnamed knob. The route crosses over a spur at mile 2.6, descending for 0.1 mile before rising again. Mile 2.9 gains the uppermost crest of Rocky Knob Ridge, a lead dropping to the north-northwest. The tread-way veers to the left (south) as it rounds the ridgetop, then slips slightly to the right of the backbone as it steadily ascends toward the main ridgeline. Climbing harder, Section 5 starts a short moderate-to-strenuous pull at mile 3.1 before becoming progressively less difficult to the cleared and towered top of Brawley Mountain (3,030 feet) at mile 3.2. The fire tower is not open to the public; the clearing, however, provides a limited open view down the power cut to Seabolt, Payne, and Picklesimer Mountains from 20 to 25 degrees. Camping is permissible at the fire tower, but there is no water nearby.

The Benton MacKaye turns right onto the fire tower road, following it for 65 yards to the usually signed and always blazed

90-degree turn to the right off the road onto ridgecrest. From here the passage descends gently on a former road surrounded by a young, all hardwood forest on or near the ridge (winter views to the left). The footpath crosses a slight saddle at mile 3.4 before ranging up and over the next knot on the spine. The downhill run, easy to moderate for 130 yards starting at mile 3.5, advances within woods where white ash saplings are unusually common. The course slants to the left of the keel at mile 3.7, beginning a trail builder's trick to reduce erosion and leg strain. Rather than routing the treadway straight down the steep crestline, the Benton MacKaye Trail Association created a sideways S configuration, half-looping the walkway away from and then back to the ridge, crossing the crest, then half-looping away and back to the ridge again.

Mile 3.8 rounds a steep-sided spur, continuing the easy walking on a well-constructed sidehill path below tall deciduous trees. The narrow passage crosses the broad ridgetop at mile 3.9, then begins the lower half-loop—a steady, no-strain grade through forest where pignut hickory and red maple rise into the overstory. The BMT briefly returns to the backbone at Garland Gap (mile 4.3; 2,420 feet). To the right (north) of the gap, a blue-blazed sidepath leads a little over 0.1 mile to a fairly reliable spring.

Once through the gap, the route drifts to the right of the ridge and ascends for 0.4 mile, traversing the upper-north flank of Garland Mountain. Here the steady easy upgrade threads through another rich wildflower and fern slope. All summer long you can spot broad beech, hay-scented, cinnamon, northern maidenhair and New York ferns on the forest floor. Starting at mile 4.5, the walking steepens for 0.1 mile—very short moderate followed by easy to moderate. The remainder of the elevation gain is gradual to the high point (2,640 feet) at mile 4.7, just below a spur north-west of Garland's apex.

The next 1.2-mile stretch drops down and down, losing 760 feet of elevation to Shallowford Bridge Road. The descent, spiced with some short moderate and longer easy-to-moderate grades, returns to the top of the fold, following a woods road into an oak-hickory forest. At mile 5.4 the track angles to the left of the keel onto a cut-in path; 0.1 mile farther, it swings to the right (west) onto a noticeably drier south-facing slope, where you can hear the shoaling Toccoa entrenched far below. The view to the left— slimmer in summer, wider in winter—focuses on the highest nearby peak across the river, 4,080-foot Big Bald at 245 degrees.

The forest becomes steadily drier as the trail loses south-slope elevation. Now short-leaf, Virginia, and white pines mix with the oaks (including southern red) and hickories. By mile 5.6 the trail ties into a roadbed

Christmas fern

flanked with white pine. Dark green Christmas ferns are among the few plants able to survive in the acidic and heavily shaded soil beneath the closely packed pines. The course bears off to the left onto a path at mile 5.7, but quickly returns to the same old road. Mile 5.9 dips to the intersection of Shallowford Bridge Road and Dial Road (1,880 feet) at their three-way intersection. Here the Benton MacKaye, faithfully following blazes, cuts straight across the intersection before returning to the woods on the right side of Shallowford Bridge Road.

Wilscot, formerly a small community near the road junction, still appears on topographical maps. This name is a shortened version of Will Scot, a nineteenth-century settler of mixed Native American and European parentage. Nearby Wilscot Mountain and Wilscot Gap were also probably named in Will's honor.

Beyond the road, the BMT enters the opening of Free Bend as the path rises toward Free Knob. Here Free Knob and its attendant ridges and spurs forced the free-flowing Toccoa River into a meandering, 6-mile-long near loop, to the west then back east to the mouth—less than a half-mile wide north to south.

Section 5 ventures west from the gap at Wilscot with one grunt to go—the overall easy-to-moderate ridgeline ascent toward Free Knob. The white diamonds lead you up and to the right off the roadbed onto a wide tread at mile 6.0. Following a short downgrade at mile 6.2, the route doglegs to the left off the crest onto a dry, oak-pine slope where blackjack and southern red oaks mingle in the diverse assemblage. Not quite a tenth-mile farther, the walkway switchbacks up and to the right to regain the spine. At mile 6.3 the BMT reaches an elevation of 2,140 feet before sinking to a slight saddle and rising to approximately the same elevation at mile 6.5.

As the ridgecrest rises straight ahead toward Free Knob (mile 6.6), the trail swerves left and down off the fold, descending an easy-to-moderate 0.6-mile grade to Shallowford Bridge Road. The woods-road track curls to the right over a spur (mile 6.9) onto a slope where most of the shadows belong to at least five species of oak. Here the river's rush becomes audible again. The course follows the top of another short spur downhill to mile 7.0, where it curves to the right off the spur and ducks into mountain laurel. A tenth-mile farther, the passage switchbacks down and to the left, remaining on roadbed as it angles toward the river. The rivulet in the ravine to the right provides potable water when filtered.

The Benton MacKaye sets foot on Shallowford Bridge Road (1,780 feet) at mile 7.2, turns right, and holds its course on the dirt-gravel as it closely parallels the Toccoa downstream. The road-walk features frequent close-up looks at the hurrying river, rippling and shoaling over rocks. Soon the road passes homes on the near upslope and across the river. It becomes paved at mile 7.6; one-tenth mile farther, the trail turns left and crosses Shallowford Bridge, iron-trussed and wooden-planked, over the gliding Toccoa. Section 5 ends across the bridge at the parking-area edge of Aska Road. Section 6 begins to the right, on the shoulder of Aska Road.

NATURE NOTES

DESPITE RELATIVELY LOW ELEVATIONS, this section's north-facing hollows and slopes support a surprisingly diverse spring wildflower display. On May 11, five species of trillium—Vasey's, large-flowered, and wake robin; Catesby's and yellow—bloomed beside BMT-5. It was the first time I had ever seen five different trilliums blossoming beside a North Georgia trail, or section of trail, on the same day. (The second time was the next year on BMT-8.) Bearing sessile blossoms (without any kind of stalk), only the yellow trillium, also known as yellow toadshade, is common. Other herbaceous wildflowers either blooming or already spent by mid-May include crested dwarf iris, foamflower, mayapple, doll's eyes, bloodroot, showy orchis, sourgrass (an oxalis or sorrel species with purple-rimmed leaves), yellow mandarin, blue cohosh, Solomon's seal and false Solomon's seal, jack-in-the-pulpit, Canada violet (exceptionally tall for a violet), whorled loosestrife, and wild geranium. The leaves of still others—black cohosh, jewelweed, Turk's-cap lily—promised color later in the year. April 20 through May 15 usually offers the maximum number of blooming wildflowers.

Relatively small clumps of mountain laurel, sweetshrub, and flame azalea (past prime) were also open in mid-May. Section 5 provides habitat for many fern species; broad beech, rattlesnake, northern maidenhair, bracken, New York, hay-scented, southern lady and Christmas are among the easiest to identify.

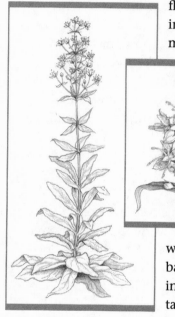

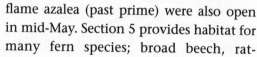

The treadway winds through at least half a dozen colonies of columbo: a distinctive, uncommon wildflower featuring an attention-grabbing basal rosette of large leaves (up to 16 inches long) and an erect stem (up to 9 feet tall) holding a panicle of small, somewhat inconspicuous corollas. Mature plants produce numerous layered leaves, narrow and unlobed, arching outward and upward. The columbo usually blooms atop its tall flowering stalk from late May until mid-June.

columbo

Basswood, a large and distinctive yet often unrecognized broadleaf, thrives in the moist hollows along this section's easternmost 0.9 mile starting from Wilscot Gap. The botanical controversy concerning the basswood's genus, *Tilia*, has waned for now. Current literature lumps all basswoods into one species—

the American basswood—with three varieties (Carolina, white, and American).

Basswood is sometimes referred to as linden, a name German settlers transferred from a *Tilia* species in Europe, or as bee-tree, because honeybees swarm to its fragrant blossoms. The common name basswood, recognized by botanists and foresters alike, stems from the bast (fibers in the tree's inner bark), which tribal Americans stripped to make rope.

basswood

This tree is identified by its large, alternate, heart-shaped leaves—sharply pointed, coarsely toothed, and usually 4 to 6 inches long and almost as wide. Bark on a maturing second-growth trunk is light to medium gray. Slight furrows rising in broken lines split the bark into vertical patterns. Especially in once- or twice-cut forests, basswoods often grow in multiboled clumps. A mature specimen can often be identified from a distance by its sapling ring—a circle of sprouts growing from the tree's base.

NORTH TO SOUTH Shallowford Bridge to Wilscot Gap

Mile 0.0—From Aska Road, cross Shallowford Bridge, turn right, then follow the road upstream beside the shoaling Toccoa River.

Mile 0.5—Section 5 turns to the left off the road and ascends toward Free Knob.

Mile 1.1—Angles up and to the right onto the crest of the spur descending eastward from Free Knob.

Miles 1.2, 1.4—Passes over two high points on the spur before descending toward Shallowford Bridge Road.

Mile 1.8—The trail dips to Shallowford Bridge Road, crosses the entrance of a side road, then re-enters the woods on the left side of the main road. The treadway gains 760 feet of elevation in the next 1.2 miles.

Mile 3.0—Advances to Garland Mountain as the track traverses its upper northern slope before descending.

Mile 3.4—Regains the ridge at Garland Gap. (To the left, north, of the gap, a blue-blazed sidepath leads a little over 0.1 mile to a spring.)

Mile 4.0—Returns to the ridgeline after gaining elevation slowly along a S-shaped trail segment.

Mile 4.5—Rises to the cleared and fire-towered top of Brawley Mountain, then descends.

Mile 5.4—Turns to the left onto FS 45, follows the road for 40 yards, then bends to the left off the road at usually signed Ledford Gap.

Mile 5.8—Passes a short sidepath up and to the right that leads to a wildlife opening.

Mile 6.4—Continues over the crown of Tipton Mountain, then descends gradually.

Mile 6.9—A sidepath to the left leads to an intermittent spring visible from the trail. Beyond the spring, Section 5 continues to descend through a series of rich hardwood hollows.

Mile 7.4—Rounds the last hollow.

Mile 7.7—Section 5 descends to and ends at Wilscot Gap on the west side of GA 60, the side across the highway from the trailhead parking area.

DIRECTIONS

SECTION 5'S WILSCOT GAP TRAILHEAD is located on the east side of GA 60 northwest of the US 19–GA 60 junction at Stonepile Gap and southeast of Morganton, Georgia. This trailhead is the northern (actually western) end of Section 4 and the southern (actually eastern) end of Section 5.

Approach from the southeast: From the US 19–GA 60 junction at Stonepile Gap north of Dahlonega, Georgia, follow GA 60 North slightly more than 26.0 miles to where the Benton Mac-Kaye crosses the highway for the second time when you are traveling in this direction. A large, half-circle parking area (partially paved) to the right side of the highway and a hiker-symbol sign mark the trailhead.

Approach from the northwest: From Morganton, Georgia, where GA 60 South turns 90 degrees to the right a short distance beyond the post office, travel GA 60 South approximately 7.5 miles to where the Benton MacKaye crosses the highway. A large, half-circle parking area (partially paved) to the left side of the highway and a hiker-symbol sign mark the trailhead.

Approach from the northeast: From the US 76–US 129 intersection in Blairsville, Georgia, where US 129 North crosses US 76 and leaves Blairsville, continue on US 76 West or turn onto US 76 West. If you approach this junction from the south, on US 129 North, circle three-quarters around the Blairsville Square, turn right to stay on US 129, then head 0.4 mile to an all-way stop. Turn right again at the stop sign and gas station, continue 0.1 mile, then turn left onto US 76 West. Once on US 76 West, drive

0.1 mile, then turn left onto signed Blue Ridge Highway (also known and signed as Old Blue Ridge Highway). Proceed on this road approximately 7.5 miles prior to turning left onto signed Skeenah Gap Road.

Stay straight ahead on Skeenah Gap Road for slightly less than 8.0 miles to its three-way intersection with GA 60. Turn right onto GA 60 and drive approximately 3.5 miles to where the Benton MacKaye crosses the highway. A large, half-circle parking area (partially paved) to the right side of the highway and a hiker-symbol sign mark the trailhead.

If you follow the Benton MacKaye to the west side of the highway (angle to the right across GA 60 from the parking area toward the gated road), the side opposite the parking area, you will be walking Section 5 toward its western end at Shallowford Bridge. If you hike with the white diamonds to the east of the highway, from the back of the parking area, you will be walking Section 4 from west to east, from Wilscot Gap to Skeenah Gap.

Shuttle: If you plan to hike this section from Wilscot Gap to Shallowford Bridge at Aska Road and plan to set a shuttle, you may want to leave a vehicle at Shallowford Bridge (follow the directions for Section 6, page 158, to the bridge), then cross the bridge, turn right, and drive Shallowford Bridge–Dial Road straight ahead (the road is known as Shallowford Bridge on one end and Dial on the other) approximately 7.2 miles (2.7 miles of dirt-gravel) to the GA 60–Dial Road junction. Turn left onto GA 60 North and travel approximately 2.8 miles to the Wilscot Gap Trailhead parking area to the right of the highway.

If you want to shorten your hike to 5.9 miles, follow the directions in the preceding paragraph, but instead of leaving a vehicle at the bridge, leave one a little closer to GA 60. Proceed 1.4 miles on Shallowford Bridge–Dial Road toward GA 60 before leaving your shuttle vehicle near the entrance of a side road to the left. Blazed with white Benton MacKaye diamonds, Section 5 drops to and crosses the entrance of this side road before re-entering the woods and completing its remaining mileage to Shallowford Bridge.

NOTES

Cinnamon fern

Shallowford Bridge to Weaver Creek Road 6

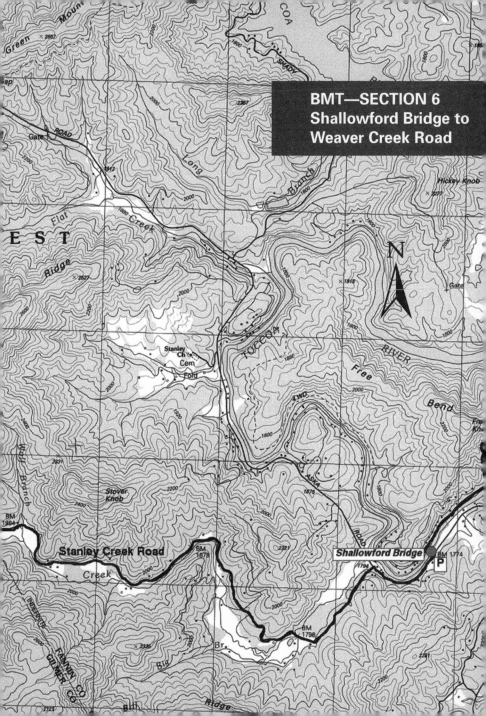

BMT—SECTION 6
Shallowford Bridge to
Weaver Creek Road

Benton MacKaye Trail, Section 6

Shallowford Bridge over the Toccoa River at Aska Road to Weaver Creek Road

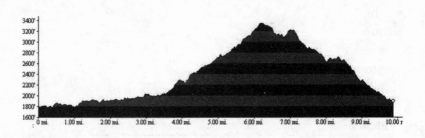

LENGTH 9.8 miles

DAYHIKING (SOUTH TO NORTH) Moderate

BACKPACKING (SOUTH TO NORTH) Moderate to Strenuous

VEHICULAR ACCESS AT EITHER END Southeastern end at Aska Road, 1,760 feet; northwestern end at Weaver Creek Road, 1,900 feet.

TRAIL JUNCTION Stanley Gap (see description)

BLAZES White diamond for Benton MacKaye; white rectangle for Stanley Gap

TOPOGRAPHIC QUADRANGLE Blue Ridge GA

DELORME MAP GA-14

COUNTIES Fannin GA, Gilmer GA

NEAREST CITIES Ellijay GA (SW), Blue Ridge GA (N), Blairsville GA (NE)

RD/NF Toccoa/Chattahoochee—except for the 3.5-mile road-walk

FEATURES Toccoa River; Fall Branch Falls; Rocky Mountain; winter views

STARTING FROM ITS southeastern end and low point at Shallowford Bridge (1,760 feet), Section 6 road-walks westward until it reaches the southeasternmost slopes of Rocky Mountain, where it changes course and heads generally north to Davenport Mountain. Beyond the turn, BMT-6 rises to its high point (3,360 feet) on the upper-north slope of Rocky Mountain. Past Davenport, the remainder of the route winds to the northwest to Weaver Creek Road. The treadway rides the western crest of the actual Blue Ridge and the Tennessee Valley Divide from south of Rocky Mountain to Scroggin Knob.

All of this segment's sustained grades are easy or easy to moderate. Its difficulty rating, however, has been bumped up a notch to reflect its 9.8-mile length and its elevation gain from low point to high—1,600 feet. Walked southeast to northwest, as described, the first 3.5 miles of this section—0.4 mile on Aska Road and the remainder on Stanley Creek Road—is a road-walk passing by houses and, occasionally, a territorial dog. Inevitably, there will be more houses and more dogs along Stanley Creek Road in the future. Walk softly and brandish a big hiking stick.

Beginning with your back to the Toccoa on the Aska Road side of Shallowford Bridge, turn right and follow Aska Road to the southwest (then northwest) and the river downstream. The normally shallow Toccoa flows fast on your right; the rest of the pavement and various buildings and businesses line the road to the left. Guided by the usual blaze throughout the road-walk, Section 6 turns left onto paved and signed Stanley Creek Road at the prominent Rich Mountain WMA sign at 0.4 mile. On the right just before the turn, Toccoa Riverside Restaurant offers sugar and salt fortifications for the open road.

The first stretch of Stanley Creek Road, which winds to the west, leads you through forested (for now) private property. By

0.7 mile the easy road-walk begins to pass houses, many of them new. The Benton MacKaye crosses over Stanley Creek at 1.0 mile. Beyond the brook, the low crest to the left above the Stanley Creek valley is Bill Ridge. At mile 1.2 you can spot the first of a few umbrella magnolias to the left of the road. By mile 1.5 the blacktop runs alongside rocky Stanley Creek to the left. The road remains fairly near the stream for almost 0.5 mile.

The pavement ends (for now) at mile 3.3, and the dirt-gravel road quickly passes beside the weathered outbuildings of the Stanley home place. In 1986, when all of the namesake road was unpaved, and cornfields filled the bottom across the road from the farmhouse, I started a long nearby trail—called Rich Mountain then—a couple of hours later than I would have liked. By the time I completed my measure-wheeling and note-taking, I knew the nearly 9-mile backtrack would lead me to trailhead and truck well after dark, home well after midnight. I had been in the mountains hiking for four days; I was hot, tired, and in a sudden hurry to head for home. I decided to hitchhike, a last resort I normally avoided.

The thumbing went fairly well once I reached a paved road, but no one picked me up on Stanley Creek Road. The further I went, the fewer chances I had, so I stashed my wheel in the woods, gave up on catching a ride, and walked fast into the summer evening. As I passed the Stanley place, just before dusk drifted out of the forest, I saw an older couple, perhaps in their mid-seventies, cooling their heels on the front porch. The man stood up, hollered out a hello, then gave me a quick, appraising glance before speaking again: "Young man you look mighty hot and thirsty. Come on up, sit a spell, and drink some lemonade." He didn't have to ask twice; the August day was still sweltering, and I had long since run out of water. I walked up to the porch, shook his hand, introduced myself, and sat in the proffered rocking chair—the best seat. While I answered their curious questions, and while we talked of the mountains, I drank and drank— most of a big pitcher of homemade lemonade. After a half hour or so, and after he asked if I needed to use his bathroom, he drove me up the darkening road to my truck.

Ever since that close encounter with kindness, when people ask me *Deliverance*-type questions, expecting the sort of hype and stereotype too willingly believed by urban readers, I counter with my stories, my experiences. Although the truth may sometimes seem too boring to sell books, I like to tell it now and then as a partial counterweight to falsehoods and sensationalism.

I have hiked several years worth of days in the Southern Appalachians, many of them alone; overall, I have come through as safe as an angel in the eye of a hurricane. I have come to no harm worse than a yellow jacket's sting. No bears have blocked my path; no rattlesnakes have struck from ambush. My rudest treatment to date has come from a very few dog owners who did not control their unruly pets when I asked—and most of them were not from the mountains. So after all my years of hiking in Highland Dixie, my only story involving the maligned mountaineers remains the one about my confrontation with uncommon kindness, about the gentle man in the mountains, Mr. Stanley, who asked a stranger—a bearded, sweaty, and smelly stranger with a pack on his back and a stout stick in his hand—up to his porch for refreshment.

BMT-6 CROSSES A SHORT wooden bridge over Fall Branch at mile 3.5 (2,000 feet), then quickly makes a usually signed and always double-blazed right turn off the road—through the Benton MacKaye parking area and back onto wildland treadway again. Here the hiking, now heading northwest, enters the riparian green of hemlock and rhododendron as it closely parallels the small-volume stream. Past the first cabin across the brook, the track begins an easy uphill grade on the rocky old roadbed. Soon you lose sight of the noisy, cascading run below.

At mile 3.7, fifty yards after the route starts an easy-to-moderate rise, a sidepath leads down and to the right a short distance to the observation deck in front of Fall Branch Falls: a twisting, 55- to 60-foot drop framed by forest. Up high and to the left the froth leaps free, quick and quivering when there is water enough. The middle is a sloshing, slanting slide to the right; the bottom pours straight down over wide rock face. There is no upstream development above the falls; you can filter water here.

BEYOND THE SIDEPATH, Section 6 accompanies the branch past the waterfall; on a sunny day you can see the bright pour of the upper falls. Mile 3.8 (2,240 feet), usually marked with at least one sign and a blaze, switchbacks sharply up and to the left, nearly doubling back on itself to the south-southeast. The BMT, now on hand-crafted sidehill footpath, gradually gains elevation to mile 4.0, where it curls 90 degrees to the right and up onto the ridgeline of a Rich Mountain spur. This southeast-facing spur is dry; Virginia pine and scarlet oak shade bracken fern and deciduous heath. After slipping below the keel onto the uppermost slope, the course bends to the left (mile 4.3) onto the main spur leading upward to the Blue Ridge. Now heading west, the Benton MacKaye makes an overall easy upridge run in the midst of an oak-pine forest; Virginia, shortleaf, and white pines compete for the canopy with hickory and at least five species of oak.

The walkway ties into the Stanley Gap Trail at the 4.6-mile mark (2,640 feet). Here the BMT turns right at the signed T-junction and shares the wider and well-worn route, additionally blazed with white rectangles and open to both hikers and bikers. The two-trail treadway slabs to the right (north) of the ridgecrest, ascending a mild grade beneath the roof of a largely hardwood forest. At mile 4.9 the passage angles up to the ridgetop—the Blue Ridge—then quickly crosses it and proceeds steadily upward in dry, south-slope woods. Where the cut-in path levels for a short distance at mile 5.0, Section 6 affords partial summer views framing 3,845-foot Cold Mountain to the left at 200 degrees.

The upslope run traverses the south side of a Rich Mountain spur; looks to the left between leafy branches show you more wild mountains wracked into buckled folds. At mile 5.2 the track swings to the right, completing a flattened half-loop over and around the uppermost pitch of the spur. Once the trail reaches the north slope, another summer-forest view opens toward your next goal: 3,460-foot Rocky Mountain, due north and only a half-mile distant. Some tall yellow poplar—gray-barked trees with re-markably straight boles—stand on the north side of the spur.

The upgrade gains the narrow crest of the Blue Ridge at mile 5.4. It then immediately bears off onto sunrise slope, rolling gen-tly with the terrain on well-constructed path. The nearly effort-less walking rounds the narrow trough of a hollow at mile 5.7, then rises over a slight spur before passing an intermittent seep-age spring at mile 5.8. Here, as the track skirts the upper slopes of Rocky Mountain to the east then north around its summit, the changes in elevation and exposure are reflected in the composi-tion and structure of the forest. Sweet birch and basswood are now common components; the oaks are significantly taller than those at the lower elevations. Where the treadway sweeps over the upper end of Bellcamp Ridge (mile 6.0; 3,260 feet)—a long Rocky Mountain lead fingering away to the east-northeast—the easy hiking enters a fern field flanking both sides of the Benton MacKaye. After a short easy-to-moderate upgrade to section high point (3,360 feet) on Rocky Mountain's uppermost north slope, the route threads through a scenic area of rock outcrops, most of them lichened gray, up and to the left of the tread.

white oak

The walkway veers onto the Rich Mountain crest north of Rocky Mountain (Rocky is a named peak on Rich Mountain) at mile 6.2. Still tending to the north, the path heads downhill on or near the ridgeline for 0.6 mile, a short, sharp pitch by far the steepest grade. The course descends into mixed hardwoods and white pine; at mile 6.4 a large fern field sprawls away downslope. After passing through a shallow saddle, Section 6 gradually gains elevation up the rocky keel to the usually signed junction at mile 6.9 (3,200 feet). Here the two trails go their own ways: Stanley Gap lights out downhill and to the right, to the northeast; good old Benton MacKaye marches forward, straight up the ridge.

Beyond the junction, the BMT eases up the spine for less than 0.1 mile to the level white oak crown of an unchristened Rich Mountain knob. From here, the next 1.1 miles make a winding descent on or near a broad ridge—the Blue Ridge and the Tennessee Valley Divide. Occasional short easy-to-moderate stretches enliven the otherwise tame walk. Without bikes and two-trail traffic, the treadway is now narrower, scarcely scuffed, and much less traveled. The route swings to the left and down off the crest onto the north-facing pitch at mile 7.0, passing through an open forest with basswood, sweet birch, yellow poplar, and black cherry surrounded by ferns. Now ranging to the northwest, the downgrade quickly returns to the ridgeline and slips onto slope before returning to the top of the fold once again. Mile 7.5 curls to the left and down off the ridgetop onto roadbed at an old homesite, marked by two rock-pile cairns to the right.

The BMT, heading southwest until the next sweeping turn, rounds an upper hollow on woods road, gains the crest, and levels beneath the dome of a forest where chestnut oak, sourwood, blackgum, and Virginia pine darken the deciduous heath below. As the course curves to the right onto slope at mile 7.9, a blue-blazed sidepath to the left leads slightly less than 0.1 mile down to water. Section 6 passes through a shallow saddle (2,630 feet) at mile 8.1, then begins its roller-coasting run to Scroggin Knob. Here the hiking rises to an unnamed knob at mile 8.2, descending moderately for a tenth of a mile to the next gap before making a generally easy upgrade to Scroggin's northernmost topknot (2,730 feet) at mile 8.5.

The Benton MacKaye angles to the right off the knob's crest, makes a short easy-to-moderate descent, curls back left over ridgeline, and starts a steady easy downgrade amidst a largely deciduous forest. From the top of Scroggin Knob, the trail loses a little over 800 feet of elevation in the next mile. This downhill stretch includes sustained easy-to-moderate grades and a few short, steeper drops. By mile 8.7 the walkway is advancing westward on a spur ridge fringed with Virginia pine and drier-site hardwoods such as southern red oak. The route swings to the left off the spur at mile 8.8, switchbacking downslope to the south. At mile 9.0 partial summer views showcase the green curve of Deadline Ridge nearby to the south. The treadway travels atop a spur for a few feet at mile 9.2 before bending to the right and down onto a predominantly hardwood slope. The sidehill path half-circles the tilted chute of a yellow poplar hollow and quickly enters oak-pine forest again.

Pushing north now, the BMT does what all good slope-traversing trails do: it crosses the interlocking splay of spur and hollow by winding over spurs in one direction and rounding hollows in the opposite direction, frequently scribing S-curves along the way. At mile 9.5 the track gains a small amount of elevation over a spur, then continues the mild descent to mile 9.7, where it crosses the north fork of Laurel Creek (1,900 feet). If you are continuing on Section 7 without reprovision, filter Laurel Creek water here before it flows into private property. The remainder of Section 6 rises slightly through young pines before dipping to the entrance of a private road at its T-intersection with two public roads. Weaver Creek Road's pavement ends at the junction; Laurel Creek Road, rough and rutted, heads downhill and to the left of the intersection. Section 6 ends at the T; Section 7 continues on unpaved Laurel Creek Road.

pink lady's-slipper

NATURE NOTES

THE PUBLIC LAND SEGMENT of this section, from Falls Branch to Weaver Creek Road, boasts a good spring wildflower display from April 20 through May 10. A partial list of herbaceous wildflowers includes pink lady's-slipper, halberd-leaved violet, foamflower, Catesby's and large-flowered trillium, dwarf and crested dwarf iris, yellow star-grass, giant chickweed, sourgrass, mayapple, whorled loosestrife, galax, Indian pipe, and bellwort. Mountain laurel and flame azalea flower in May.

The lady's-slipper colonies win best of show along this BMT section. Don't wait too late, though. During a recent cool, rainy spring, the vein-etched slippers were ready to wear on April 30, but many were faded and deflated by May 10.

With the exception of one small colony of interrupted fern growing on an east-facing slope of this section, the easily recognized cinnamon fern is the tallest fern beside the BMT from Springer Mountain to the Ocoee River. The cinnamon, usually found on moist, nearly wet sites, is most abundant on north-facing slopes and at the heads of north-facing hollows. Here on Section 6, however, this graceful fern is often common on the upper east-facing slopes of Rich Mountain. This common nonflowering plant forms clumps of 2- to 4-foot-tall fronds that arch backwards in a circular spray. During the spring, several fertile stalks bearing thousands of cinnamon-

cinnamon fern

colored spore cases rise from the center of the spray. Nearly as tall as the sterile fronds and completely lacking leaf tissue, these fertile fronds release their spores in late spring and early summer, then wither and die back.

The alternate pinnae, blunt tipped along the edges and deeply lobed, have distinctive, fuzzy tufts of light reddish brown hairs on their lower bases. This cinnamon-colored fuzz is also prominent along the stem, especially near the ground. Hummingbirds weave the downy fuzz into their nests.

After mile 7.5, where the track leaves the Rich Mountain ridgeline, the Virginia pine is especially abundant and easily recognized along several stretches of treadway. The Virginia is the only pine

Virginia pine

standing beside the BMT south of the Ocoee River that always bears two needles per bundle. It also displays the shortest needles (1½ to 3 inches) of any pine found in the Benton MacKaye corridor. The dull yellow-green to gray-green needles are stout, slightly flattened, and often somewhat twisted.

This conifer's cones, bark, and thickly branched growth habit are also distinctive. The diminutive, reddish brown cones are only 1½ to 2¾ inches long. The bark covering a mature bole is orangish brown and shaggy, with small, thin, scaly plates that flake off easily when touched. (The bark of the straight-trunked shortleaf pine has roughly rectangular plates that are much larger and smoother.) Especially in the open canopy of sunny ridges, this evergreen often develops numerous twisting limbs, quite different from those of white and shortleaf pines. Unlike many others in its genus, the Virginia's lower limbs often persist for years, even after the branches are dead.

The Virginia, an early succession species also known as scrub pine, competes best and is most common on dry, low-elevation ridges. It is intolerant of heavy shade and soon dies after other trees block the sun. Many stands of Virginia pine are dying along the Benton MacKaye from pine beetle infestations, a natural occurrence.

NORTH TO SOUTH
Weaver Creek Road to Shallowford Bridge

Mile 0.0—From the three-way T-intersection at the paved end of Weaver Creek Road, where Laurel Creek Road (unpaved as of now) continues straight ahead, follow the BMT into the woods to the right side of the private drive's entrance. Heading uphill, the dirt-gravel private road is the tail of the T.

Mile 0.1—Section 6 crosses the north fork of Laurel Creek (water safe to filter).

Mile 0.5—Half-circles the tilted notch of a yellow poplar hollow.

Mile 1.3—Gains the northern high point of Scroggin Knob.

Mile 1.6—Ranges across Scroggin's southern high point.

Mile 1.9—Where the course curves to the left onto ridgecrest, a sidepath to the right leads slightly less than 0.1 mile to water.

Mile 2.3—BMT-6 slants up and to the right onto ridgetop, then ascends more sharply.

Mile 2.8—Levels on the white oak crown of an unchristened Rich Mountain peak.

Mile 2.9—The route reaches the Benton MacKaye–Stanley Gap junction; the two trails share the same treadway for the next 2.3 miles.

Mile 3.8—Slabs to the left off the crest north of Rocky
    Mountain, then rises over the upper-elevation end of
    Bellcamp Ridge at mile 3.8.
Mile 4.4—Descends to the narrow keel of the Blue Ridge before
    quickly bearing to the right onto slope.
Mile 4.9—Crosses over the crest of the Blue Ridge.
Mile 5.2—Forks away from the Stanley Gap Trail
    at the junction.
Mile 5.8—Follows a modified switchback down and to the left
    off a spur onto east-facing slope.
Mile 6.0—Curls down and to the right beside Fall Branch.
Mile 6.1—Passes a sidepath leading down and to the left to Fall
    Branch Falls (water safe to filter).
Mile 6.3—Turns to the left onto Stanley Creek Road.
Mile 6.5—Begins paved portion of road-walk.
Mile 7.8 to 8.3—Follows the blacktop alongside rocky Stanley
    Creek for nearly 0.5 mile.
Mile 8.8—Crosses a bridge over Stanley Creek.
Mile 9.4—Arrives at the Stanley Creek Road–Aska Road
    intersection, then turns right onto Aska Road and
    follows the Toccoa River upstream.
Mile 9.8—Section 6 ends at the Shallowford Bridge over the
    Toccoa River.

DIRECTIONS

SECTION 6'S SHALLOWFORD BRIDGE Trailhead is located off
Aska Road southeast of Blue Ridge, Georgia. This trailhead is the
northern (actually western) end of Section 5 and the southern
(actually southeastern) end of Section 6.

Approach from the northwest: From the four-way US 76–GA 5–GA 2 intersection at the northern edge of Blue Ridge (McDonald's on the corner), travel US 76 East for 0.7 mile to the signed right turn onto Windy Ridge Road. Proceed 0.1 mile on Windy Ridge Road to the three-way stop, then turn left and continue 0.2 mile to the signed right turn onto Aska Road (cemetery to left after turn). Follow Aska Road for approximately 8.5 miles to the iron-sided Shallowford Bridge and the pull-in parking to the left of the road.

Approach from the northeast: Follow the directions for Section 5, approach from the northeast (see page 139), from Blairsville to the GA 60–Skeenah Gap Road junction. Turn right onto GA 60, advancing for 0.8 mile before turning sharply down and to the left onto signed Dial Road. Remain on Dial–Shallowford Bridge Road for approximately 7.2 miles to the parking area off Aska Road. The pavement ends after 4.4 miles, and the road parallels the shoaling Toccoa River at its Shallowford Bridge Road end. The pavement begins again before you turn left and cross Shallowford Bridge over the river to the Aska Road parking area.

Approach from the southeast: From the US 19–GA 60 junction at Stonepile Gap north of Dahlonega, Georgia, travel GA 60 North slightly less than 23.5 miles before turning sharply down and to the left onto signed Dial Road. (Look for Dial Road 0.6 mile beyond signed Doublehead Gap Road, also on the left side of the highway.) Once on Dial Road, follow the approach from the northeast directions.

If you stand at the edge of Aska Road with your back to the bridge, then walk Aska Road to your right, southwest and downstream, you will be on Section 6 heading toward Weaver Creek Road. If you cross Shallowford Bridge and turn right, northeast and upstream, you will be walking Section 5 toward GA 60 at Wilscot Gap.

Shuttle: If you plan to set a shuttle and hike this section from south to north (actually southeast to northwest), from Shallowford Bridge to Weaver Creek Road, your shuttle is fairly easy traveling from the northwest but somewhat longer traveling from the northeast and the southeast. If you are driving from the northwest (Blue Ridge), follow Section 7's directions (see page 178) to the Weaver Creek Road Trailhead, backtrack out to Aska Road, then turn right and finish the approximately 7.5 miles on Aska Road to Shallowford Bridge over the Toccoa River.

If you are traveling from the northeast (Blairsville) or the southeast (Stonepile Gap), cross Shallowford Bridge, turn right onto Aska Road, then proceed approximately 7.5 miles on that road before turning left onto Weaver Creek Road. Follow Section 7's directions to the Weaver Creek Road Trailhead, then backtrack to Shallowford Bridge.

NOTES

*Covered bridge
over Cherry Log Creek*

Weaver Creek Road
to Bushy Head Gap 7

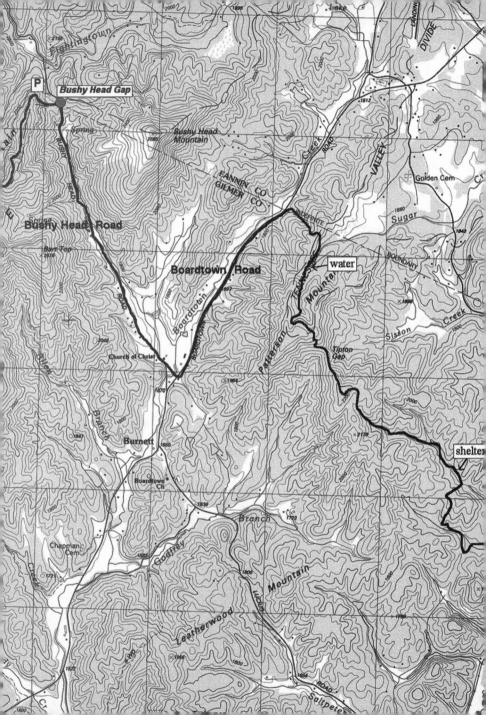

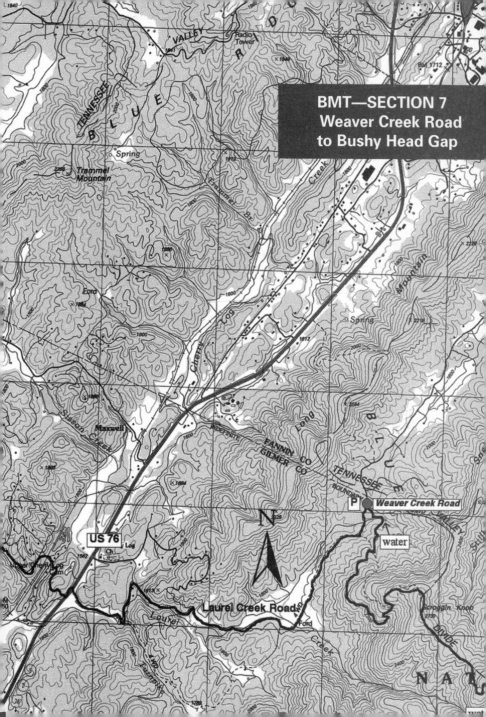

BMT—SECTION 7
Weaver Creek Road
to Bushy Head Gap

Benton MacKaye Trail, Section 7

*Weaver Creek Road to Bushy Head Gap
at Bushy Head Road*

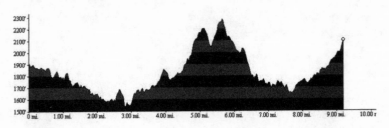

LENGTH 9.0 miles

DAYHIKING (SOUTH TO NORTH) Easy to Moderate

BACKPACKING (SOUTH TO NORTH) Moderate

VEHICULAR ACCESS AT EITHER END Southeastern end
at Weaver Creek Road, 1,900 feet; northwestern end
at Bushy Head Road, 2,090 feet.

TRAIL JUNCTION Old Benton MacKaye Trail (see
description)

BLAZES White diamond for Benton MacKaye; blue
diamond for Old Benton MacKaye

TOPOGRAPHIC QUADRANGLES Blue Ridge GA,
Cashes Valley GA

DELORME MAP GA-14

COUNTIES Gilmer GA, Fannin GA

NEAREST CITIES Ellijay GA (SW), Blue Ridge GA (NE)

RD/NF Toccoa/Chattahoochee (The 0.4 mile nearest
Weaver Creek Road passes through Forest Service

property. The remainder of the Section follows public and private roads or paths through private property.)
FEATURES Open views from roads; cascades on Laurel Creek; winter views; ponds; covered bridges

W HILE IT BEARS THE SAME NAME and blaze, Section 7 of the Benton MacKaye is notably different from the other sections in this guide. It offers more easy road-walking than all of the other segments combined. It begins with a 2.5-mile road-walk and ends with a 2.6-mile road-walk; the middle stretch alternates between short road-walks and footpaths of varying widths and origins. Except for the 0.4 mile nearest Weaver Creek Road—Forest Service property to either side of the lane—all of the remaining distance traverses private property.

In addition to the expected houses and cabins, Section 7 also passes near three ponds you can sit beside (on the Sisson property), at least two picnic tables you can sit at, and a trail shelter you can sleep in. The treadway also winds past a church and a chapel, follows nostalgia through two covered bridges, and makes several turns at or near split-rail fences.

Overall, the trail travels northwest from Weaver Creek Road to Boardtown Road. From its first Boardtown Road junction, the course leads walkers to the southwest before turning to the northwest onto Bushy Head Road and finishing the walk in that direction. This section's southeastern end at Weaver Creek Road, its first intersection with Boardtown Road, and its northwestern end at Bushy Head Gap are all located close to the Gilmer–Fannin County line.

Starting at Weaver Creek Road (1,900 feet), this stretch gradually loses elevation to its Cherry Log Creek crossing at mile 2.9

(1,540 feet, the lowest BMT point in Georgia) before slowly rising to section high point at mile 5.6, where the trail crosses Patterson Mountain at 2,260 feet. The track then descends again, this time to the Boardtown–Bushy Head Road intersection (1,670 feet) at mile 7.3. The final road-walk leg ascends to 2,090 feet at Bushy Head Gap.

Weaver Creek Road ends at the Fannin–Gilmer County line, where its two paved lanes narrow to a single dirt track—rough and rutted Laurel Creek Road. From the end of Weaver Creek Road, Section 7 follows the gentle grades of Laurel Creek Road, a pickup truck or four-wheel drive vehicle route. This rural road walk, which heads southwest for its first 0.8 mile, fords the north fork of its namesake stream at 0.1 mile, a simple rock-step crossing at normal water levels. After heavy rains, low-lying, poorly drained places along the road fill up with long troughs of water, easily skirted if you're afoot.

THE TRAIL QUICKLY LEAVES national forest land, numerically dominated by Virginia pine, and enters fenced private property: pastures actively grazed and former pastures succeeding to saplings. Views to the right, to the southwestern end of Long Mountain, will continue as long as open pasture remains. Mile 0.8 fords Laurel Creek's south fork, another stacked-rock stepover at normal flow. Beyond the south fork, the course leads generally westward to the Appalachian Highway. The country lane darkens through shady woods again, then passes beside more old pastures grown over with new forest.

The road-trail crosses a bridge over Laurel Creek at mile 1.2 and travels uphill. As the road widens, it becomes sunnier and more heavily graveled. It passes houses, primarily on the left, and signed side roads leading to cabins on the slopes of Long Mountain. (Ignore signed Laurel Creek Road to the right.) The BMT curls left with the main road at mile 1.5, descends a short easy-to-moderate grade, then runs alongside hemlock-shaded Laurel Creek, sliding and sloshing down the tilted chutes of its ravine.

Mile 1.9 turns left and down onto single-track County Road 158, usually marked with two signs—Benton MacKaye and county road. The gravel road bends sharply to the right in front of a house and proceeds past a grassy field on the left and upslope woods to the right, reaching the eastern edge of the divided four-lane Appalachian Highway (1,590 feet) at mile 2.5. (If your thru-hiker food fantasies are getting the better of you, you can find convenience stores and fast food restaurants to the right along the highway, a mere five miles away on the outskirts of Blue Ridge.) Here Section 7 crosses the highway's four lanes to the BMT sign on the far side, turns left, and follows the west side of the highway for slightly less than 0.1 mile (green and white hiker-symbol sign) to a short dead-end slab of perpendicular pavement. Turn right at this stub of blacktop, walk 25 yards to the fence (don't continue straight where you first reach the wire), turn left and tag along the highway side of the barrier for a little less than 40 yards, then turn right through the signed gap in the fence. From this entrance, the trail angles northwestward across the Sisson property for nearly four miles.

Here the treadway makes an easy switchbacking ascent through a young low-elevation forest to mile 2.7, where it crosses a road just uphill from a church. Across the road, the narrow sidehill path slants downslope (very short moderate the steepest grade) toward the moist, year-round green of white pine, hemlock, and rhododendron. After veering left and down at the double blaze, the route crosses Cherry Log Creek beneath the arch of a covered bridge at mile 2.9. Once through the shady wicket, the Benton MacKaye follows the road straight ahead, across the railroad tracks. Almost immediately past the railroad grade, the trail turns to the left off the road, then parallels the tracks for nearly 0.1 mile before swinging alongside Conley Branch.

From here the footpath quickly passes an old-growth beech (if it is still alive) and closely accompanies the branch, a Cherry Log Creek feeder, up its V-shaped ravine. The white blazes soon lead you to the bridge over the brook (mile 3.1) downstream from a normally gentle, thin-water falls. During high flow this gradual, 8- to 10-foot drop is a rollicking cascade; at low levels it is a mild slide down mostly smooth rock. Generally easygoing, the course continues to escort the branch upstream beneath a forest of hemlock and moist-site hardwoods, including sweet birch. The trail, heading northwest, rises beyond the upper section of the cascade and soon reaches a bankside picnic table. The Benton MacKaye makes a second bridged crossing at mile 3.3, ascends toward Sisson Road, dips back down to the branch, then pops back up to the road at mile 3.4.

THE SISSON PROPERTY walking tour turns left onto the road, following it to the left and down at the fork, where the signed side road Chapman Lake Trail leads straight ahead. Guided by white diamonds, the roadway ramble descends to and crosses Conley Branch again at mile 3.5 before heading uphill past homes and side roads on Granny Branch Drive. At mile 3.7, opposite Dupont Drive, the route bears off to the right onto a road descending into a dry forest where spindly shortleaf pines are common. The roadbed narrows to single lane, rising gently and crossing a beginning branch, a Conley Branch tributary, at mile 3.8. One-tenth mile farther, the walkway swings up and to the right at the fork, then curls up and to the right again on the way to Cherry Lake dam (1,740 feet) at mile 3.9. A small, weathered-wood chapel stands to the left on the far side of the dam.

Turn right and climb steps to the lake's observation deck before following the boardwalk out to Cherry Lake Drive. Bend left onto the road and stroll (stay straight on the main road at the fork) to the signed Cherry Lake Drive–Indian Rock Road intersection at mile 4.1. The trail curves to the right onto Indian Rock Road and skirts its right shoulder for 25 yards before dropping to the right off the road onto path. It then dips to and crosses a road, easing down into rhododendron and bridging a small stream at mile 4.2 (the longer north fork of Conley Branch). Now mostly effortless hiking, the passage accompanies the flow through mountain laurel to mile 4.4, where a short sidepath leads to Indian Rock Shelter: the only overnight shelter along the Benton MacKaye Trail north of Springer Mountain.

Fifty yards past the shelter, Section 7 spans the stream again—on a single sawn plank—and quickly bears right onto Indian Rock Road again. The flat road walk soon passes lake number three, Indian Rock, appointed with a bench and picnic table rather than a deck and chapel. Mile 4.5 travels over the branch again, this time through the shade of the second covered bridge. Twenty-five yards beyond the covered bridge, to the left about 10 feet off its namesake road, stands the vertical breach of Indian Rock, narrow side facing the road. Easily seen in winter, the rock—close to 9 feet high on its covered bridge side—resembles a giant gravestone, a large thumb protruding from a rock hand still buried below, or a tall rounded fin. You decide.

Where Indian Rock Road swerves to the right, the route switches to a narrower road, straight ahead to the northwest. Further on, as the road veers to the right near a house at mile 4.6, the trail holds course straight ahead onto an ascending woods road at the split-rail fence. Here the track works its way up the cove, up the watershed of the southern prong of the stream's final snake-tongue fork. After a

short easy-to-moderate grade, the BMT ramps up more gradually beside the small branch tumbling down the cove's cleft. The forest overhead, cupped within the sheltering slopes, becomes increasingly moist—habitat for sweet birch, tall yellow poplar, beech by the brook, even a few black cherries. The blue-diamond-blazed path tying into the Benton MacKaye's left

sweet birch

side (south) at mile 4.7 is known to BMTA members as the Old Benton MacKaye Trail. Most recently the entrance to that route, which reportedly leads a little more than a mile to Lucius Road, was signed JT's Trail.

The walkway makes a 50-yard, moderate-to-strenuous surge at mile 4.8 before settling down to lesser gradients. Here white pines have joined the increasingly larger oak complement; the uppermost fork is now a barely flowing rivulet. The path maintains its mild uphill run, past flanking cabins, past where the water no longer courses in the cove's furrow. At mile 5.1 you cross a road at a left angle, then ascend to an oak-picketed ridgecrest (2,210 feet) close to the road.

One-tenth mile beyond the last road, you come to another road, essentially a short driveway leading downhill to houses. Turn right onto the wide path beside the road, then descend gently on the road straight ahead close beside the homes. At mile 5.3 you begin losing elevation, sometimes sharply, down a rocky roadbed on a hardwood ridge. After passing through Tipton Gap (2,090 feet), turn right onto a wide paved road (mile 5.4). Walk this road for slightly less than 0.1 mile, then cross the ditch and slant to the right and upslope onto the wide treadway. Fifty feet beyond the ditch, take the narrow sidehill fork to the left, ascending through woods where chestnut oaks thrive. After swinging up and to the right away from the road, the passage climbs up a hardwood hollow (65 yards of moderate to strenuous) before curling left onto slope and gaining elevation more slowly.

At mile 5.6 the frequently turning ramble crosses straight over Patterson Mountain's ridgeline and the Tennessee Valley Divide at a shallow saddle (2,260 feet, section high point). Now descending to the north, the cut-in path passes above a grove of yellow poplar in a hollow to the right, and continues on the unexacting stretch to mile 5.8, where it rounds an upper hollow and begins to dip more sharply (easy to moderate, one very short moderate grade). At mile 6.1, at a double blaze, the trail swerves down and to the left off the woods road, then drops into another hollow. The now mild grade quickly ties back into old roadbed, paralleling Sugar Creek's beginning run—the outflow from Patterson's northwestern flank—down and to the left. Interweaving with the evergreen of white pine and mountain laurel, the broadleafs, including black cherry, sweetgum, umbrella magnolia, spicebush, and sweetshrub, add their particular colors, textures, and patterns to the tapestry of the forest. After hopping over the rivulet onto path at mile 6.2, the track regains the woods road and ranges down the cove to the left of the incipient creek.

Section 7 sinks to the sunlight of Boardtown Road (signed Sugar Creek Road for a short distance before its name changes to Boardtown) at mile 6.4 (1,730 feet), turns left, and follows the occasional blazes along the right side of the road to the southwest. Here the flat road-walk runs parallel to Boardtown Creek, down and to the right in the bottom of the valley. Most of the homes to the right are set far back off the road near the stream. At mile 7.3 (1,670 feet), where you should see a double blaze painted on the right side of the pavement, the route turns onto the first public road to the right—Bushy Head Road. If the road sign is missing, look for the dilapidated wooden shed to the inside of the turn and the blazes, including the guiding white diamonds on Bushy Head Road.

Sixty-five yards beyond the turn, the mountain road bridges Boardtown Creek. Not far after the road starts its first upgrade, it offers an open view of conical Bushy Head Mountain, up ahead at a narrow angle to the right of the road. If you about-face 180 degrees, you will see Patterson Mountain to the east across Boardtown Road. The easy grades, most of them uphill, proceed to mile 8.0, where the pavement ends (for now) and the dirt-gravel begins. A small branch flows under the road at mile 8.4. This rivulet rises from a spring not far up the steep slope to the left of the road. If the water is clear, and there is no obvious development beside the run, this is the easiest place to filter water since upper Sugar Creek.

BMT-7's final few tenths mile make a steady easy-to-moderate ascent to the road's high point (2,090 feet) at Bushy Head Gap. The gap is marked with a Benton MacKaye sign to the right (east) and two signed side roads: Cub Trail to the left and Bushy Head Lane to the right. The continuing end of Section 8, a cut-in path angling up the left bank, enters the forest less than 100 feet beyond Cub Trail.

NATURE NOTES

SEVERAL SEGMENTS of this road-bound section—all on the Sisson property—feature surprisingly good spring wildflower displays. Large numbers of Catesby's trillium bloom during mid-April from the Appalachian Highway up to the road crossing above the church (mile 2.7). During the same time of year, rue anemone, giant chickweed, long-spurred violets, and more Catesby's trillium enliven the stretch from the church road down to the covered bridge over Cherry Log Creek (mile 2.9). In the stream valley (mile 3.1) just above the railroad tracks, the species already mentioned plus jack–in–the–pulpit, wake robin, foamflower, halberd-leaved violet, and Vasey's trillium blossom from mid-April through mid-May. Large and showy, the Vasey's trillium usually reaches peak between May 5 and May 15.

Extensive mayapple colonies (flowering usually begins during the second half of April) cover the forest floor where the treadway rises up a hollow from mile 4.6 to mile 5.1. Other spring ephemerals include dwarf and crested dwarf iris, large-flowered trillium, doll's eyes, and Indian cucumber-root.

Sweetshrub and flowering dogwood add their colors to the woods by mid-April. Walk this stretch between May 5 and May 15 to see both flame azalea and mountain laurel.

As Section 7 winds its way through the Sisson property, it traverses several areas where the spindly shortleaf pine is a common component of the dry, low-elevation oak-pine forest. A mature shortleaf is readily identified by its distinctive bark, relatively short needles, and growth habit. This conifer's dull orange-brown bark is broken into roughly rectangular plates—often approximately 2 inches wide by 3 inches long—with thin, flat scales. These scales are brittle; even a squirrel's scramble can knock a few of them off.

shortleaf pine

While their 2¾- to 5-inch-long needles are relatively short, they are noticeably longer than the very short, often twisted needles of the Virginia (see description on page 156), another pine that inhabits dry ridges. The shortleaf's dark yellow-green needles occur in bundles of two or three to the sheath.

This pine's clean, telephone-pole-straight trunk remains clear of branches for much of its height. Its pyramidal crown, short and somewhat narrow, is sparsely branched.

The mayapple is a common, widespread, and well-known wildflower, often growing in ground-covering colonies of 20 to 150 plants. Also known as mandrake, this species is most abundant in moist, largely hardwood forests, where its familiar leaves rise 10 to 18 inches above the soil. The umbrellalike leaves, most often 7 to 12 inches across while the plant is in bloom, are deeply cleft into 5 to 7 lobes. Single-leaved mayapples do not bear flowers; only the two-leaved specimens produce the solitary corollas, easily identified by their waxy white petals and yellow stamens. Usually 1 to 2 inches wide, the blossoms stem from the fork between the two leaves and hang beneath their shade. Look for the flowers from mid-April through early May. This herb was once a fertility symbol: some people believed that young women who picked the mandrake's flowers would soon become pregnant.

mayapple

Despite this plant's common name, the mature fruit looks more like a yellowish green egg than an apple. When fully ripe, the berries are edible in small doses. Mountain families once canned jellies from the fruits. A few too many can act as a swift and sure laxative. Unripened fruit and the rest of the plant are poisonous; large amounts can be toxic and potentially deadly.

The Cherokee and their botany students—the early settlers—concocted mayapple medicine to cure numerous complaints, among them liver troubles, warts, and hearing loss. Modern research has proven this native perennial's medicinal prowess. Today, drugs derived from this species are employed in the treatment of cancer and venereal disease.

NORTH TO SOUTH
Bushy Head Gap to Weaver Creek Road

Mile 0.0—From Bushy Head Gap, walk Bushy Head Road (the main road) to the south toward Boardtown Road.

Mile 1.0—Section 7 continues on Bushy Head Road where the pavement begins (as of now).

Mile 1.7—Turns to the left onto Boardtown Road.

Mile 2.6—Bends sharply up and to the right off the pavement (now Sugar Creek Road) into woods, ascends.

Mile 2.8—Hops over Sugar Creek's beginning run (water safe to filter).

Mile 2.9—Veers up and to the right onto a woods road at a double blaze, ascends.

Mile 3.4—Continues over Patterson Mountain's ridgeline at shallow saddle, descends.

Mile 3.9—Crosses road and enters upper hollow, then descends.

Mile 4.4—After descending a branch-furrowed cove on a woods road, the trail passes a split-rail fence before entering the road straight ahead. The route soon ties into Indian Rock Road.

Mile 4.5—BMT-7 passes under the arch of a covered bridge.

Mile 4.6—Passes a short sidepath to the left that leads to Indian Rock Shelter.

Mile 4.9—Reaches signed Cherry Lake Drive–Indian Rock Road intersection, curls to the left onto Cherry Lake Drive.

Mile 5.1—Turns to the right off Cherry Lake Drive, follows a boardwalk to the observation deck and Cherry Lake dam, descends.

Mile 5.3—Turns to the left opposite Dupont Drive and heads downhill onto Granny Branch Drive.

Mile 5.6—After the road-walk bridges a culverted branch, the trail curves to the right onto Sisson Road at the fork. At mile 5.6 the BMT drops to the right and down off Sisson Road toward the branch.

Mile 5.9—Bridges a branch downstream from a cascade (mile 5.9), parallels the railroad tracks, turns to the right and down onto a road, then crosses the tracks.

Mile 6.1—Passes over Cherry Log Creek through the wicket of a covered bridge, proceeds straight ahead uphill into woods.

Mile 6.3—Continues across a road just uphill from a church.

Mile 6.4—After descending to the Appalachian Highway at mile 6.4, the Benton MacKaye turns left, follows the northwestern shoulder of the highway for slightly less than 0.1 mile, then crosses the divided highway before following County Road 158.

Mile 7.1—The trail swings to the right onto Laurel Creek Road at the usually signed three-way intersection and continues on this road for the remainder of the section.

Mile 7.8—Crosses a bridge over Laurel Creek.

Mile 8.2—Fords the south fork of Laurel Creek—a rock-step crossing at normal water levels.

Mile 8.9—Fords the north fork of Laurel Creek—a rock-step crossing at normal water levels (water safe to filter here).

Mile 9.0—Section 7 ends at the three-way intersection with paved Weaver Creek Road (straight ahead) and a dirt-gravel private drive (up and to the right).

DIRECTIONS

SECTION 7'S WEAVER CREEK ROAD Trailhead is located south of Blue Ridge, Georgia, at the end of paved Weaver Creek Road. This trailhead is the northern (actually northwestern) end of Section 6 and the southern (actually southeastern) end of Section 7.

Approach from Blue Ridge: From the four-way US 76–GA 5 –GA 2 intersection at the northern edge of Blue Ridge (McDonald's on the corner), travel US 76 East for 0.7 mile to the signed right turn onto Windy Ridge Road. Proceed 0.1 mile on Windy Ridge Road to the three-way stop, then turn left and continue 0.2 mile to the signed right turn onto Aska Road (cemetery to left after turn). Follow Aska Road for approximately 1.0 mile before turning right onto signed Weaver Creek Road. Take Weaver Creek Road straight ahead for approximately 3.7 miles to the end of the pavement (for now) at the Fannin–Gilmer County line. There is a small parking area to the right where the blacktop ends. A private dirt-gravel road heads up and to the left from the end of Weaver Creek Road. Laurel Creek Road—a single-track lane, muddy and rutted after heavy rain—continues straight ahead into Gilmer County from the end of Weaver Creek Road.

If you walk Laurel Creek Road straight ahead from the end of Weaver Creek Road, you will be on Section 7 heading toward Bushy Head Gap. If you follow the white-blazed path just inside and to the right of the private road's entrance, you will be hiking Section 6 toward Shallowford Bridge at Aska Road.

Shuttle: If you plan to set a shuttle and hike this section from south to north (actually southeast to northwest), from Weaver

Creek Road to Bushy Head Gap, your options are limited and you cannot drop a vehicle off on your way to the starting trailhead. Follow Section 8's directions (see page 200) to Bushy Head Gap and leave a vehicle. Backtrack to US 76, then turn left onto US 76 East and proceed approximately 6.4 miles to the four-way US 76–GA 5–GA 2 intersection at the northern edge of Blue Ridge (McDonald's on the corner). From this intersection follow the approach from Blue Ridge directions to the Weaver Creek Road Trailhead.

NOTES

Large-flowered trillium

Bushy Head Gap to Dyer Gap

8

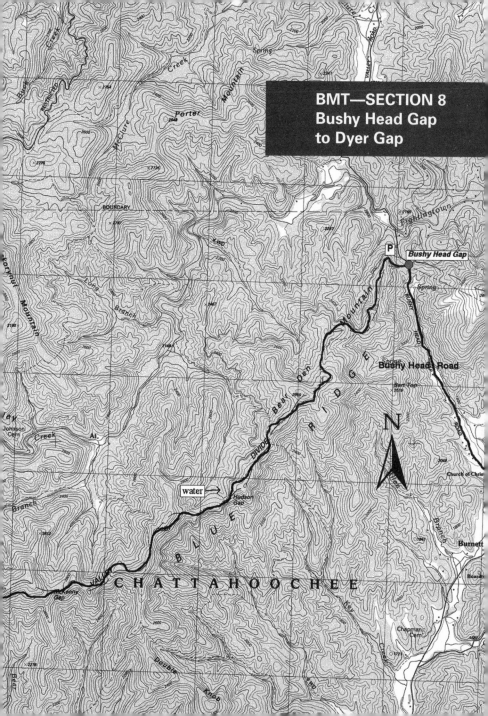

**BMT—SECTION 8
Bushy Head Gap
to Dyer Gap**

Benton MacKaye Trail, Section 8

*Bushy Head Gap at Bushy Head Road
to Dyer Gap at FS 64*

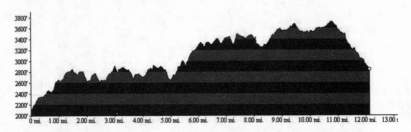

LENGTH 12.7 miles

DAYHIKING (SOUTH TO NORTH) Moderate

BACKPACKING (SOUTH TO NORTH) Moderate to Strenuous

VEHICULAR ACCESS AT EITHER END Eastern end at Bushy
Head Road, 2,090 feet; western end at FS 64, 2,870 feet

TRAIL JUNCTIONS None

BLAZE White diamond

TOPOGRAPHIC QUADRANGLES Cashes Valley GA,
Dyer Gap GA

DELORME MAP GA-14

COUNTIES Gilmer GA, Fannin GA

NEAREST CITIES Ellijay GA (S), Blue Ridge GA (E)

RD/NF Armuchee-Cohutta/Chattahoochee

FEATURES Remote trail; numerous winter views; wildlife
opening; Flat Top Mountain; rock outcrops; extensive
fern colonies and spring wildflower displays

ECTION 8 IS LONG AND REMOTE and lonely. At 12.7 miles, this segment between roaded gaps is the longest detailed in this guide. It is just right for a leisurely paced two- or three-day backpack trip, or a fast-paced dayhike for the fit and firm of knee. This stretch roams through big woods—the Benton MacKaye's most remote run outside of the Cohutta–Big Frog Wilderness. For nearly ten miles, from mile 2.6 to mile 12.4, the route does not cross a single Forest Service system road. North of Fowler Mountain (mile 6.6), the trail often follows the southeastern perimeter of the 95,200-acre Cohutta WMA.

If the BMT's corridor is protected, and if ORV's are kept off the treadway, this section has the potential to become one of Georgia's premier hikes: a wild walk where the accomplishment of mileage slowly earned rewards you with a rhythm for which your body and mind are thankful. This stretch needs the tromp of more hikers to help the Benton MacKaye Trail Association keep the treadway open and well defined.

From Bushy Head Gap to the summit of Fowler Mountain, the walkway winds to the west-southwest on or near the western arm of the Blue Ridge, which doubles as the Tennessee Valley Divide. After turning sharply atop Fowler, the remainder of the section wends north-northwest, again following the Blue Ridge. BMT-8, primarily a ridgetop and upper-slope route, frequently undulates up and down, but most of the grades are easy or easy to moderate. Bushy Head to Dyer also includes miles of gentle walking, flat or close to it. Judged by Southern Appalachian standards, this link does not present hikers with any long, sustained grades of even moderate difficulty.

From section low point at Bushy Head Gap, the trail slants up the road bank and rises into a diverse oak-hickory forest. After a short dip, the track skirts Cub Trail (a road) on the left, and continues its mild ascent on sidehill path: a Benton MacKaye specialty—a narrow tread, intimate and slightly winding, laboriously cut into slope. The walking ducks into a thicket of mountain laurel below a predominantly oak canopy at 0.2 mile. By 0.4 mile the BMT parallels the ridgeline of Bear Den Mountain, just up and to the left. The trail gradually gains elevation to mile 0.6 (2,420 feet), where it turns to the right onto the undemanding gradient of a woods road.

At 0.8 mile the course comes to a configuration of roads that might prove confusing were it not for the guiding white diamonds. A short distance beyond an ORV road that drops to the right, the BMT forks to the right away from the main woods road, which proceeds straight ahead. Now on sidehill path again, the passage curls upward with the help of a pair of modified switchbacks—rounded to prevent erosion and shortcutting—through a stand of mature oaks. The steep slope offers steady partial summer views and good winter prospects of the abiding Appalachians. Past a short easy-to-moderate stretch, the walkway ramps up and over a slight spur, maintaining the slow-climbing ascent amidst a north-facing forest above an open understory of ferns and herbaceous wildflowers. The upgrade (easy to moderate) crests Bear Den Mountain and the western arm of the Blue Ridge at mile 1.0.

After rising to the top of a knob (2,680 feet) at mile 1.1, the trail angles to the left, following the ridge gently downhill to a shallow saddle, where it heads up toward the next bump on Bear Den. The overall easy ascent remains on the oak-hickory ridgetop until mile 1.3, where it bears to the left off the woods road track and slabs onto slope. Here, as the land rises toward the next peak, the route begins its end run around the knob's uppermost southeastern flank. The footpath reaches 2,840 feet at mile 1.5, dips for a short distance, drifts left of the crest, then gradually gains elevation over a spur at mile 1.6. Just down from the spur, the nearly effortless walking passes a gap-in-the-trees view (to the left until the forest closes it) framing Leatherwood Mountain a little over two miles away.

At mile 1.7 the trail regains the ridgeline and descends into mature timber; yellow poplar and white oak now hold sway in the canopy. The roadbed treadway holds its course straight ahead where another woods road curls to the right and down at mile 1.8. From here the BMT slips to the right of Bear Den's backbone (mile 1.9), sticking to the gradual downgrade on the wide woods road. Often white pine saplings and an occasional hemlock represent the entire conifer component in the otherwise broadleaf woods.

THE TRACK LEVELS ATOP the fold at mile 2.1 before beginning the slow ascent toward the next knob. At mile 2.3, where the ridge rises more sharply, the white diamonds direct you to the right of the keel and down toward the next saddle. Following a steady no-sweat descent, the course slants back to the crest and crosses FS 793 in Hudson Gap (2,630 feet) at mile 2.6. The outflow of a spring is located approximately 0.1 mile to the right (north) of the gap.

Beyond the gap, Section 8 advances, on or near the Blue Ridge for the most part, to the west-southwest toward Fowler Mountain. Here, as the elevations rise steadily higher, the established pattern continues: the trail often remains on the ridgetop through saddles and where the walking is relatively easy, but when the land lifts toward a steep-sided peak, the walkway leaves the crest and swings around the high point on upper slope. After heading uphill from Hudson Gap (short easy to moderate the most difficult), the wildwood path slips to the left of the backbone (mile 2.9), climbing as it passes around the upper southern pitch of the next rise. At mile 3.0 a gap in the trees to the left allows you another glimpse of Leatherwood Mountain at 130 degrees. The Benton MacKaye crests the spine at mile 3.1 and quickly gains the top of the next hump (2,940 feet) before riding the ridge downward (easy to moderate the sharpest).

At mile 3.5 the passage slabs to the right off the ridgecrest, beginning a particularly enjoyable stretch as it bypasses yet another prominence. Here on north-facing slope, where you can often see far down the fall, white ash and black cherry, basswood, sweet birch, and tall hickories shade fern and wildflower. BMT-8 rolls through a saddle (2,700 feet) at mile 3.8 before ramping up to the next rise. Skirting the moist side of the ridge again, the route snakes through moderately rich habitat supporting a diverse, though not abundant, fern population that includes broad beech, southern lady, northern maidenhair, and rattlesnake. By mile 3.9 the treadway is back atop the fold and climbing (60 yards of moderate difficulty) to the crown of a 2,860-foot knob, which it reaches at mile 4.0.

THE NEXT DOWNHILL, also moderate for a short distance, runs straight ahead on the ridgetop (guided by a double blaze and possibly a carsonite sign) where the roadbed veers left and down onto slope. Once through McKenny Gap (2,780 feet) at mile 4.2, the track doglegs to the left of the crest as it begins another end-around, this one skirting south of Cooks Knob, 3,120 feet high. The lonely path—down a little, up a little, generally easy up—rolls here and winds there to match the topography of the steep mountainside. Mile 4.3 offers winter views to the left. Sassafras is particularly plentiful in the predominantly oak-hickory forest. At mile 4.5 the trail files below a whaleback breach of gray outcrop rock, 8 to 10 feet high in one spot. A tenth-mile farther, a break in the trees to the left affords a look at Walnut Mountain nearly nine miles away.

After tying into road grade and ascending moderately for a few rods, the walking rises to the ridgeline at mile 4.8 (2,920 feet, the highest elevation from McKenny Gap to Hatley Gap) and starts down. It then quickly curls to the right off the keel and begins a descending half-loop to the north around the next minor swell. The way soon parallels a ferny ravine; by mile 4.9 the water of a Burnett Branch feeder flows over rocks to the right nearby. This is the first of the essential fluid seen from this section. During late September of a recent drought year, the rill was trickling thinly, but enough for easy filtering. A colony of spicebush flanked the rivulet; the berries, oblong and bright green during most of the summer, were turning to October's shiny red.

The roadbed route continues to lose elevation (several short easy-to-moderate grades) among white pine saplings and broadleafs, including an occasional shagbark hickory. The Benton MacKaye regains the ridge just before dropping to Hatley Gap (2,650 feet) at mile 5.3. Here at Hatley, where the Blue Ridge rises sharply straight ahead, and where the climb to Fowler Mountain begins, the track slips to the right of the crest and heads uphill much more gradually on slope. Through the scrim of bare branches, winter views open to Horse Ridge a mile to the north. The walking, a steady easy upgrade, meanders on moist, north-facing slope supporting a diverse hardwood assemblage. Mile 5.4 rounds the furrow of a hollow; after rain, a rivulet tumbles down the rocky notch.

Angling steadily upslope (one very short moderate pull, another short easy to moderate), the course heads up a hollow, higher ground to both sides. At mile 5.6 the treadway curves hard to the left, leaving the hollow and entering drier woods of chestnut oak, blackgum, and sassafras. It then half-circles over a spur and rises toward the notch of the next hollow—tall, arrow-straight yellow poplars tower above the intricate fern forms—before curling around the upper hollow and sweeping back to the main ridgecrest (3,040 feet) at mile 5.8.

The southwestward path, often snaking side to side rather than running straight up, continues the ridgetop climb in an oak-hickory forest. By mile 5.9 the walkway starts up harder—moderate, very short moderate to strenuous, then easy to moderate—before leveling to an undemanding stretch at mile 6.0. Section 8 heads uphill harder again at mile 6.2 (a short moderate grade the most difficult), threading through a woods where mountain winterberry, a deciduous holly red-berried in the fall, is abundant. Mile 6.3 reaches the easternmost wave (3,370 feet) of Fowler Mountain's three-pronged peak. Following a slight downgrade to a shallow saddle, the route rises to Fowler's middle and highest hump (3,390 feet at mile 6.6).

Atop Fowler, the BMT changes course; beyond where it bends to the right below the summit, the primary direction of travel for the remaining mileage in Georgia is north. From Fowler to mile 8.3, where the trail curls onto slope, the Benton MacKaye arches and rolls with the ridgeline. Beyond Fowler, the track descends to a saddle (3,300 feet) at mile 6.8, rises on roadbed to where it crosses the sunset edge of a knob (3,430 feet) at mile 7.0, then loses elevation to the next shallow gap at mile 7.1. As you will notice, sweet birch and yellow poplar are more common along the north-facing downgrades.

F OR THE NEXT HALF MILE, from 7.1 to 7.6, the tread undulates on grades mild as milk. It crosses a small bump at mile 7.5 before dipping 0.1 mile to a slight saddle. The uplift at mile 7.8 (3,540 feet) is the high point of Horse Ridge—a lead fingering down to the east between two streams. The roller-coaster ride continues, downhill to the gap (3,410 feet) at mile 8.1 and back up (short moderate) to Douglas Knob at mile 8.2 (3,483 feet at the benchmark). After curling onto slope at mile 8.3, the footpath descends (short easy to moderate) back to Blue Ridge backbone in Halloway Gap (3,250 feet) at mile 8.6. In the gap, a blue blaze leads to the right (northeast) a little less than 0.2 mile to water. The sidepath from Halloway Gap leads to an excellent campsite; in addition to water it affords beauty, solitude, and the moral rectitude of adhering to environmental guidelines. Nine-tenths mile beyond Halloway, trailside water is available just before the wildlife opening.

Past Halloway Gap, the hiking ascends (except for one short downhill stretch) the ridgecrest into an even-age stand of yellow poplar. Following a short easy-to-moderate elevation gain, mile 8.9 slants up and to the right onto sidehill, where the contour lines on the map bunch tighter toward the next rise, 3,660-foot Dominy Knob. Back to its old tricks, the Benton MacKaye swings around the peak on its eastern pitch. Here the upgrade gradually works its way back toward the spine north of the knob's apex, where the crest descends toward the rising path. Mile 9.0 passes a three-foot-high shark-fin outcrop immediately to the right of the tread. Near the end of the upslope, you can look through winter's stick-figure hardwoods to the closest peak to the right (30 degrees)—an unchristened, double-humped knob, highest heave to the left, 3,560 feet.

witch-hazel

By mile 9.2 the wide passage, now back on the keel, quickly descends through an area of low outcrop rock. Two-tenths mile after topping the ridge, Section 8 swerves to the left onto a gentle-slope woods road. Here witch-hazel, which begins blooming by October 20, arches over the roadbed. A spring-run rivulet is soon visible in the nearby ravine to the left. As always, filter or treat your water; hog wallows big as bathtubs often muck up the spring. The route dips to and skirts the southern edge of a wildlife opening at mile 9.6 before starting uphill through oak-hickory forest on the rocky, washed-out access road. One-tenth mile past the grassy clearing, at a double blaze, BMT-8 angles to the left off the road onto path. If you miss this turn, you will come to another opening fairly quickly.

You may camp in the wildlife opening; however, the Forest Service requests that you do not have a fire nor build a fire ring. If you start a fire without a ring, you might, under the right conditions, burn the field and start a forest fire. If you build a fire ring, your rocks, soon hidden in the tall grass, can damage the mowers.

After a short ascent in the shadows of an oak–yellow poplar canopy, the BMT rambles downhill on the crest, winding around a broken line of outcrop rock. It leaves the crease of the fold at mile 9.9, and descends somewhat harder (overall easy) toward hemlock and rhododendron, a good sign that water is nearby. At mile 10.1 the track turns nearly 90 degrees to the left where the roadbed continues straight ahead, then drops 65 yards to its rock-step crossing (3,540 feet) of a permanent headwater branch of the South Fork Jacks River. Beyond this section's first stream crossing, the walking rises and falls on easygoing roadbed grades in a hemlock and hardwood forest; several old-growth hemlocks still grace the ravine to the left. The track, following a short easy-to-moderate downgrade, crosses a rocky seepage run at mile 10.4. The no-sweat walking roams through woods where beech trees, including many saplings, are much more common than usual along the BMT.

After another short easy-to-moderate dip, the roadbed levels at mile 10.6, where a double blaze signals the Benton MacKaye's bend onto the footpath to the left. Eighty yards downhill from the turn, the trail rock-hops a second South Fork feeder (3,520 feet), this one wider and with a higher-volume flow. It then ascends to ridgeline, slips onto sunset slope at mile 10.8, and after another tenth of a mile rejoins the crest of Flat Top Mountain, wide and often nearly level side to side. Here the easy hiking beneath mature hardwoods, their boles well spaced on the fern-green floor, is particularly pleasant. Mile 11.3 passes a poor-form, old-growth white oak (if it is still alive) in a steadily shrinking clearing to the right of the trail. The soon-to-disappear opening—Flat Top's 3,730-foot summit—is the site of a former fire tower. Here at Flat Top, the Benton MacKaye gains its highest elevation since its southern terminus at Springer Mountain. The BMT does not rise above 3,700 feet again until the climb to Big Frog, north of the Tennessee border.

Forty yards past the oak, at a double-blazed post, the treadway doglegs down and to the left off the main roadbed into young woods. The course curves to the right and down around the end of a wall-like line of outcrop at mile 11.4, entering older forest. Now losing elevation on western slope, the scenic sidehill path offers partial summer and impressive winter views of the Cohutta Mountains looming high and rounded on the horizon to the west and west-northwest. Due west, Bald Mountain lifts its forest-covered pate to 4,005 feet slightly less than seven miles away; closer in at 300 degrees, Cowpen Mountain bows up to a respectable 4,150 feet.

Although it occasionally ducks down more sharply, the grade is generally easy as it traverses a forest where mature oaks hold the overstory. The route drops moderately to an eight-foot-tall outcrop at mile 11.5, then sinks more gradually to the wide, fern-floored gap (3,500 feet) at mile 11.7. Here, where the land sweeps up toward Flat Top's northernmost knob, the BMT swings to the left and descends on rocky slope. Mile 11.8 makes a rounded, modified switchback down and to the right onto rock steps, another BMTA specialty. The scenic footpath continues the generally easy downgrade beneath tall broadleafs; more partial summer and good winter outlooks stretch to the buckled folds of the Cohuttas. Rock steps ease the descent at the end of a short sharp pitch at mile 12.1.

The narrow walkway proceeds downhill on an open hardwood slope; at mile 12.4 the route sidles onto a ridgetop saddle (3,020 feet) before quickly bending to the right out to FS 64A. The remainder of Section 8 turns left onto FS 64A, following the rough and rocky road downhill to the three-way FS 64–FS 64A intersection (large Cohutta WMA sign and usually a small BMT sign) at Dyer Gap. Section 9 continues to the left on FS 64.

NATURE NOTES

DUE TO A NUMBER of factors—length and variety of habitat and exposure the most obvious—Section 8 affords an excellent spring wildflower display, especially colorful from April 20 through May 10. Along this section, as well as beside BMT 5, you can spot at least five trillium species, blooms faded or fresh, on a single day's hike. On May 10 of a recent rainy spring, the large carmine corollas of the Vasey's trillium were at

Vasey's trillium

peak, Catesby's were faded pink, large-flowered were pink and frayed, and the white color-morphs of the wake robin (also known as purple or red trillium) looked shopworn. The yellow trillium, a sessile-flowered species also known as yellow toadshade, was abundant and still vibrantly hued along several miles of trail. On that day a friend and I, with where-to-look-help from BMT botany expert Mike Christison, noted nearly forty-five different wildflowers (not counting the obscure or inconspicuous) that had already bloomed, were blooming, or would blossom before spring's end.

A short roll call of the species (omitting plants that occur beside nearly every other BMT section, or plants that are too rare too mention) includes doll's eyes, lousewort, speckled wood lily, wild geranium, yellow mandarin, showy orchis, sourgrass, bell-wort, and squawroot. Still others, such as Turk's-cap lily and black cohosh, offered hope of more beauty during summer's heat.

On May 10, sweetshrub bloomed in large numbers, mountain laurel was just starting to open its corsages at the lowest elevations, and the occasional flame azalea was not quite at peak.

chestnut oak

In September, after it cools down again, lobelia, gentian, and assorted asters, including white snakeroot, add their grace to the turning forest. By late October and early November, as the last of the herbaceous wildflowers crumple and brown, the witch-hazel begins to unfurl its yellow sprays of twisting, slender petals. Witch-hazel, a small, often multiple-boled tree, is abundant beside the rivulet near the wildlife opening.

The chestnut oak—mainly a mountain tree of the Appalachi-ans—is one of the most common ridge and dry-slope hardwoods within the Benton MacKaye corridor. Alongside Section 8, *Quercus montana* (*Quercus* is Latin for beautiful tree) is most abundant on south-facing ridgelines and south- and west-facing slopes. It is often numerically dominant on west-facing slopes, especially if those pitches are rocky and full of mountain laurel. The chestnut oak greatly increased its share of the canopy after the chestnut blight and is now a major component of the oak-pine and oak-hickory forests. Another common name for this species is moun-tain oak. In fact, Scouts and other children are taught to remember this name by folding a leaf's width in half along the midrib to see the silhouette of the mountains.

This oak received its accepted common name because its leaves superficially resemble those of the American chestnut, a species no longer able to survive in most of its range beyond sapling stage. The foliage of the two trees, however, is easy to tell apart. Noticeably narrower than the chestnut oak leaf, the chestnut leaf is distinguished by its prominent, sharp-pointed teeth. The chestnut oak leaf—4 to 9 inches long—has margins with rounded, wavy lobes, no points and no bristles. No other large Southern Appalachian broadleaf bears this type of leaf.

Only two ferns—the hay-scented and the New York—establish extensive colonies of thousands and thousands of ground-blanketing plants beside the Benton MacKaye. Like the New York (see description on page 90), the hay-scented breaks ground at regular intervals, creating a uniform symmetry similar to an agricultural crop. Two factors account for the hay-scented's patterned appearance and abundance. Its underground rhizomes produce evenly spaced, cloned colonies. And like the New York fern, this pteridophyte promotes its domination by poisoning many other plants, an evolutionary advantage that allows it to spread over acres of the forest floor.

hay-scented fern

The hay-scented is the second most common fern in the Benton MacKaye corridor. (The New York is first.) When Henry David

Thoreau wrote, "God created ferns to show what He could do with leaves," he could have been referring to the finely cut, feathery fronds of this fern. The alternate pinnae—thin-textured, yellow-green, and delicate—produce the light, sweet scent of newly mown hay. Its arching, deciduous fronds are usually 15 to 30 inches high. Because beds of hay-scented and New York ferns are often intermixed, it would appear that the two species have developed at least partial immunity to each other's poison.

NORTH TO SOUTH Dyer Gap to Bushy Head Gap

Mile 0.0—From the three-way, T-intersection of FS 64 and FS 64A, follow FS 64A—usually marked with a brown carsonite sign, a small BMT sign, and a large Cohutta WMA sign—uphill to the southeast.

Mile 0.3—Section 8 angles to the right off FS 64A into woods and ascends the rocky, southwestern slope of Flat Top Mountain's northernmost peak.

Mile 1.0—Passes through a wide, fern-floored gap, slabs to the right of the crest, ascends.

Mile 1.4—Arrives at Flat Top's level high point, site of a former fire tower.

Mile 2.1—Crosses a South Fork Jacks River tributary branch, rises for 80 yards, then turns to the right onto roadbed at a double blaze.

Mile 2.6—Rock-steps across another South Fork feeder, rises for 65 yards, then bears 90 degrees to the right.

Mile 3.0—BMT-8 turns to the right onto a woods road (mile 3.0), descends 0.1 mile to where it passes the southern edge

of a wildlife opening, then quickly parallels the
outflow of a spring to the right.

Mile 3.5—The trail slants to the left of the rising ridgeline and
slabs onto sidehill around the eastern pitch of
Dominy Knob.

Mile 3.8—Regains the crest and descends to Halloway Gap at
mile 4.1 (water to left of gap).

Mile 4.5—Rises to the top of Douglas Knob, descends toward the
next gap.

Mile 4.9—Reaches the high point of Horse Ridge, descends
easily.

Mile 5.7—Traverses the western edge of Fowler Mountain's
northern peak.

Mile 6.1—Ranges across Fowler's middle hump, the mountain's
highest point.

Mile 6.4—Ascends to the easternmost uplift of Fowler's three-
pronged crown, descends.

Mile 6.9—Doglegs to the left off the main ridge, descends on
slope to Hatley Gap at mile 7.4.

Mile 7.8—Passes a headwater rivulet of Burnett Branch flowing
nearby to the left of the trail.

Mile 8.5—Proceeds through McKenny Gap.

Mile 8.7—Ascends to the high point of a knob.

Mile 8.9—Rolls through a saddle, slips to the left of the spine.

Mile 9.2—Returns to the crest.

Mile 9.6—Swings to the right off the ridge and skirts the upper
southeastern pitch of a knob.

Mile 10.1—Crosses FS 793 in Hudson Gap (spring located
approximately 0.1 mile to the left, north, of the gap).

Mile 10.6—Levels atop the fold before slabbing to the left onto slope and gaining elevation toward the next knob on Bear Den Mountain.

Mile 11.1—Crosses over a spur.

Mile 11.7—Leaves the ridgeline of Bear Den Mountain.

Mile 12.1—Turns to the left from a woods road onto path at a double blaze.

Mile 12.7—Section 8 ends at Bushy Head Gap at Bushy Head Road.

DIRECTIONS

SECTION 8'S BUSHY HEAD GAP Trailhead is located off Bushy Head Road west of Blue Ridge, Georgia. This trailhead is the northern (actually northwestern) end of Section 7 and the southern (actually eastern) end of Section 8.

Approach from the east: From the four-way US 76–GA 5–GA 2 intersection at the northern edge of Blue Ridge (McDonald's on the corner), travel US 76 West toward Ellijay, Georgia, for approximately 6.4 miles, then turn right onto signed Lucius Road. Proceed approximately 2.8 miles on Lucius Road before turning right onto Boardtown Road at the T-intersection. Continue on Boardtown Road for 0.4 mile, then turn left onto signed Bushy Head Road. Remain on Bushy Head Road (pavement ends after 0.7 mile as of now) for approximately 1.7 miles to the high point of the road at Bushy Head Gap, marked by a four-way intersection (Cub Trail to the left, Bushy Head Lane to the right) and a Benton MacKaye sign to the right of the main road. There is no parking at the exact point where the trail re-enters the woods.

Continue straight ahead and down (on the road you drove in on) less than 100 yards to the entrance of a Forest Service road to the left. Enter that road and park along its shoulder.

Approach from the south: From the US 76–GA 2–GA 282–GA 5 intersection in East Ellijay, Georgia, travel US 76 East toward Blue Ridge for approximately 9.9 miles to the signed left turn (across two lanes of traffic) onto Lucius Road. (See the preceding approach for directions from Lucius Road.)

At Bushy Head Gap, the BMT re-enters the woods 20 yards past Cub Trail. If you angle up the western bank of the road (to your left and on the Cub Trail side traveling from either the east or south approach), you will be hiking Section 8 toward its Dyer Gap end at FS 64. If you tread Bushy Head Road to the south from the gap (opposite from the way you drove in to the gap), you will be road-walking Section 7 toward its Weaver Creek Road end.

Shuttle: If you wish to walk this section from south to north, from Bushy Head Gap to Dyer Gap, and want to set a shuttle, follow directions for Section 9 (see page 215) to Dyer Gap. From Dyer Gap backtrack on FS 64 to Watson Gap, turn right onto Old State Route 2, and proceed approximately 6.3 miles on that road (it becomes paved after a little over 1.0 mile) before turning right onto signed Cashes Valley Road. Travel straight ahead on the main road (it changes names and after 2.6 miles becomes dirt-gravel) for approximately 3.3 miles to the high point of Bushy Head Gap, which is marked by a four-way intersection, Bushy Head Lane to the left, Cub Trail to the right.

*Shadow Falls on South Fork
Jacks River*

Dyer Gap to Watson Gap 9

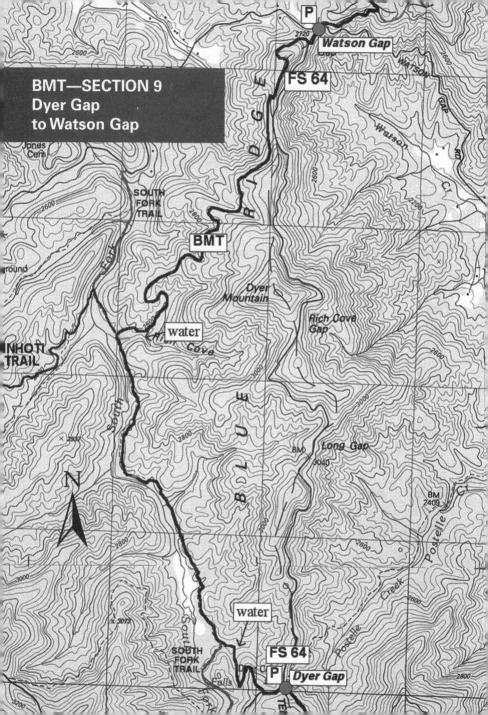

BMT—SECTION 9
Dyer Gap
to Watson Gap

Benton MacKaye Trail, Section 9

*Dyer Gap at FS 64 to Watson Gap
at the four-way intersection of FS 22, FS 64,
Old Highway 2, and County Road 187*

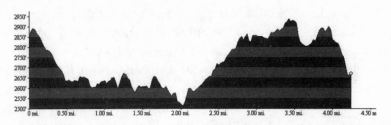

LENGTH 4.5 miles

DAYHIKING (SOUTH TO NORTH) Easy to Moderate

BACKPACKING (SOUTH TO NORTH) Moderate

VEHICULAR ACCESS AT EITHER END Southern end at FS 64,
2,870 feet; northern end at Watson Gap's four-way
intersection, 2,730 feet

TRAIL JUNCTIONS South Fork (see description), Pinhoti (see
note on page 211)

BLAZE White diamond for Benton MacKaye; South Fork
currently unblazed

TOPOGRAPHIC QUADRANGLES Dyer Gap GA, Hemp Top GA-
TN

DELORME MAP GA-14

COUNTY Fannin GA

NEAREST CITIES Ellijay GA (S), Blue Ridge GA (E),
Ducktown TN (NE)

RD/NF Armuchee-Cohutta/Chattahoochee
FEATURES South Fork Jacks River; Shadow Falls (see
description)

SCENIC WHERE IT CLOSELY PARALLELS the South Fork Jacks River, Section 9 is the second shortest Benton MacKaye link in Georgia. Because the northern end of Section 10 (Georgia's shortest section at 4.1 miles) is 1.0 mile away from vehicular access, BMT-9's total walking distance is the least in Georgia for those hiking the trail one section at a time. This segment's length and difficulty rank it the easiest in Georgia. From Dyer Gap (2,870 feet), the route gradually drops to section low point (2,500 feet) at mile 2.1 before steadily working its way to high point (2,960 feet)—the top of a Blue Ridge knob at mile 4.2.

The western crest of the Blue Ridge anchors this segment's two ends, which are in north-south alignment. But instead of rising and falling along the famous fold due north from Dyer Gap, the track descends to the northwest and closely accompanies the South Fork Jacks River to Rich Cove; it then ascends northeastward back to the Blue Ridge near Watson Gap. BMT-9 threads through Georgia's premier bear country: the 95,200-acre Cohutta Wildlife Management Area.

Section 9 shares 1.6 miles of its treadway with the South Fork Trail. Open to hikers and horse riders, the South Fork is much more heavily used than the Benton MacKaye. From mile 0.6 to mile 2.2, portions of the trailside forest, especially upslope and between South Fork side streams, were logged between 1980 and 1990. Although these cuts are rapidly regenerating, they will have the look and feel of young third-growth for a few more decades. The rest of the forest, especially downslope from the grade near the river and flanking the upslope tributaries, is increasingly impressive second growth.

Starting at the three-way FS 64–FS 64A intersection at Dyer Gap, the route follows FS 64 generally westward (away from the cemetery) for 0.1 mile, to the blazed and usually signed right turn off the road onto obvious treadway. Here the well-constructed footpath descends below a largely hardwood roof. White pine saplings and slow-growing hemlock are stuck in the understory for now; blackgums are a major component of the mid-canopy. After gradually losing elevation atop a ridgeline for a short distance, the track doglegs to the left off the crest onto northwest slope at 0.2 mile. The mild grade heads down into the deeper shade of

blackgum

hemlock and mountain laurel. At 0.3 mile the Benton MacKaye bends 90 degrees to the right and down at the double blaze, paralleling the ferny cleft of a hollow.

By 0.5 mile the easy walking accompanies the hollow's rivulet toward the South Fork Jacks River. Rosebay rhododendron flank the unnamed and unmapped watercourse; white pine and mature hemlock add their year-round green to the riparian forest. The hike crosses the beginning branch—shallow, clear, a little more than a stride wide—then closely follows its flow to 0.6 mile, where Section 9 makes a signed right turn onto the South Fork Trail (2,630 feet). The two trails share the same treadway, a woods road, for the next 1.6 miles. Heavy usage right after rain mucks up the low-lying spots along this stretch.

If you turn left onto the South Fork Trail, away from the Benton MacKaye, a side trip of slightly over 0.2 mile (one way) leads you to the steep path dropping to the bottom of 20-foot-high Shadow Falls. Across the catch pool, the South Fork of the Jacks River foams in a straightforward swath of sharply slanting white over mossy rock.

Back on the BMT and traveling generally north-northwest, the shared treadway immediately rock-steps the branch (the one it just followed) as it parallels the South Fork Jacks River downstream. Here the wide walkway gently undulates with the terrain in or near the South Fork's narrow floodplain. The trail passes by an old beaver swamp, the result of a dammed side stream in the flat to the left. An occasional umbrella magnolia, readily identified by its whorls of jungle-sized leaves, adds a tropical look to the trailside vegetation. In one of the older upslope cuts, this one probably logged in the late 1970s, white pine saplings have grown three to four feet per year. One particularly ambitious solar-powered specimen gained at least 17 feet in height (each whorl of branches represents a year's growth) in five years.

Barely roller-coasting, the passage proceeds under a canopy of white pine, hemlock, and mixed hardwoods. The track frequently tunnels through rhododendron breezeways. Mile 0.9 crosses a small branch, the first of at least half a dozen step-over or rock-step crossings along the two-trail route. Usually hidden down and to the left behind the evergreen screen, the South Fork most often remains within earshot. But if you look closely, you can occasionally catch glimpses of the river through the rhododendron. A short sidepath at mile 1.3 leads to an open view of the clear, quick water sloshing over low ledges. The forest, which includes white pines well over 100 feet tall, is often dark, especially during cloudy summer days.

The road grade rounds a slight hollow after 1.8 miles; two-tenths mile farther it reaches the second bankside look at the river. The route crosses a shallow branch (section low point at 2,500 feet) flowing out of Rich Cove at mile 2.1. One-tenth mile beyond the crossing, the trails split apart at an obvious signed junction. South Fork Trail remains on the old road straight ahead; the white diamonds lead up and to the right away from the roadbed.

AFTER THE TRAILS GO THEIR SEPARATE WAYS, the remainder of Section 9 winds to the northeast, back to the Dyer Mountain crest, back to the Blue Ridge. Fifty-five yards beyond the split, the path swerves up and to the right onto a fern-lined woods road, beginning the rolling ascent on Dyer's lower-west slope. The walkway curls to the right around a slight hollow sheltering a New York fern colony at mile 2.3, then continues the easy grade. One-tenth mile beyond the hollow, this section's thickest tree—a modest-sized yellow poplar 10 feet 2 inches around—is rooted (if it is still alive) 30 feet to the left of the tread.

Past a beginning branch to the right, the uphill hiking tops out at easy to moderate before gearing back to gentler grades. Mile 2.7 levels through the site of a former clearing quickly regenerating to sourwood and two pine species, white and Virginia. The route rises into young third-growth woods before dipping slightly to the spine of a Dyer Mountain spur (2,760 feet) at mile 2.9. Here the Benton MacKaye quickly crosses the spur, maintaining course on undemanding grades, most of them up. Where the slope faces north, the forest becomes moister; sweet birch, hemlock, and yellow poplar mingle with red maple and the oaks. The trail bends down and to the right with the former logging road (mile 3.3) into older forest dominated by pole-timber yellow poplar. One-tenth mile farther, the roadbed treadway half-circles a culverted hollow (intermittent rivulet) moist enough for basswood.

Beyond the hollow, the track crosses over another spur; the downslope ravine is now to your left. The trail wanders above another hollow before curving to the right (mile 3.5) into larger timber—northwest-slope hardwoods lording over hemlock and white pine saplings. Mile 3.8 makes a double-blazed turn to the left and down off the old road onto narrow path. If you miss this dogleg, you will reach FS 64 after 80 yards. In the future, after more feet have defined the treadway, this turn will be much easier to spot.

After the turn, the shady, sidehill footpath descends for 0.1 mile before gaining elevation to mile 4.0, where it swings left onto the crest of the Blue Ridge. The next 0.2 mile ascends (overall easy) on or near the oak-pine–forested ridgeline to section high point—the cap of an unchristened knob (2,960 feet). The remainder of the route veers to the left off the knob onto slope, switchbacks to the right, then steadily descends (easy to moderate grades the most difficult) to Watson Gap (2,730 feet). The final downhill grade passes beside tall hardwoods, mostly oak, to FS 64 and the Benton MacKaye Trail sign. Section 9 turns left and follows FS 64 for 80 yards to its end in front of the large Cohutta WMA sign. Section 10 perseveres straight ahead through the four-way intersection, toward Dally Gap on FS 22.

Note: *Walked south to north, BMT-9 splits away from the South Fork Trail at mile 2.2. This signed junction is now also the northern terminus of the Pinhoti Trail, another long-distance route. The Pinhoti's current southern terminus is located off Highway 77 in the southern portion of Alabama's Talladega National Forest. When completed, the Pinhoti Trail will span approximately 250 to 275 miles; Georgia's share of that distance is currently listed as 151 miles.*

NATURE NOTES

DESPITE THE LENGTH of its conifer- and rhododendron-shaded segment, BMT-9 features a surprisingly diverse spring wildflower display. While early spring hikers might see trout lily and blood-root in bloom, walking this section from April 20 through May 5 gives you the best opportunity to observe the most species in blossom. In addition to the nearly ubiquitous Catesby's trillium, you might spot yellowroot, blue cohosh, mayapple, Solomon's seal and false Solomon's seal, showy orchis, dwarf and crested dwarf iris, foamflower, wild geranium, pink lady's-slipper, tooth-wort, giant chickweed, and at least five species of violets—halberd-leaved and birdfoot among them.

Two extensive wild geranium colonies bloom downslope from FS 64 (the southernmost 0.1 mile starting from Dyer Gap) start-ing around April 20. Galax and partridgeberry flower later in the spring. The inconspicuous corollas of the false hellebore—the early spring perennial greening the moist slopes with their large, prominently pleated basal leaves—do not usually open until July. If you are hiking in the fall, look for the grass-of-Parnassus, whose rounded, kidney-shaped leaves are decidedly ungrasslike.

It is unusually common in the South Fork's watershed. Showy, five-petaled, and delicately veined with green, the single cream-colored flowers usually break bud sometime between September 1 and September 20. A roughly circular spray of golden flower parts helps complete the easy identification.

umbrella magnolia

Sweetshrub adds its scent to the air by April 20; flame azalea (not common) and mountain laurel open in May. The rosebay rhododendron flanking the South Fork and its feeders was in full white flower on July 8 of a recent year.

From Section 6 northward through Section 12, the aptly named umbrella magnolia is a minor component of the understory forest along or near low-elevation streams. Although somewhat scarce, this deciduous magnolia—bearing the largest noncompound leaf of any tree in the Southern Blue Ridge—is conspicuous and easily identified. The tropical-sized leaves—10 to 20 inches long, 5 to 10 inches wide (for mature trees), and broadest beyond the midpoint—are whorled in umbrella fashion near the end of branch stems. Each leaf is pointed at both ends. Like most broadleafs, saplings often exhibit significantly larger leaves than mature trees.

The Fraser magnolia, which has the second largest noncompound leaf of any Southern Highland tree, is much more common than the umbrella magnolia alongside the Benton MacKaye corridor. Unlike the umbrella magnolia, the Fraser (see illustration on page 262) has whorled leaves with distinctively eared bases. Despite its leaf-size ranking, this hardwood is by far the smallest of the three deciduous magnolias found beside the BMT. (The cucumbertree is the third.) The umbrella's maximum height, which it attains in the Southern Appalachians, is listed as 30 to 40 feet. Usually, however, it is much shorter and often has several shrubby trunks.

Especially abundant beside this section, the Catesby's trillium is impossible to miss during its early spring flowering season. Catesby's, also known as rose trillium, is easily distinguished from the other trillium species found near the Benton MacKaye. Much smaller than the wake robin, the large-flowered, or the Vasey's, this native perennial is usually between 4 to 12 inches in height. Its characteristic three leaves are relatively short, only 2 to 4 inches long, and often wavy edged.

Catesby's trillium

The strongly recurved flowers, which almost always hang at or below leaf level, range from white tinged with pink, to pink, to dark pinkish red. The corollas become deeper pink or darker pink-red as they age. Like the leaves, the petals of the 1- to 1¾-inch-wide blossoms are wavy margined. Curling, bright yellow anthers in the center of the nodding bloom confirm the identification. During a recent spring, most of the Catesby's beside this section were in bloom or opening by April 23.

NORTH TO SOUTH Watson Gap to Dyer Gap

Mile 0.0—Facing the large WMA sign at Watson Gap's four-way intersection, follow the right side of the road to your left, FS 64, for 80 yards before angling up and to the right into the woods.

Mile 0.3—Section 9 gains the high point of an unnamed knob.

Mile 0.5—Slips to the right off the Blue Ridge crest.

Mile 0.7—Bears to the right onto an old roadbed at the double blaze.

Mile 1.1—Half-circles a hollow with an intermittent rivulet.

Mile 1.6—Crosses over a Dyer Mountain spur.

Mile 2.3—The BMT ties into the South Fork Trail at an obvious junction. The two trails share the same wide treadway for the next 1.6 miles.

Mile 2.4—Section 9 crosses a shallow branch flowing out of Rich Cove.

Mile 2.5—Nears the South Fork Jacks River for a bankside view.

Mile 3.2—Passes a short sidepath that leads to an open view of the South Fork.

Mile 3.9—The trails split apart at a signed junction. The BMT turns to the left and follows a small branch upstream. (See the detailed south-to-north narrative for information concerning the waterfall on the South Fork.)

Mile 4.4—Turns to the left onto FS 64.

Mile 4.5—Section 9 ends at Dyer Gap's three-way FS 64–FS 64A intersection.

DIRECTIONS

SECTION 9's DYER GAP Trailhead is located at the three-way FS 64–FS 64A intersection southeast of the Cohutta Wilderness. This trailhead is the northern (actually western) end of Section 8 and the southern end of Section 9.

Approach from the east: From the four-way US 76–GA 5–GA 2 intersection at the northern edge of Blue Ridge, Georgia (McDonald's on the corner), travel GA 5 North approximately 3.7 miles before turning left onto Old SR 2. Up to three signs may mark this turn: one for Watson Gap, another for Old SR 2, and a Highway 2 street sign.

Approach from the northeast: From the three-way TN 68–GA 60–GA 5 intersection in McCaysville, on the Georgia-Tennessee border, take GA 5 South approximately 6.5 miles to the right turn onto Old SR 2, marked with any combination of signs—Watson Gap, Old SR 2, Highway 2.

From Old State Route 2: Proceed on the main road for approximately 10.3 miles (the pavement ends after approximately 9.0 miles) to Watson Gap's four-way intersection and large Cohutta WMA sign. (If you wish to leave a shuttle car at Section 9's northern end—Watson Gap—leave it at the four-way intersection before continuing to Dyer Gap.) At Watson Gap, turn left onto FS 64 and remain on that road for approximately 3.3 miles to its three-way intersection with FS 64A, located at Dyer Gap just past the Dyer Mountain Cemetery. This junction is usually further marked by three signs: a large Cohutta WMA sign at the entrance of FS 64A, a small Benton MacKaye sign, and a carsonite sign for FS 64A. You will find limited, pull-in parking opposite the entrance to FS 64A.

If you walk FS 64 to the west, in the same direction you drove to reach the trailhead from Watson Gap, you will be on Section 9 heading toward the four-way intersection at Watson Gap. If you follow FS 64A uphill, opposite the parking area, you will be hiking Section 8 toward Bushy Head Gap.

NOTES

Wild boar near the BMT

Watson Gap to Spanish Oak Gap 10

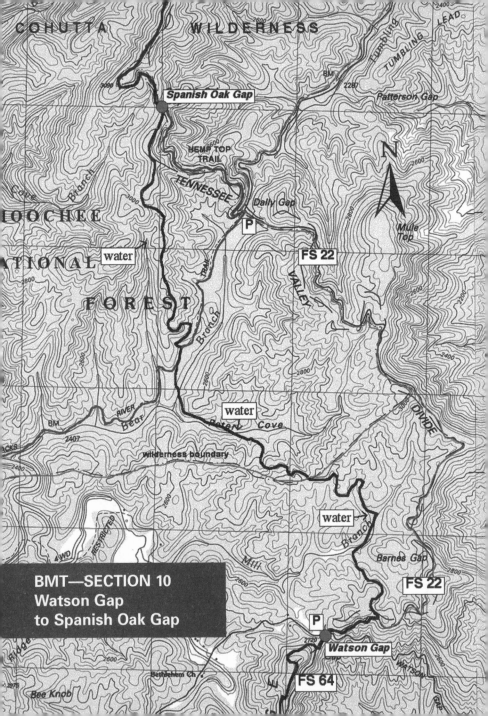

BMT—SECTION 10
Watson Gap
to Spanish Oak Gap

Benton MacKaye Trail, Section 10

*Watson Gap at the four-way intersection
of FS 22, FS 64, Old Highway 2, and County Road 187
to Spanish Oak Gap at Hemp Top Trail*

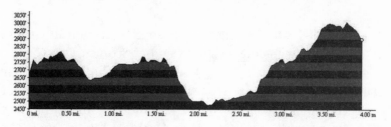

LENGTH 4.1 miles (see description)

DAYHIKING (SOUTH TO NORTH) Easy to Moderate

BACKPACKING (SOUTH TO NORTH) Moderate

VEHICULAR ACCESS AT ONE END ONLY Southern end at
Watson Gap's four-way intersection, 2,730 feet, has
vehicular access. Northern end at Spanish Oak Gap,
2,940 feet, does not have vehicular access. The nearest
access requires a 1.0-mile walk on Hemp Top Trail from
Dally Gap to reach the Benton MacKaye–Hemp Top
junction.

TRAIL JUNCTIONS Jacks River (see description), Hemp Top
(see description)

BLAZE White diamond until Section 10 enters Cohutta
Wilderness at mile 1.4. The Benton MacKaye Trail is
not blazed within the Cohutta Wilderness.

TOPOGRAPHIC QUADRANGLE Hemp Top GA-TN

DELORME MAP GA-14

COUNTY Fannin GA
NEAREST CITIES Ellijay GA (S), Blue Ridge GA (E),
Ducktown TN (NE)
RD/NF Armuchee-Cohutta/Chattahoochee
FEATURES Wilderness; mountain streams; fern colonies;
large white pine

BMT-10, at 4.1 miles, is the shortest section in Georgia. This segment's northern end at Spanish Oak Gap is a 1.0-mile walk from its nearest vehicular access point, Dally Gap. If you wish to set a shuttle and hike BMT-10 one way between vehicles, you will walk the additional mile either to or away from Spanish Oak Gap. Once Section 10 veers off FS 22 at 0.3 mile, it begins the Benton MacKaye's longest roadless stretch south of US 64: 16.1 remote miles between open Forest Service roads. Starting at mile 1.4, the route embarks on a 13.6-mile trek through the combined 45,059-acre Cohutta–Big Frog Wilderness. All of this section lies within the 95,200-acre Cohutta WMA, Georgia's largest wildlife management area.

Approximately 0.6 mile of this segment, the first 0.3 mile and the last 0.3, closely follows the western crest of the Blue Ridge, which doubles as the Tennessee Valley Divide. Starting at Watson Gap, BMT-10 takes FS 22 to the east-northeast for the first 0.3 mile, leaves road and ridge, then lights out generally northwest for the remainder of its distance. The wildwood path descends to the west of the famous ridge and crosses headwater streams of the Jacks River, including section low point (2,460 feet) at Bear Branch, before rising back to the Blue Ridge. With 0.3 mile remaining, the walkway regains the western crest atop an unchristened knob, section high point at 3,020 feet.

Walked south to north from its Watson Gap end, Section 10 begins in front of the large Cohutta WMA sign at the gap's four-way intersection. From this middle-of-nowhere junction, follow carsonite-signed FS 22—its narrow entrance also blazed with a BMT diamond and signed for Dally Gap—to the east-northeast. Crunch the easy upgrade of dirt-gravel FS 22 for 0.3 mile, to the bend-back left turn (2,810 feet) off the road and up into young hardwoods. Wide wooden steps, a trail sign, and the in-creasingly familiar white blaze make this change in direction impossible to miss for all but the most stumble-footed daydreamers. The footpath quickly gains the top of a spur, re-mains on the crest for less than 100

sourwood

feet, then angles to the right and down off the spine. The track rises into an oak-hickory community, where blackgum, chestnut oak, sourwood, pignut hickory, and red maple share sunlight with saplings of white pine and American chestnut.

Now in a forest of older, larger trees, the route returns to level ridgetop at 0.4 mile. It then slants to the right and down off the keel onto dry southeastern slope supporting a dense understory of deciduous heath, whose ripened berries attract bear in July and August. Following a downgrade with several very short, steep dips, the treadway reaches a slight saddle, where it curls to the right and down off the spur again. Now the hiking heads down a shallow hollow to the Mill Branch floodplain. The base of an old home-place chimney is located 13 paces to the right of the trail in the upper part of the flat. You will have much better luck finding the stacked rocks if you search in winter or early spring before the tangle of vegetation blankets the bottomland. Mile 0.8 makes a bridged crossing over Mill Branch (2,635 feet).

Across the narrow stream, BMT-10 begins a gradual elevation gain on the old lane, still remarkably open and aislelike, that once led to the homesite. Fence wire used to corral the formerly cleared bottomland is plainly visible to the right. The no-strain stroll occasionally tunnels through the heavy shade of overarching hemlock, mountain laurel, and rosebay rhododendron. At mile 1.0 the roadbed sinks to and crosses a step-over rivulet before switchbacking up and to the left. The nearly effortless walking parallels hollows and slowly works its way uphill below an oak-pine canopy that includes occasional tall Virginia pines. After curving left and crossing over a spur, the course rounds an upper hollow at mile 1.3. The easy ascent reaches a ridgecrest (2,790 feet)—the black-and-white signed Cohutta Wilderness boundary—at mile 1.4. Blazes are not allowed within the wilderness; the rest of this section and all of the next one inside the Cohutta–Big Frog Wilderness are unblazed. Signs, often destroyed by bears or vandals, mark trail junctions—and that's it. Wilderness map and compass are essential for Section 11.

O VER THE RIDGELINE and now in wilderness, the Benton MacKaye makes a curving, 0.6-mile descent to a fork of Bear Branch flowing out of Peter Cove. The grade, undemanding hiking interspersed with a few short moderate stretches, often runs alongside hollows before half-circling their heads. These hollows are generally north facing and moist for their relatively low (2,520 to 2,720 feet) elevation. Ferns, especially the densely colonial New York fern, abound in most of the hollows; the most extensive fern field flanks the path for a full tenth of a mile. As is usual in low-elevation, second-growth hollows, straight-boled yellow poplars have won the competition toward the sun.

The wilderness walkway doglegs to the right off the old road, heading downslope beside hemlock on another, narrower woods road. It crosses a shallow, 10- to 12-foot-wide tributary of Bear Branch (2,490 feet) at mile 2.0. Once across, the track bends to the west and parallels the brook downstream on gentle grades well above the water. The fork soon pools as it slowly flows through a string of old beaver ponds. Most of the dams are grassed over; the gray snags, once woodpecker high-rises, have fallen; open water is decreasing year to year. The treadway drops with the stream toward its meeting with Bear Branch. As the footpath approaches the confluence, it swings to the north, crossing the larger Bear Branch—20 feet wide and usually rock-step shallow by mid-June—at mile 2.4 (2,460 feet).

Just to the left of the trail across the stream stands an old-growth hemlock (if it is still alive), approximately 11 feet 6 inches around. Here the BMT makes a short easy-to-moderate up-hill run before gaining the nearly level crest of a low ridge. Mature white pine, many in the 8- to 10-foot circumference range, tower several tiers above the other ridgetop trees. The route slabs down and to the left off the spine, dipping to a prominent trail junction at mile 2.6. Guided by a sign, Section 10 turns to the right onto the wide, boot-worn Jacks River Trail. It shares the JRT's tread for 90 yards before veering up and to the left (northwest) onto a narrow path at the second sign.

Marching solo again, the wildland trail pushes forward up a hollow and bears off to the right through a forest featuring more impressive trailside white pines. Rising steadily, the track swings to the left above a small side hollow filled with ferns before rounding its dry notch at mile 2.8. The route, flanked by mountain laurel and deciduous heath, sweeps up and to the right onto ridgecrest at mile 3.0. Here the Benton MacKaye makes a ridgetop ascent (the first 120 yards are moderate) to the crown (2,800 feet) of the first in a series of unnamed knobs at mile 3.1.

With one exception, the final mile before the Hemp Top junction follows a north-south-trending ridgeline that rolls through shallow gaps and arches over nearly identical knobs. You can find water to the left of a shallow saddle at mile 3.4. If this source is unsigned, however, it may be difficult to find. If you are planning to hike ahead on Section 11 without pause for reprovision, make sure you load up on water at Bear Branch. The next trailside water—Double Spring Gap—is at mile 4.4 on Section 11.

After an overall easy-to-moderate downhill from another knob, the track rises easily to mile 3.6, where it slabs to the left off the crest and crosses the fern-floored notch of an upper hollow. BMT-10 regains the main ridge at mile 3.7, then rises to the peak of the next unlabeled rumple (mile 3.8), section high point at 3,020 feet. Now riding the western keel of the Blue Ridge again, the course loses elevation before climbing over the last oak-wrapped bump at mile 3.9. It then descends on old-road grade to its tie-in with Hemp Top Trail at the south end of Spanish Oak Gap (2,940 feet). Easy to moderate overall, the final stretch traverses woods where the often short-lived Virginia pine has reached the overstory.

The southernmost 3.1 miles of Section 11 share the former Forest Service road treadway with the Hemp Top Trail. If you turn left at the usually signed junction, you will be walking north on BMT-11. If you turn right onto Hemp Top Trail, you will reach the Dally Gap Trailhead off FS 22 after one mile of slightly down-hill hiking.

NATURE NOTES

ALTHOUGH THIS SECTION does not support large numbers of individual spring wildflowers, it does offer a diversity of species. A few of the early bloomers include Solomon's seal and false Solomon's seal, dwarf and crested dwarf iris, Catesby's trillium, wild geranium, bloodroot, mayapple, foamflower, trailing arbutus, trout lily, bellwort,

partridgeberry

pink lady's-slipper, and halberd-leaved violet. April 20 through May 5 is the best time to see the largest number of herbaceous wildflowers in blossom.

Mountain laurel should start opening in mid-May. Indian cucumber-root, partridgeberry, and galax bloom from late May into June. By the middle of July rattlesnake plantain, phlox, and rosebay rhododendron add their contributions to the warm-season show. From early September well into October assorted asters and grass-of-Parnassus enliven the understory beneath the turning forest.

Look for the evergreen partridgeberry colonies along the descending stretch of hemlock-shaded woods before crossing the Bear Branch tributary at mile 2.0. Except for the size of its trailing beds, which occasionally cover hundreds of square feet, everything else about the partridgeberry is diminutive. This recumbent herb usually starts blooming by mid-May and continues through much of June. The fragrant white or pinkish flowers—trumpet shaped and fringed inside—always occur in joined pairs. These small (only ½ to ⅔ of an inch long) corollas share fused ovaries that produce a single berrylike fruit with two closely set, eyelike indentations, one from each ovary.

The bright red fruits are especially noticeable from midsummer through autumn. As the common name implies, ruffed grouse eat the fruits. Grouse and turkey, however, eat these colorful but flavorless fruits only as a last resort, which explains why many of these bright fruits last through winter and a few remain until the next flowering season.

Even without berry or bloom, clusters of partridgeberry are easy to identify by their small, shiny, dark green leaves—opposite and prominently veined. The ovate evergreen leaves are ½ to ¾ of an inch long.

The snow-white blooms of the bloodroot are occasional to common along much of the Benton MacKaye south of the Ocoee River. To many, the bloodroot epitomizes the beauty and fragility of spring wildflowers. Closing at night and during cloudy weather, its petals normally drop off in a mere two to five days. A hard rain, however, can plaster all the frail petals to the forest floor before their short allowance of days is over, and that is it until the next year.

This native perennial is one of the Benton MacKaye's earliest bloomers. In fact, its corollas have flared and fallen before most hikers lace up their boots for the first walk of the new year. Picking one weekend to find blooming bloodroot is a hit-or-miss proposition. Unlike more reliable wildflowers that start blooming within a narrow, predictable time span and last longer, this early bird waits for a spate of warm sunny days in late winter or very early spring, then pops up despite the cold weather to come.

Bloodroot blossoms are the largest and showiest of the very early spring wildflowers along the Benton MacKaye. Their single, bright white corollas—usually 1¼ to 2¼ inches wide—are impossible to miss against the brown thatch of last year's leaves. Eight to twelve (normally eight) petals encircle the prominent yellow stamens in the center.

Unlike the leaves of many other wild-flowers, bloodroot leaves are large, distinctive, and easily recognized long after its blooms have fallen. Roughly circular in outline, the deeply divided, palmately scalloped leaf has five to nine lobes. The thick, slightly leathery leaf grows substantially after early spring, reaching 4 to 7 inches across by mid-June.

This native perennial forms colonies by means of rhizomatous runners. Usually small, these colonies most often occur in open, predominantly deciduous forests up to at least

bloodroot

4,000 feet. As long as there is plenty of early spring light, you will find this species on a variety of sites—high slopes and ridges, hardwood coves, and sunny woods above streams where rhododendron and hemlock are absent.

A member of the Poppy family, the bloodroot is the only member of its genus. As its name suggests, this plant's root bleeds acrid, orange-red sap. Tribal Americans utilized its somewhat poisonous juice for war paint, dye, and insect repellent.

NORTH TO SOUTH Spanish Oak Gap to Watson Gap

Mile 0.0—After walking 1.0 mile on Hemp Top Trail from its Dally Gap Trailhead, turn left onto the northern end of Section 10 at the usually signed Benton MacKaye–Hemp Top junction at the southern end of Spanish Oak Gap.

Mile 0.3—Section 10 gains elevation to the top of the highest knob, the second in a series of unnamed knuckles.

Mile 0.4—Leaves the ridgeline for 0.1 mile.

Mile 0.7—Reaches shallow saddle (usually signed water source to the right, west).

Mile 1.0—Rises over the last knob, then slants down and to the left off the ridgetop 0.1 mile farther.

Mile 1.4—Usually guided by a sign, the BMT turns to the right onto the Jacks River Trail, shares its wide treadway for 90 yards, then doglegs left off the JRT at the second signed junction.

Mile 1.7—The trail crosses Bear Branch.

Mile 2.1—Crosses a shallow Bear Branch feeder flowing out of Peter Cove.

Mile 2.7—Exits the Cohutta Wilderness at the black-and-white signed ridgetop boundary (blazing resumes).

Mile 3.3—Makes a bridged crossing over Mill Creek.

Mile 3.8—Turns right onto FS 22 and finishes the route on that road.

Mile 4.1—Section 10 ends at Watson Gap's four-way intersection.

DIRECTIONS

SECTION 10'S WATSON GAP Trailhead is located at the four-way intersection—FS 22–FS 64–Old Highway 2–County Road 187—near the eastern boundary of the Cohutta Wilderness. This trailhead is the northern end of Section 9 and the southern end of Section 10. As you enter the four-way intersection from Old Highway 2, the narrow roadway of FS 22, the usually signed way to Dally Gap, is uphill to the right; FS 64 is to the left.

Follow the directions for Section 9 (see page 215) to the four-way intersection at Watson Gap. If you walk FS 22 from Watson Gap and turn into the woods after 0.3 mile, you will be hiking on Section 10 heading toward its junction with the Hemp Top Trail. If you walk the right shoulder of FS 64 for 80 yards past the Cohutta WMA sign before angling to the right into forest, you will be hiking Section 9 toward Dyer Gap.

Shuttle: If you wish to set a shuttle and walk Section 10 from south to north (Watson Gap to Hemp Top Trail to Dally Gap), you will have to take FS 22 for approximately 3.5 miles to Dally Gap, leave a vehicle, then backtrack to Watson Gap. The trailhead at Dally Gap is obvious: bulletin board, trail signs, pull-in parking to the left and right. Two signed and gated trails—Jacks River and Hemp Top—begin to the left side of the road at Dally Gap. Jacks River leads downhill past the bulletin board; Hemp Top, where you will either begin or end, heads uphill to the right of the Jacks River Trail.

Rhododendron tunnel

Spanish Oak Gap
to Chestnut Ridge

11

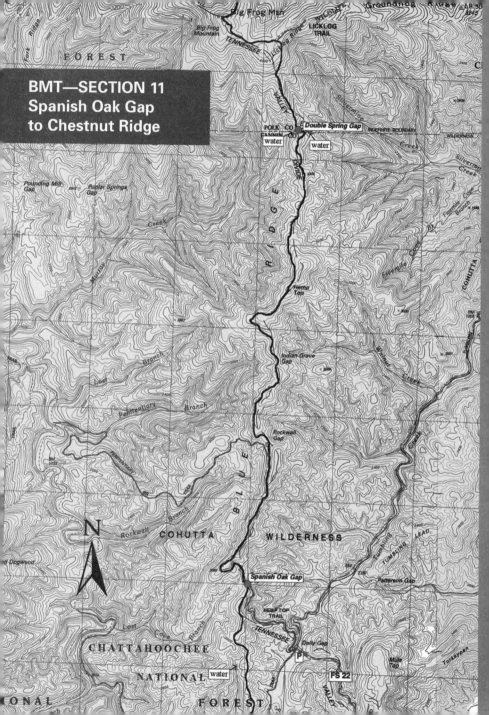

BMT—SECTION 11
Spanish Oak Gap
to Chestnut Ridge

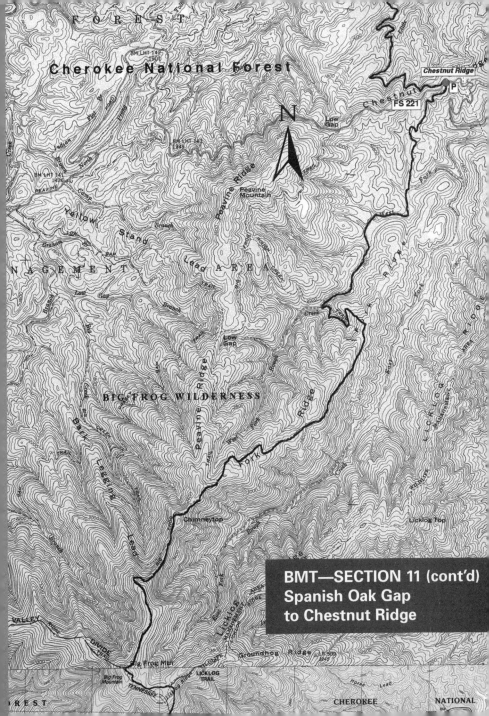

BMT—SECTION 11 (cont'd)
Spanish Oak Gap
to Chestnut Ridge

Benton MacKaye Trail, Section 11

*Spanish Oak Gap at Hemp Top Trail
to Chestnut Ridge at FS 221*

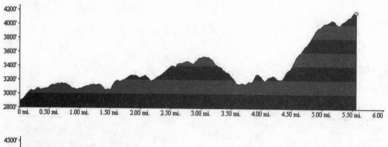

LENGTH 12.3 miles (see description)

DAYHIKING (SOUTH TO NORTH) Moderate

BACKPACKING (SOUTH TO NORTH) Moderate to Strenuous

VEHICULAR ACCESS AT ONE END ONLY Southern end at
Spanish Oak Gap, 2,940 feet, does not have vehicular
access. The nearest access requires a 1.0-mile walk on
Hemp Top Trail from Dally Gap to reach the Benton
MacKaye–Hemp Top junction. Northern end at FS 221,
1,900 feet, has vehicular access.

Trail Junctions Hemp Top, Penitentiary Branch, Licklog
Ridge, Wolf Ridge, Big Frog, Big Creek, Fork Ridge,
Rough Creek, West Fork (see description for all
junctions)

Blaze White diamond after Section 11 leaves the Big Frog
Wilderness near its northern, Chestnut Ridge end.
The Benton MacKaye Trail is not blazed within the
Cohutta–Big Frog Wilderness.

Topographic Quadrangles Hemp Top GA-TN, Caney
Creek TN, Ducktown TN

DeLorme Maps GA-14, TN-26

Counties Fannin GA, Polk TN

Nearest Cities Ellijay GA (S), Blue Ridge GA (SE),
Ducktown TN (E), Cleveland TN (W)

RD/NF Armuchee-Cohutta/Chattahoochee,
Ocoee/Cherokee

Features Wilderness; winter views; Big Frog Mountain;
wildflower displays; West Fork Rough Creek

A FAST-PACED DAYHIKE FOR THE FIT or a more leisurely
two- or three-day backpack trip, Section 11 is the wildest and highest of the southernmost twelve BMT sections. All but its northernmost 1.4 miles wind through the
combined 45,059-acre Cohutta–Big Frog Wilderness: the largest
national forest wilderness or combined wilderness east of the Mississippi. This segment does not touch or cross an active road for its
entire length. Section high point, 4,220 feet atop Big Frog Mountain, is by far the loftiest Benton MacKaye elevation from Springer
Mountain to the Ocoee River. BMT-11 also boasts the greatest

elevation differential (2,560 feet) between high and low points of any section detailed in this guide. Although it is 0.4 mile shorter than Section 8, Section 11's southern end requires a 1.0-mile walk from the nearest vehicular access, which increases its distance to 13.3 miles for hikers beginning or ending at Dally Gap.

Starting from its southern end at Spanish Oak Gap, this link follows the Blue Ridge due north to the Hemp Top–Licklog Ridge junction (mile 5.2), where the route angles west-northwest to Big Frog's summit (mile 5.7). Here, atop The Frog, the track leaves the Blue Ridge and rambles to the north-northeast toward its FS 221 end.

From Spanish Oak Gap, where the BMT ties into Hemp Top Trail, Section 11's entire length—through the two-state wilderness and out to FS 221—shares its tread with segments of six different trails, all of which were built before the Benton MacKaye. Neither the BMT nor any of the other path-sharing trails are blazed within the wildernesses. Junctions are not always signed, especially in the Big Frog Wilderness, where bears regularly rip them to kindling. After a bear pulls down a sign, all you have is a post and other treadways to mark an intersection. You need a good, comprehensive map—preferably the "Cohutta and Big Frog Wilderness Georgia-Tennessee" map—and a compass to verify various junctions and direction of travel.

BMT-11's southern end is located at the Benton MacKaye–Hemp Top junction near Spanish Oak Gap, a 1.0-mile walk northwest from Dally Gap. Section 11, walked south to north, continues straight ahead on Hemp Top Trail.

This section's initial 3.1 miles to Hemp Top (the mountain) are as easy to walk as they are to describe. The route accompanies the crest and upper slope of the Blue Ridge northward on the smooth track of former FS 73, closed when the Georgia Wilderness Bill of

1986 added 2,900 acres to the Cohutta Wilderness. All of the grades on this first stretch, both up and down, are easy, and each time the former road leaves the ridgeline, it slants onto the western slope, the drier side road builders always prefer.

Beyond the Penitentiary Branch junction, Benton MacKaye's Hemp Top segment becomes one of the least traveled links of trail in the Cohutta Wilderness, especially in summer. The forest is still in the process of filling in the road's former light gap. And where there is light in the mountains, there are briers, saplings, and tall herbaceous plants, especially asters. Although the Benton MacKaye maintainers usually do an excellent job of brushing out the route, you may still encounter thick vegetation during the summer.

From the Benton MacKaye–Hemp Top junction at Spanish Oak Gap, Section 11 presses northward on an easy upgrade into a diverse, second-growth forest: a predominantly hardwood canopy above white pine saplings and occasional hemlocks. Succession species, such as black locust, flank the former light gap, and occasional pockets of Virginia pine indicate a southern or southwestern exposure. Slowly gaining elevation, the nearly effortless walking often slabs onto upper sunset slope before returning to ridgetop. Mile 1.4 arrives at the signed Penitentiary Branch junction (3,080 feet) just south of Rockwall Gap. Penitentiary Branch Trail slants downhill to the left; the Benton MacKaye continues straight ahead.

BEYOND THE PENITENTIARY BRANCH connection, the second of many to come, the course becomes narrower and more pathlike. The wilderness walkway regains the keel through Rockwall Gap before angling back onto the western sidehill, where it continues the gradual elevation gain to the next named gap, Indian Grave. Here, as the trail swings around the crest's next high point, the effects of elevation and exposure become more and more noticeable. As the track half-loops west, north, then east back to the top of the Blue Ridge, it traverses south- and southwest-facing slopes, west-facing slopes, and northwest- and north-facing slopes, sometimes in quick succession. The drier southwest pitches support oak-pine forests; the slightly moister western slants tend to be oak-hickory; and the slopes oriented toward the north provide habitat for species requiring higher moisture levels for good growth—black cherry, white ash, basswood, and sweet birch. Fern fields are increasingly common on the higher northwest-facing flanks.

The BMT advances through Indian Grave Gap (3,220 feet) at mile 2.1, continuing the gradual ascent on the upper-west side of the mountain. After curling over a Hemp Top spur at mile 2.6, the wildland path works its way back to the ridgecrest and gently rises to the crown of Hemp Top (3,580 feet) at mile 3.1. Along the way it passes an open grove of shagbark hickory to the left. Until 1985, old FS 73 dead-ended at the turnaround trailhead parking area on the summit, the site of a former fire tower now reclaimed by saplings branching toward the sun.

Still heading northward, the path veers to the left and down off the mountaintop, making a sharp 80-yard pitch to an old woods road below. The descent proceeds on milder grades (mostly easy, short easy to moderate) within a largely oak-hickory forest shading occasional clumps of bear-food huckleberry. The downhill run bottoms out at a stand of yellow poplar in a shallow saddle (3,180 feet) at mile 3.7. Now the Benton MacKaye arches and rolls with the Blue Ridge crest—rising over low knobs, dipping to slight gaps—before dropping on steeper grades to the belt of white pine in Double Spring Gap (3,210 feet) at mile 4.4. The highest heave along the way lifts your soles to 3,305 feet.

Double Spring Gap is situated at the intersection of an east-west-running man-made boundary and a north-south-running natural barrier. The political border separates states, national forests, counties, wildernesses (east of the trail), and WMAs. The geographical boundary is the Tennessee Valley Divide, which separates major drainages.

True to its name, the gap features two springs, one to the right and the other to the left. What its name doesn't tell you, however, is that the clear flows from these two springs, starting only a few rods apart, take vastly different journeys to the sea. The spring to the left (west) feeds one of Murray Creek's headwater prongs. Its flow chart is a list of Amerindian names: Jacks River (named after a tribal American named Jack), Conasauga River, the Oostanaula, the Coosa, the Alabama, and the Tensaw Rivers to the Gulf of Mexico at Mobile Bay. The sister spring to the east of the gap takes a slightly less direct route to the Gulf: Silvermine Creek, Tumbling Creek, Ocoee River, the Hiwassee, the Tennessee, the Ohio, and finally down the mighty Mississippi.

These two springs are Section 11's first trailside water sources north of Spanish Oak Gap. If usually reliable Elderberry Spring, 0.1 mile below the top of Big Frog, is drought dry, this gap is your last water until at or near West Fork Rough Creek at mile 10.0. The spring to the right (east) has a wider path and more water; it also receives much more use, occasionally even from horses. Therefore, it is safer to duck through the rhododendron and filter the Mobile Bay–bound water nearby to the left.

Immediately beyond the deep gap, where a sign traditionally welcomes hikers to Tennessee's Cherokee National Forest,

Section 11 starts up through the narrow swath of tall white pine. The next 0.8-mile segment to the Licklog Ridge junction, while not easy, is definitely straightforward: it climbs without relent, gaining 820 feet of elevation in 0.8 mile. The benchmark of hard Southern Appalachian hiking is a sustained elevation rise of 100 feet per 0.1 mile of run—close to a 20 percent grade. Moderate to strenuous for dayhikers and a solid strenuous for backpackers, this grunt is the BMT's steepest long upgrade from Springer Mountain to the Ocoee River.

B EYOND THE GAP, the path closely straddles the boundary between the Cohutta and Big Frog Wildernesses. Benton MacKaye–Hemp Top is the only route that connects the trail systems of the two wildernesses. Generally following a former WMA boundary jeep road (a few signs are still embedded in the trailside trees), the pull ascends the ridge into a south-facing forest where oaks and other sunny-site broadleafs have the upper branch. As the footpath, now more winding and much narrower than in years past, nears 3,800 feet, sugar maples become increasingly common. Here, on Big Frog's island of high habitat, northbound hikers first encounter the sugar maple—a northern hardwood—as a common component of the forest.

By mile 4.9 the passage slips to the right of the broad crest and ascends more gradually to the usually signed, three-way junction with the Licklog Ridge Trail (4,030 feet) at mile 5.2. Where Hemp Top Trail ends in a shallow saddle on Licklog Ridge, Section 11 turns left (west), sharing treadway with the uppermost 0.5 mile of Licklog Ridge Trail to the top of Big Frog. Still riding the Blue Ridge and still near the boundary between the two wildernesses, the course rises gently in the midst of open hardwoods on the upper-north slope of a 4,090-foot knob. The understory, especially during a wet year, is lush with ferns and herbaceous wildflowers. The walkway dips to a saddle at mile 5.4, then heads up the keel for a short distance before slanting back onto the north slope again. Overhead, the well-spaced forest includes yellow buckeye, black cherry, white oak, and the Benton MacKaye's southernmost yellow birches. A little more than 200 yards below the summit, the track passes Elderberry Spring—a small, picturesque, rocked-in basin to the left.

yellow buckeye

The slow-climbing ascent to Big Frog Mountain ends with an easy-to-moderate upgrade to the usually signed, three-way intersection (mile 5.7; 4,220 feet) atop the crown. Big Frog's exact high point (4,224 feet) is 30 to 35 yards directly ahead to the northwest. Three trails—Licklog Ridge, Wolf Ridge, Big Frog—converge at the junction. Even if the sign is missing from its post, as it sometimes is, making the correct turn is fairly easy. The BMT, leaving the Blue Ridge, curves to the right onto the Big Frog Trail and shares its treadway downhill to the north-northeast. Wolf Ridge, which travels west-northwest away from the mountain, is to your left across the campsite. Benton MacKaye–Licklog Ridge ties almost seamlessly into the Big Frog Trail.

From the top of Big Frog, Section 11 begins its long descent to the northeast through the heart of the Big Frog Wilderness. The first 3.8 miles of this stretch, to the first Rough Creek junction, remain on or near the crest of Fork Ridge: a major lead dropping from Big Frog to the northeasternmost perimeter of the wilderness. Although the route loses 1,960 feet in those 3.8 miles, it does so with remarkable ease and steadiness. The occasional easy-to-moderate downs are the sharpest grades of sustained length.

The initial elevation loss, nearly effortless, wends beneath ridgeline hardwoods, wind-dwarfed and rounded. Clumps of autumn-blooming witch-hazel arch above the walkway. Occasionally following the dark tread along the narrow, rocky keel, the slow-dropping descent works its way to mile 6.2, where it starts down with a somewhat renewed sense of purpose. By mile 6.3 the blazeless path slabs slightly to the right (east) of the spine onto sidehill.

Mile 6.5 crosses the crest and switches sides, this time slipping to the left (west) of the fold. Here, where Bark Legging Lead meets Fork Ridge, the trail builders crafted a half loop that is difficult to recognize until you see the route drawn across the contour lines of a map. (The name Bark Legging Lead comes from the old logging days. Especially when limbing felled trees in the middle of nowhere, axemen found it prudent to protect their shins from bloody gashes; tree bark was abundant, cheap as the effort to pick it up, and worked well enough.) Rather than taking the straighter, shorter, and much steeper way down Fork Ridge, the track swerves to the northwest, descending the uppermost lead before curving back to the east to rejoin Fork Ridge. Benton MacKaye–Big Frog begins the roundabout by tunneling through a long archway of rhododendron. After winding over the lead, it dips downhill on a north-facing wildflower slope, open and rich.

By mile 6.7 the passage is back atop Fork Ridge, snaking down into a mostly deciduous forest still short from the thin soil and stunting wind. Until the trees block the opening, a gap to the right offers a good view of nearby Licklog Ridge across the deeply incised valley of East Fork Rough Creek. Big Creek Trail, occasionally signed and usually cairned, ties into the left (west) side of the BMT at mile 6.9 (3,660 feet). Beyond this junction, the course continues straight ahead, nearly level, on a hardwood-forested fold where white oaks are common. After heavy rain, you can hear the East Fork's crashing cascades way downhill to the right.

Mile 7.0 slants onto sunset slope where mountain winterberry, a deciduous holly red-berried in the fall, thrives in the understory. The no-strain walking travels on sidehill path as the route skirts the upper-west tilt of Chimneytop, a named knob on Fork Ridge. Section 11 switchbacks to the right over a Chimneytop spur at mile 7.2, angling back toward the main ridgeline in the shade of a moist forest of buckeye, basswood, and sugar maple. The grade regains the keel at mile 7.3, ranges gently downhill on narrow ridgeline, then drifts to the right (east) of the fold just downslope from a saddle. The top and east side of Fork Ridge afford occasional partial summer and good winter views of Licklog Ridge, running parallel to the southeast.

The forest reflects the loss of elevation and the change of exposure to nearly south; now white and Virginia pines rise above mountain laurel and deciduous heath. The hiking swings around the upper, southeastern slant of the next knob, this one formed by the convergence of Peavine and Fork Ridges. One-tenth mile beyond where the footpath joins the spine again, the BMT arrives at the Big Frog–Fork Ridge Trail junction—rest-stop open and usually signed—at mile 7.6 (3,380 feet). Here, where the Big Frog Trail dives to the left and down, the Benton MacKaye switches treadways, pushing straight ahead with the crest onto Fork Ridge Trail.

Forty yards beyond the junction, BMT-FRT veers to the left onto slope, continuing the mild downgrade through a forest harboring occasional large chestnut oaks and sweetshrub colonies. Partial views to the left are of nearby Peavine Ridge, one of the many leads splaying downward from Big Frog. A high-range easy

galax

descent ramps you into a rich, north-facing hollow wooded with tall yellow poplar, overstory-height red maples, and multi-boled clumps of light-skinned Fraser magnolias. Mile 7.9 rounds the hollow's notch, graced with the sprays of tall cinnamon ferns in season. The narrow footpath winds over a spur at mile 8.1; one-tenth mile farther it half-circles the head of a smaller hollow, this one not as lush as the magnolia hollow. The walkway returns to the ridge at mile 8.3, slides onto the northwestern pitch for a short distance, then regains the crest for more easy walking.

Mile 8.5 passes through a shallow saddle (2,820 feet) before quickly slanting to the right (southeast) side of the ridge, which rises straight ahead toward the next knob. Here mature Virginia pine, some of them thicker than average for their species, signal the drier conditions of the oak-pine forest. Scarlet and chestnut oak, sassafras, sourwood, and white pine join the short-needled Virginia pine above galax and deciduous heath. The wilderness trek steadily loses elevation on a sidehill path. In this lower and drier habitat, a few dogwoods have escaped the anthracnose disease that has decimated many of them in the moister areas of the Southern Appalachians, including Big Frog Mountain.

THE ROUTE TIES BACK INTO the descending spine at mile 9.4; one-tenth mile farther, it T's into the three-way intersection with Rough Creek Trail (2,260 feet)—a small, often poorly marked loafing spot in a slight gap. Here, at the lower-elevation end of Fork Ridge Trail, BMT-11 turns left (300 degrees) onto Rough Creek Trail and shares its treadway as it descends to the northwest. One hundred and thirty yards from the junction, the downhill hiking begins to lose elevation (short easy to moderate the sharpest grade) on a dry spur. The track bears off down and to the left of the spur at mile 9.6, working its way toward water in the notch below.

The descent comes to an abrupt edge in the forest as the course ducks into a dark belt of hemlock. Now on old roadbed, the walkway makes a rounded switchback to the right (mile 9.7) into a northwest-facing hollow. Here the tread, passing several tall yellow poplars, accompanies the rocky cleft of the hollow. It then curls to the right again and crosses the hollow's usually dry notch at mile 9.9. On the other side of the furrow, look to your left to see if the old-growth yellow poplar is still alive; its fluted gray bole rises through the rhododendron 40 to 45 yards away.

The BMT-RCT rock-steps (usually dry shod) across the West Fork Rough Creek at mile 10.0. Once across this small stream, the route rises to a former system road that was closed when this area was added to the Big Frog Wilderness in 1986. As time passes, the road will narrow steadily to footpath; doghobble thickets and hemlock saplings are already filling the light gap. Thirty-five yards after turning right onto the road grade, you reach the Rough Creek–West Fork intersection (still mile 10.0; 1,880 feet), usually marked with some combination of post, sign, or cairn. West Fork Trail ends at this junction; Rough Creek continues uphill to the left on path. Switching treadways for the final time, Section 11 ventures straight ahead on the woods road, now sharing the track with the West Fork Trail.

Except for the two crossings, the next 1.3 miles, paralleling the West Fork to the north-northeast, offer the Benton MacKaye's mildest wildland hiking of this length. The often nearly level route affords occasional summer views of the clear-water creek. The riparian forest, second growth and scenic, is tall and straight and diverse. Here low-elevation species such as sycamore, sweetgum, and umbrella magnolia mingle with a host of other hardwoods and a conifer component of hemlock and white pine.

At mile 10.4 the roadbed walkway runs alongside the creek close enough for a good view. Mile 10.6 drops to and rock-steps across the West Fork at the site of a former bridge. The track pitches down a steep bank and rock-steps the creek for the final time at mile 10.7. Just after the course leaves the Big Frog Wilderness, it crosses over a culverted rivulet at mile 10.9. Four-tenths mile farther along the west side of the stream, the easygoing stretch passes over another culverted branch (section low point at 1,660 feet). Stop daydreaming here; a sharp turn is coming up soon. Forty-five yards beyond this culvert, you will cross over still another one. Forty feet past this culvert, the BMT-WFT turns 90 degrees to the left and up where the road continues straight ahead. Usually unsigned, this turn is marked with a double blaze (blazes resume outside of the wilderness), a rock-step entrance to the path, and perhaps a cairn that sometimes shape-shifts into a fire ring.

The next half-mile leads northward up the eastern slope of a steep-sided, south-facing hollow, its rivulet becoming smaller and smaller until the notch is dry. Generally easy, the sidehill path does what it must to traverse the terrain: wiggles side to side, dips occasionally, rises more sharply for a few feet when necessary. This section is lush with rhododendron and hemlock, dark green and shiny on sunny days before spring's bud break. Several of the nearby hemlocks are old growth—over 10 feet in circumference.

The trail angles out of the hollow, picking up a woods road in a saddle (1,820 feet) at mile 11.8. Gaining elevation gradually, the wide grade soon enters a forest thick with thin trees. Mile 12.1 rounds an upper hollow with a tall conifer-broadleaf canopy. Much of this forest—skinny hardwoods, even skinnier pines, mostly Virginia—is regenerating from cuts made in the late 1980s and early 1990s. Winter views to the right across the West Fork valley provide a last look at Licklog Ridge; the peak due south along the crest is Licklog Top. Section 11 ends on Chestnut Ridge (1,900 feet) at the West Fork Trailhead beside FS 221. Section 12 pushes forward on the gated road (old FS 45) directly across FS 221.

NATURE NOTES

SECTION 11'S PROTECTED STATUS, length, and over 2,500-foot elevation differential—its varying exposures and numerous environments from ridgetop to riverine—all help support a diverse wildflower display. The first spring wildflowers begin opening during late March and early April at the lowest elevations. The color slowly climbs to Big Frog's broad crown, where spring's final pulse of herbaceous perennials does not fade until the end of May. Asters and many others bloom throughout summer and early autumn.

The steadily shrinking light gap of the former road on

BMT–Hemp Top still lets in enough sun for three seasons of asters, plus summer bloomers such as lobelia, phlox, mountain mint, and spotted touch-me-not. A loose colony of yellow-fringed orchid usually flowers sometime between August 12 and August 27.

lily-of-the-valley

The high-elevation BMT–Licklog Ridge segment is open forested and lush with herbaceous wildflowers in late summer and early fall. Late in the summer of a recent wet year, this stretch was crowded with asters such as white snakeroot. Purple hyssop, a square-stemmed mint 5 to 7 feet tall, blossoms near the treadway from late August into September.

May is the month for wildflowers atop Big Frog. Lily-of-the-valley and Catesby's trillium bloom in large numbers along the upper ridgecrest of BMT–Big Frog from May 5 to May 25. Wood lilies and others unfold in lesser numbers. Further downhill, along the moist north-facing slopes, scattered colonies of wake robin trillium whiten the forest floor during the first half of May. Later in the year, during late August and September, the bright orange berries of yellow mandarin and the cowled lavender corollas of monkshood enliven the same slopes.

Where BMT–Fork Ridge slants onto a drier southeastern pitch, the white wands of galax, a glossy-leaved evergreen herb, often flank the track from mid-May into June. Further north, on the old-road segment of BMT–West Fork, the arching shrub doghobble dangles its diminutive flowers, urn-shaped and white, from late April through early June. After BMT–West Fork turns 90 degrees to the left and up off the old roadbed, look for the waxy white Indian pipe in the steep-sided hollow during late May and June.

In addition to doghobble, other flowering shrubs—mountain laurel, flame azalea, sweetshrub, rosebay rhododendron—hold their own pageant starting in early May. The rhododendron begins blooming in July and usually lasts well into August. Flame azalea catches your eye along some part of BMT–Fork Ridge during the last half of May and reaches Big Frog's peak by the end of the month. When you are hiking Section 11 from south

sugar maple

to north, the BMT turns to the left from the end of Hemp Top onto Licklog Ridge. If you turn to the right onto Licklog Ridge Trail, taking a short detour off the Benton MacKaye, and follow the 0.5 mile of treadway nearest the junction, you can see a gaudy flame azalea show during the last half of May and perhaps into June.

The sugar maple and yellow birch, both near the southern limit of their extensive ranges across northernmost Georgia, stand beside only one section of the BMT from Springer Mountain to the Ocoee River. And along Section 11, they are found together in abundance only alongside a short run of treadway centered upon the 4,224-foot Big Frog Mountain. These two northern hardwoods, herded down the Appalachians by the cold from the last glaciation, are simple to identify because they are distinctive and because their Benton MacKaye corridor habitat is limited. The yellow birch, which survives on an island of high-country habitat atop Big Frog, requires slightly cooler weather than the sugar maple, which strays further down Big Frog's slopes.

yellow birch

Here, atop the mountain, the sugar maple's familiar leaf—the silhouette gracing the Canadian flag—is unmistakable. It has long, pointed lobes, green stems, and smooth, unserrated margins. The sugar maple exhibits the most brilliant fall leaf display in eastern North America; red, yellow, and orange often light up the same tree, occasionally even the same branch.

The curling bark of the yellow birch sets it apart from sapling stage to maturity. The yellowish silver to yellowish bronze bark peels into long thin-layered strips. Mature specimens, those over the century mark, lose their youthful curls except on their upper branches. The papery strips work well as a fire starter, even when wet.

Paired at the end of short branchlets, the toothed leaves of this tree turn bright butter yellow in autumn. The aroma of wintergreen that emanates from its cracked twigs is pleasant, though not as noticeable as the noseful wafting from sweet birch.

Bear sign is often all too obvious during late summer, especially on the segment from the Penitentiary Branch Trail junction to Double Spring Gap. The answer to the old rhetorical question about what a bear does in the woods is an emphatic yes. Berry-eating bears deposit large piles of scat on the trail. Every now and then, if you sit still for awhile, you can hear bears cracking black cherry branches as they gorge on the juicy fruit.

Over the years, trail maintainers and other hikers have played a game—flip-the-rock—with the Cohutta bears. Noticing a fairly large flat rock on the treadway, a hiker flips the rock one flop, bottomside now top, off the middle of the path. That night, or another, a foraging bear pads along the middle of the track. Looking for grub beneath the rock, the bruin hooks a long-clawed paw to the outside edge of the rock, flipping it one flop back toward the middle of the tread. There appears to be one informal rule, which the bears almost always abide by: only one bottom-over-top flip per passing. This slow-paced game is at its subtle best when, through a sequence of bear and backpacker flips, the rock travels from one side of the trail to the other and back again.

NORTH TO SOUTH Chestnut Ridge to Spanish Oak Gap

Mile 0.0—From the usually signed West Fork Trailhead off FS 221, follow the Benton MacKaye–West Fork Trail to the south (the side opposite the parking area and gated road) toward West Fork Rough Creek.

Mile 0.5—Section 11 angles to the right and down from the roadbed onto a narrow path descending into a hollow.

Mile 1.0—Bears 90 degrees to the right onto a former system road, follows the easy grade parallel to West Fork Rough Creek.

Mile 1.6—Rock-steps West Fork Rough Creek.

Mile 1.7—Crosses the West Fork again.

Mile 2.3—The route passes the usually signed West Fork–Rough Creek junction; the BMT now shares the treadway with Rough Creek Trail. Section 11 continues straight ahead past the junction for 35 yards, turns left and rock-steps the West Fork for the final time, then ascends.

Mile 2.8—At the occasionally signed, three-way Rough Creek–Fork Ridge junction in a slight gap, the Benton MacKaye turns up and to the right onto the lower-elevation end of Fork Ridge Trail.

Mile 2.9—Slips to the left of the ascending ridgeline, rises on the sidehill.

Mile 3.8—Ranges through a shallow saddle on Fork Ridge and switches to the other side of the crest.

Mile 4.4—Half-circles the head of a smaller hollow, then rounds a moist hollow where Fraser magnolia is common.

Mile 4.7—The trail arrives at the Big Frog–Fork Ridge junction, usually signed and rest-stop open. Here the BMT switches to the Big Frog Trail and proceeds straight ahead, upridge, toward Big Frog Mountain.

Mile 5.1—Switchbacks to the left over a Chimneytop spur.

Mile 5.4—Passes Big Creek Trail, occasionally signed and usually cairned, where it ties into the right side (west) of the BMT–BFT.

Mile 6.6—The treadway gradually gains elevation to the usually signed Licklog Ridge–Wolf Ridge–Big Frog junction atop Big Frog Mountain. Here the BMT curls down and to the left onto upper Licklog Ridge Trail and descends.

Mile 6.7—Passes rocked-in Elderberry Spring to the right.

Mile 7.1—Arrives at the usually signed three-way Licklog Ridge–Hemp Top junction, then bends to the right and down onto Hemp Top Trail.

Mile 7.9—Passes through Double Spring Gap (water to either side of the saddle).

Mile 8.6—Bottoms out in a stand of yellow poplar at a shallow gap.

Mile 9.2—Gains Hemp Top's crown.

Mile 9.7—Curves over a Hemp Top spur.

Mile 10.2—Holds its course through Indian Grave Gap.

Mile 10.9—Reaches the signed Penitentiary Branch junction just south of Rockwall Gap and advances straight ahead on former system road.

Mile 12.3—Section 11 ends at the usually signed Benton MacKaye–Hemp Top junction. If you turn to the right, you will be on the northern end of Section 10; if you continue straight ahead on the former road, you will cruise into Dally Gap after another 1.0 mile of easy walking.

DIRECTIONS

SECTION 11'S DALLY GAP Trailhead is located off FS 22 on the eastern border of the Cohutta Wilderness. This trailhead is a one-mile walk from the northern end of Section 10 and the southern end of Section 11.

Follow the directions for Section 9 (see page 215) to the four-way intersection at Watson Gap. From Watson Gap, turn right and uphill onto narrow FS 22, usually marked with a sign for

Dally Gap. Proceed on FS 22 for approximately 3.5 miles to the trailhead at Dally Gap, obvious with its bulletin board, trail signs, and pull-in parking to the left and right. Two signed and gated trails—Jacks River and Hemp Top—begin to the left side of the road at Dally Gap. Jacks River leads downhill past the bulletin board; Hemp Top, the route that leads to Section 11, heads uphill to the right of the Jacks River Trail.

Starting at Dally Gap, a 1.0-mile walk takes you to the usually signed Benton MacKaye–Hemp Top junction. If you turn left onto the Benton MacKaye Trail, you will be walking Section 10 north to south toward Watson Gap. If you continue walking Benton MacKaye–Hemp Top straight ahead on the former road, you will be hiking Section 11 toward its northern end at Chestnut Ridge (FS 221).

Shuttle: If you are planning to set a shuttle, taking the Forest Service roads approximately 16.5 miles between trailheads is much shorter and quicker than going back out on the highways. If you want to hike this section north to south, from Chestnut Ridge to Dally Gap, leave a car at Dally Gap, then take FS 22, FS 65, and FS 221 to the Chestnut Ridge (West Fork) Trailhead. If you want to walk south to north, from Dally Gap to Chestnut Ridge, follow directions for Section 12 (see page 265) to the Chestnut Ridge Trailhead, leave a car there, then continue straight ahead on FS 221, FS 65, and FS 22 to Dally Gap.

The three Forest Service roads tie into one another without turn or trouble. Follow these three roads as they form their segment of the loop around the Cohutta–Big Frog Wilderness. Keep the wilderness to your left or right, depending upon your direction of travel, and you will remain on the correct route.

Late winter snowfall

Chestnut Ridge
to Ocoee River 12

Benton MacKaye Trail, Section 12

Chestnut Ridge at FS 221
to Ocoee River at US 64

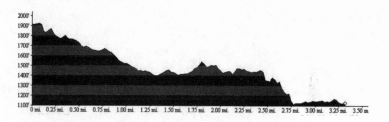

LENGTH 3.3 miles

DAYHIKING (SOUTH TO NORTH) Easy

BACKPACKING (SOUTH TO NORTH) Easy to Moderate

VEHICULAR ACCESS AT EITHER END Southern end at FS 221,
1,900 feet; northern end at US 64, 1,130 feet.

TRAIL JUNCTIONS Chestnut Mountain Loop,
Thunder Rock, West Fork

BLAZES White diamond for Benton MacKaye;
double tan blaze for Chestnut Mountain Loop

TOPOGRAPHIC QUADRANGLE Ducktown TN

DELORME MAP TN-26

COUNTY Polk TN

NEAREST CITIES Blue Ridge GA (SE), Ducktown TN (SE),
Cleveland TN (W)

RD/NF Ocoee/Cherokee

FEATURES Hardwood hollows; winter views; Ocoee River

BMT-12 IS THE SHORTEST and easiest section described in this guide; it is also the first full section to be completed within Tennessee's Cherokee National Forest. Trod south to north, this stretch is an easy downhill stroll from ridge to river, from high point (1,900 feet) on Chestnut Ridge to low point (1,120 feet) along the Ocoee River. This segment follows a circuitous route—west, then north, then back east—to reach its Ocoee River bridge destination. Despite this section's 3.3-mile length, the straight-line gap between its two ends, which are slightly aslant of north-south alignment, measures only 1¼ miles wide. Section 12 shares segments of its treadway with three other trails: Chestnut Mountain Loop Bike and Hike for the first 0.4 mile; West Fork (footpath #302) for the first 1.7 miles; and Thunder Rock, also a footpath, for the final 1.2 miles down to the campground.

Starting on the north side of FS 221, across the road from the southern segment of the West Fork Trail (signed trail #303), the track follows the gated road (old FS 45) angling downhill and to the west off Chestnut Ridge. Here the Benton MacKaye shares the roadbed with the tan-blazed bike and hike trail (mostly bike) and the northern segment of the West Fork Trail (#302). The Chestnut Mountain Loop is part of a larger bike and hike network: the Tanasi Trail System. The walkway descends gradually on gravel tread. Overhead, a second-growth mesophytic forest rises straight and tall: diverse, north-slope hardwoods control the canopy, hemlock and white pine saplings remain in the understory for now. You can easily identify black cherry, silverbell, sweet birch, red maple, Fraser magnolia, American holly, witch-hazel, white ash, pignut hickory, yellow poplar, sassafras, sourwood, basswood, black locust, blackgum, and three species of oak before you round the first hollow at 0.2 mile. At trailside, an umbrella magnolia sapling super-sized its whorled foliage, the largest leaf measuring 22 inches long minus the short stem—gigantic for the temperate zone.

Several mature yellow poplars (8 to 10 feet in circumference) rise out of the second hollow, a tenth mile beyond the first. At the 0.4-mile mark, the BMT turns left onto another road grade, this one less traveled. Here, where Section 12 veers off the main track, the Chestnut Mountain Loop proceeds straight ahead, splitting away from the white blazes. The two-trail treadway maintains its mild downgrade beneath the shade of hemlock and mixed hardwoods; Christmas fern colonies frequently

black cherry

grace the high-side bank. One-tenth mile beyond where the woods road swings around another north-falling hollow at 0.6 mile, an extensive colony of northern maidenhair fern adds its delicate, circular symmetry to the upslope bank below a prominent rock cut.

By 0.8 mile the treadway has turned to the north, now paralleling a ravine down and to the right. By mile 1.1, if the water is high enough, you can hear a rill—the middle prong of Little Gassaway Creek. After curling around a hollow and winding over a slight spur, the gentle downhill course crosses the terrain between prongs and accompanies the western fork of Little Gassaway. At mile 1.4 (1,410 feet) the wide passage ascends for the first time, switchbacking to the right across the western fork and continuing easy up. The ravine and water and rhododendron are now down and to the right. The undemanding incline quickly enters drier habitat, where young hardwoods and Virginia pine are regenerating from a cut made around 1990.

Mile 1.7 crosses FS 45 (1,500 feet). As the carsonite sign indicates, BMT-12 shares its route with the Cherokee National Forest's Thunder Rock Trail from FS 45 down to the campground beside the Ocoee. Beyond the road, the nearly effortless walking advances on narrow sidehill path below an oak-pine overstory darkened by three pine species: Virginia, shortleaf, and white. At mile 1.9 the track makes a usually signed right turn onto old roadbed. Now heading downhill again, just below and to the right of a spur, the grade offers partial summer and leafless winter views of Chestnut Ridge to the right (120 degrees). One-tenth mile past the turn onto the woods road, after ranging through a stand of Virginia pine, the course ties into another woods road and bends to the right with the blazes onto a dry slope where chestnut oaks are common.

The no-strain hiking crests a ridgeline at mile 2.1, crosses to the sunset side, quickly angles back to the ridgetop, then slips to the right of the keel before rising over a spur at mile 2.2. Once over the spur, the BMT begins its descent to the river on cut-in path, running alongside a ravine to the right where hardwoods overshadow hemlocks. The trail makes a curling switchback at mile 2.4, continuing to parallel the rhododendron-lined ravine steeply entrenched to the right. At mile 2.6 the BMT heads down harder, soon beginning a series of switchbacks that wind into the Ocoee's gorge. Short moderate downgrades are the sharpest; wooden steps prevent erosion and help hikers negotiate the steepest pitches. Above the first switchback, winter's latticework allows good looks to the right, to the flex-and-fold uplift of the two tallest ridgelines in the Little Frog Wilderness: Dry Pond Lead and Little Frog Mountain at 60 to 70 degrees. The two crests converge at Sassafras Knob, the highest peak in the wilderness at 3,320 feet.

BEYOND A FOOTBRIDGE AT MILE 2.8, the Benton MacKaye quickly reaches the south bank of the Ocoee—a large river at least 50 yards wide when water is released for paddle-sport boaters on warm-weather weekends. Ocoee is the English-tongue attempt at the Cherokee word for "Apricot Place," derived from the apricot vine, today known as passionflower or maypop. The name came from an important Cherokee settlement, once located near the river's confluence with the Hiwassee. From here, at the lowest elevation (1,120 feet) along the Benton MacKaye's southernmost twelve sections, the trail turns right and heads upstream into a floodplain forest, which includes mature sweetgums and even river birch, a tree found this far north in the Appalachians only along large, low-elevation rivers. The treadway gradually pulls away from the river; at mile 2.9, guided by a blaze, it forks to the right further away from the rushing water. The walkway enters Thunder Rock Campground (still mile 2.9) at a trail sign and bulletin board.

Traveling solo again, the BMT turns right onto the campground road, soon passing restrooms and potable water. (Restrooms are locked during the closed season, but hand-pump water and porta-toilet remain available.) It continues straight ahead on the campground road to the three-way intersection at the beginning of FS 45 (mile 3.2). Here the remainder of Section 12 turns left at the junction, passes Ocoee #3 Powerhouse, crosses the bridge over the Ocoee, then ends at the edge of US 64 East. The BMTA now has permission to move forward in the Cherokee National Forest. Section 13, which will begin across the highway at the Dry Pond Lead sign, is scheduled to open in the near future. For more up-to-date information, contact the BMTA. (See page 275.)

Fraser magnolia

NATURE NOTES

ESPECIALLY IN THE HARDWOOD hollows at its higher-elevation southern end, Section 12 features a surprisingly good wildflower display from April 15 to May 5. On April 15 of a recent year, flowering dogwood, Carolina silverbell, and Fraser magnolia were starting to bloom above the spring ephemerals along the southernmost 0.4 mile of treadway. A partial list of the herbaceous wildflowers in blossom, bud, or leaf on that day include rue anemone, giant chickweed, bloodroot, dwarf and crested dwarf iris, yellow star-grass, both the false and regular Solomon's seal, long-spurred and halberd-leaved violets, foamflower, blue cohosh, doll's eyes, and wake robin trillium.

The low-arching shrub doghobble begins blooming at the lower-elevation northern end during mid-April. Mountain laurel starts whitening the woods in late April and lasts well into May.

The Fraser magnolia is especially noticeable along the southernmost end of this section during early spring. Its fragrant flowers—pale yellow and usually 6 to 9 inches in diameter—are conspicuous in the April woods. One of three deciduous magnolias found beside the Benton MacKaye (umbrella magnolia and cucumbertree are the other two), the Fraser is also easy to identify after its flowers have faded and fallen. This Southern Appalachian endemic grows into a small- to medium-sized tree with smooth (almost as smooth as the beech), light gray or light gray-brown bark. Its leaves—6 to 18 inches long and 3 to 8 inches wide, the second largest noncompound tree leaf in the Southern Highlands—are crowded into whorls at branch ends. The richer the habitat, the larger the leaf. Saplings occasionally sport jungle-sized leaves 7 to 9 inches wide and up to 20 inches long. The noticeably eared base of the Fraser magnolia leaf is diagnostic. The magnolia with the longer, uneared leaf—the umbrella (see page 212 for description)—is much less common beside the BMT.

dwarf iris

Two native irises with nearly identical corollas, the dwarf iris and the crested dwarf iris, bloom at approximately the same time along the Benton MacKaye corridor. These small, rhizomatous perennials, however, are readily distinguished by habitat, by leaf shape, and by their sepals, which are either crested or uncrested. The dwarf iris is occasional to common in the drier oak-pine forest. The crested dwarf iris is common to abundant in the moister habitats of coves, north slopes, and stream margins. The dwarf iris has much longer, narrower leaves, uncrested sepals, and most often occurs in clusters of half a dozen to twenty plants. The crested dwarf iris has shorter, wider leaves, crested sepals, and often grows in dense, extensive colonies (see page 89 for illustration).

In the oak-pine forest north of FS 45, the dwarf iris opens well before the canopy closes. Some flowers were already faded by April 15 of a recent spring. The colorful blossoms, which have three sepals and three petals, appear singly atop stems usually only 3 to 4½ inches high. The flame-orange honey guides—landing strips for pollinating insects—flicker out of the center of the sepals. The orange streaks of the dwarf iris lack the fuzzy, raised tufts that characterize the crested dwarf iris. At 2 to 2¾ inches wide, dwarf iris blooms are slightly larger and richer in color than the crested species. Corolla colors range from washed-out violet and pale yellow-orange to a vibrant blue that becomes deep purple near the flame-colored honey guides.

After the blossoms disappear, this wildflower can be identified by its essentially straight, swordlike leaves—more or less 12 inches long and less than ½ inch wide.

NORTH TO SOUTH Ocoee River to Chestnut Ridge

Mile 0.0—From the southern shoulder of US 64, the BMT crosses the Ocoee #3 Powerhouse bridge over the Ocoee River, then turns right onto the campground road at its three-way intersection with FS 45.

Mile 0.4—Section 12 angles to the left onto path at the trail sign and bulletin board (shares the treadway with Thunder Rock Trail to FS 45), then quickly reaches the floodplain forest near the riverbank.

Mile 0.5—Crosses a footbridge and begins the ascent out of the Ocoee gorge, then parallels a steeply entrenched ravine to the left.

Mile 0.9—Makes a curling, modified switchback.

Mile 1.6—Crosses FS 45.

Mile 1.9—Switchbacks to the left across the western fork of Little Gassoway Creek.

Mile 2.5—After paralleling a hollow down and to the left, the route bears to the east.

Mile 2.9—Turns to the right onto a more heavily used road grade and shares the track with a bike trail.

Mile 3.3—Section 12 ends at FS 221—at Chestnut Ridge.

DIRECTIONS

SECTION 12's CHESTNUT RIDGE Trailhead is located in Tennessee off FS 221 just north of the Big Frog Wilderness. This trailhead is the northern end of Section 11 and the southern end of Section 12.

Approach from the east: From the US 64–TN 68 intersection near Ducktown, Tennessee, travel US 64 West for approximately 7.5 miles before turning left onto FS 45 at TVA's Ocoee No. 3 Powerhouse. The turn is additionally marked with a sign for nearby Thunder Rock Campground.

Approach from the west: From the US 411–US 64 intersection near Ocoee, Tennessee, follow US 64 East for approximately 18.5 miles to the right turn onto FS 45 at TVA's Ocoee No. 3 Powerhouse. The turn is additionally marked with a sign for nearby Thunder Rock Campground.

From FS 45: Forest Service 45 crosses over the Ocoee River, passes close beside the powerhouse, then proceeds straight ahead, uphill, at the signed junction for Thunder Rock Campground, which is nearby to the right. (If you wish to leave a shuttle car at the lower-elevation northern end—the campground end—turn right into Thunder Rock Campground and leave a vehicle at the parking area to the left of the road a short distance beyond the turn off FS 45.) Continue on this steep, winding Forest Service road (the pavement ends just past the powerhouse) for slightly less than 3.0 miles to its three-way intersection with FS 221. Turn left onto FS 221 and travel 0.4 mile to the usually signed Chestnut Ridge Trailhead, marked with a West Fork Trail sign to the right side of the road and at least one sign for multiple trails (including the West Fork) to the left side of the road. Section 12's southern end is the gated Forest Service road angling downhill and to the left from the way you approached the trailhead. Limited parking is located on the left side of the road. Section 11's northern end shares its treadway with only the West Fork Trail to the right side of FS 221, opposite the gated road's entrance. The Forest Service asks that you not block access through the gate.

NOTES

Environmental Guidelines

THE BENTON MACKAYE Trail Association and the Forest Service formally endorse the Leave-No-Trace (LNT) principles for hiking and camping. The following guidelines adhere to the philosophy of the Leave-No-Trace movement. For more information visit the LNT website: www.lnt.org.

Leave-No-Trace guidelines recommend that you camp 200 feet (65 yards) away from a trail. LNT proponents readily acknowledge, however, that Southern Appalachian ridge-and-slope trails often make the 200-foot standard unrealistic.

Before the Hike

■ Limit group size to no more than ten for backpacking and no more than twelve for dayhiking.

■ Split large organized groups into two or three smaller parties, allowing the groups to hike on different sections, travel opposite directions on the same section, stagger their starts, or do whatever it takes to avoid overwhelming everyone and everything in their path.

■ Educate large groups, especially children, about the evils of littering and cutting across switchbacks before they leave the trailhead.

■ Take a lightweight backpacking stove so you won't have to build fires for cooking.

■ Repackage food supplies in sealable bags or plastic bottles so there will be fewer boxes and tinfoil pouches to burn or carry.

On the Trail

■ Travel quietly. And, if you can, take your long breaks away from the trail to preserve solitude and to keep other hikers from having to hopscotch over and around your gear.

■ Don't litter—not even the smallest of candy wrappers or cigarette butts. If you pack it in, pack it out—all of it.

■ And don't be a hider—a person whose conscience is caught midway between right and wrong. The undersides of rocks should be salamander sanctuaries and tree hollows should be wildlife dens—not beer can repositories.

■ Remember that organic scraps are definitely litter. Orange peels, peanut hulls, apple cores, and campsite compost piles crowned with eggshells and spaghetti noodles are not welcome sights along the trail. Carry these organic scraps out or, if you are planning on having a fire anyway, burn them. If there is no way you are going to carry out an apple core, at least give it a good downslope heave well out of sight of the trail. And no one wants to see your misfired banana peel draped over the flame azalea.

■ Carry a plastic bag with you. Help pick up what those uncaring louts have left behind. Take only pictures and litter; leave only footprints and good karma.

■ Take your dump du jour at least 100 feet from the trail and at least 150 feet from a campsite or water source. Dig a cat hole with boot heel or plastic trowel, then cover everything up completely—please.

■ Stay on the main trail while hiking, and do not cut across switchbacks. Cutting across switchbacks tramples vegetation, starts erosion, and encourages more shortcut taking.

■ Step to the high side of the trail so you don't cave in the lower side when moving aside to let other hikers or backpackers pass.

■ Don't feed, follow, approach, harass, or pick up any animal. This precept especially includes snakes; needlessly bludgeoning the head of a snake definitely falls into the category of harassment.

■ Don't pick, pluck, dig up, or cut up any flowers, plants, or trees—not even the tiny ones you think no one will miss. Let offenders know of your disapproval gently and tactfully, at least at first.

Leave-No-Trace Camping

■ Don't use worn-out campsites. Let areas of bare earth with eroding soil, damaged trees, and exposed roots heal. Use existing, well-established campsites in acceptable condition. Better yet, move well away from the trail and make a no-trace camp that will rarely, if ever, be used again.

■ Do your best to camp at least 100 feet away from trail or stream. Be creative and exert some effort in this regard. Where the trail rounds a spur, you can often find good sites on the spur well off the trail. Many ridgelines are plenty wide and flat enough for you to camp 200 or more feet off the treadway. The Benton MacKaye frequently skirts the high points of knobs and named mountains. Instead of following the track as it slabs off the crest, continue straight ahead, through the woods, to the top of the knob, often only a 40- to 80-foot elevation gain. If you have a topographic map, and know where you are, it is relatively easy to find a flat-topped knob that is neither too high above nor too far away from the trail.

If you want to camp near a creek flowing parallel to the trail, try crossing the creek and tucking in on the other side. That way your camp will be well over 100 feet from the path and maybe even 100 feet away from the stream.

■ Don't cut standing trees or pull up or beat down vegetation to make room for your tent or tents. Fit in, tuck in—don't hack in.

■ Don't enlarge an existing campsite. There is no need for large groups to circle the wagons against the night. Again, fit in and tuck in.

■ Absolutely no campsite construction—leave the blueprints and hard hats at home: no boot bulldozing, trenching, digging latrines, hammering nails in trees, etc.

■ Use biodegradable soap and dispose of waste water at least 100 feet from camp and 150 feet from any water source.

■ Don't wash dirty dishes directly in a spring or stream. Don't use soap on yourself or your clothes directly in a spring or stream.

■ Don't bury trash or food scraps. Animals will dig them up.

■ Don't spit your toothpaste on campsite vegetation. After a month of drought, heavily used sites look like bird roosts.

■ Make your campsite look as natural as when you found it. Replace branches, twigs, and leaves cleared for the sleeping area.

■ Keep length of stay to one or two nights, if possible.

■ Wear soft-soled shoes in camp.

■ Avoid building campfires. Take a lightweight backpacking stove for cooking. If you do start a fire, keep it small and use only dead and down wood. Leave the saws and axes at home.

■ Erase all evidence of a campfire built with no fire ring. Scatter the ashes, replace the duff, and camouflage the burned area.

■ Don't build fire rings—tear them down.

■ Never build a fire on a dry, windy day.

Backcountry Courtesy

■ Leave radios and CD players at home or bring headsets.

■ Don't take a dog with you unless it is well trained. Even then, carry a leash so you can control your animal when necessary. Leave behind dogs that may growl or bark at other hikers. Do not take aggressive dogs—canine weapons—into the wilds for protection. Creating stress for other hikers is unconscionable.

■ Take consideration—do nothing that will interfere with someone else's enjoyment.

■ Keep as quiet as possible. Drunken parties, war whoops, and loud radios are frowned upon, and downright rude.

■ Remember that campsites are first come, first served. Don't whine, argue, or try to crowd in if someone already has the campsite you really wanted.

■ Help preserve the illusion of solitude, for yourself and others. Make yourself as unobtrusive, as invisible, as possible. Use earth-tone tents and tarps and, if possible, camp far enough off the trail so that other hikers can't see you and vice versa. Never camp smack on the trail so that other hikers have to wind through your sprawling encampment just to follow the trail. Also, if possible, take lunch and long rest breaks off the trail.

Usage Rules
for the Cohutta–Big Frog Wilderness

THE FOREST SERVICE HAS established a set of stricter regulations to help alleviate overuse and sloppy use in the Cohutta–Big Frog Wilderness. The following rules, enforced by wilderness rangers, apply to Benton MacKaye Trail hikers within the wilderness.

■ The maximum group size, for both dayhiking and backpacking, is twelve.

■ The campsite size limit is 400 square feet, roughly 20 feet by 20 feet. No more than four tents are allowed within your 400-square-foot campsite. If your group of twelve or fewer people has more than four tents, you must split your crew up between different campsites. Campsites must be at least 300 feet apart.

■ You must camp at least 50 feet away from any water source—spring, branch, creek, or river.

■ Only one fire ring with a maximum diameter of 18 inches is allowed per campsite. The Forest Service recommends that you not build any fire rings.

Addresses and Maps

IN GEORGIA, all of the Benton MacKaye's public-land tread-way traverses the Chattahoochee National Forest. From Springer Mountain to Weaver Creek Road (Sections 1–6), the BMT's public-land route ranges across the Toccoa Ranger District. From Bushy Head Gap to Double Spring Gap (Sections 8–10 and 11 south of the Tennessee border), the trail passes through the Armuchee-Cohutta Ranger District.

All of the Benton MacKaye Trail currently completed in Tennessee, from Double Spring Gap to US 64 (Section 11 north of the Tennessee border and Section 12), travels northward into the Cherokee National Forest's Ocoee Ranger District.

For more information, contact the following offices:

Chattahoochee National Forest

USDA Forest Service
Supervisor's Office
1755 Cleveland Highway
Gainesville, GA 30501
(770) 297-3000
www.fs.fed.us/conf

USDA Forest Service
Toccoa Ranger District
6050 Appalachian Highway
Blue Ridge, GA 30513
(706) 632-3031

USDA Forest Service
Armuchee-Cohutta Ranger District
3941 Highway 76
Chatsworth, GA 30705
(706) 695-6736

Cherokee National Forest

USDA Forest Service
Supervisor's Office
P.O. Box 2010
Cleveland, TN 37320
(423) 476-9700
www.southernregion.fs.fed.us/cherokee

USDA Forest Service
Ocoee Ranger District
3171 Highway 64 East
Benton, TN 37307
(423) 338-5201

Maps of the two national forests and the Cohutta–Big Frog Wilderness are available from the Forest Service offices for a small fee. The combined wilderness map is entitled *Cohutta and Big Frog Wilderness Georgia-Tennessee.*

Topographic quadrangles (1:24,000) are available from the United States Geological Survey. Call 1-888-ASK-USGS or order online (http://earthexplorer.usgs.gov). Nongovernmental online sources—view for free, download for a nominal fee—include www.topozone.com and http://terraserver. homeadvisor.msn.com.

The Benton MacKaye Trail Association

THE BMTA WELCOMES NEW MEMBERS who are interested in constructing and maintaining their trail—the Benton MacKaye. The BMTA website includes current membership fees and additional pertinent information. Members receive a monthly newsletter, which provides progress reports on past trips and details concerning upcoming work trips and events.

Group work trips are always scheduled for the second Saturday of each month. After members are trained in approved techniques, many of them volunteer to maintain their own short segments of the treadway. The BMTA furnishes the necessary tools and instruction.

Benton MacKaye Trail Association
P.O. Box 53271
Atlanta, GA 30355-1271
www.bmta.org

BMTA Donors

The Benton Mackaye Trail Association, Peachtree Publishers, and the author thank the following people for their generous contributions. Without their financial support, this first BMT guidebook would not have been possible.

Anonymous
Martha C. Black, in memory of Flo Westin,
    mother of David Sherman
David and Linda Blount
Claire Broadwell

Edwin Dale
Darcy Douglas
John Dowling
Sam Evans
Jane and Tom Keene
Victoria Lynn Kelsey and David John Kelsey Sr.
Terry Miller
Tony Oldfield
David Pullen
Tom Rhodes
Bill Ross the Younger
Nancy Shofner
Debbie Tuten

Index of Nature Illustrations

Other Books by Tim Homan

Hiking Trails of the Southern Nantahala Wilderness, the Ellicott Rock Wilderness, and the Chattooga National Wild and Scenic River

Hiking Trails of the Cohutta and Big Frog Wildernesses

Hiking Trails of the Joyce Kilmer–Slickrock and Citico Creek Wildernesses

The Hiking Trails of North Georgia

A Yearning Toward Wildness: Environmental Quotations from the Writings of Henry David Thoreau